Body Image

Body Image
Nursing concepts and care

Bob Price SRN, BA (Hons), MSc.,
Cert. Ed.

Prentice Hall
New York London Toronto Sydney Tokyo Singapore

First published 1990 by
Prentice Hall International (UK) Ltd,
66 Wood Lane End, Hemel Hempstead,
Hertfordshire, HP2 4RG
A division of
Simon & Schuster International Group

Printed and bound in Great Britain by
BPCC Wheatons Ltd, Exeter

British Library Cataloguing in Publication Data

Price, Bob
  Body image nursing concepts and care.
  1. Medicine. Nursing. Psychological aspects
  I. Title
  610.73019

  ISBN 0-13-023367-6

---

1 2 3 4 5   94 93 92 91 90

This book is dedicated to
Helen, Lorna and Andrew
*who have lived **Body Image** for more than a year*

Contents

Acknowledgements

I would like to gratefully acknowledge the assistance of Grace Rose and her librarian colleagues. Without their invaluable help this book would not have been possible.

I would also like to record my thanks to my teaching colleagues and my students, many of whom have become involved in body image exercises or discussions.

Preface

A few decades ago the idea of a nursing textbook on aspects of altered body image would have seemed ludicrous. More recently, many nurses would have felt such a book appropriate only to the psychiatric nurse. Today it is important that the whole profession considers the wide range of problems associated with an altered body image and the nursing interventions that may be used to solve such problems. This developing nursing concern with how we think we look, particularly when our body has changed or been changed in some way, stems from a number of modern trends.

The first trend is a professional nursing commitment to the philosophy of holistic care: a nursing intervention that is designed to address the person as a being with psycho-social and spiritual as well as physical domains. Such a philosophy recognises that health problems may arise in any of these four domains and that when it does, it frequently affects the patient and significant others in one or more of the other domains. A nursing intervention designed to help the patient must therefore address all the relevant problems, not just one of them.

Without this first trend of a widely held holistic philosophy, we could not conceive of altered body image as a subject, for it is in the meeting of the physical, psychological and social aspects of ourselves that we have the material to form such notions as normal and altered body image. To have a body image (normal or altered) implies that we have a physical body and series of attitudes or feelings toward it. Disorders of the body or our feelings could both give rise to an altered body image. This in turn might prove problematic for social life, spiritual well-being and even physical health if it led to attempted suicide.

The second contributing factor is mankind's capacity to change the appearance of the human body. This can now be done in an almost infinite number of ways, some intentional, some unintentional, some therapeutic and some downright destructive. One needs only mention the effects of motor car accidents, advances in plastic surgery, developments in anti-cancer treatments and the modern interest in adjustment of body appendages to make the point. Modern man has become increasingly interested in 'body alteration' and this has usually involved both nurses and doctors who have become agents of change, as well as agents of cure and caring.

A third trend is probably society's greater appreciation of mental health. People say we live in a stressful world, that 'it's not good for you'. When this sentiment is expressed they are usually talking about psychological as well as physical well-being. We have tried to understand the ingredients of contentment, of happiness. There are trained psychiatrists, psychotherapists and counsellors to help in this quest. One of the things that has been found repeatedly is that to be happy you have to be tolerant (at the very least) of the body you live within. Just as psychological problems may cause physical pathology and symptoms, so the reverse may be true. It is amusing to note that Florence Nightingale had discovered this many years before the counselling couch came into full use:

> Volumes are now written and spoken upon the effect of the mind on the body. Much of it is true. But I wish a little more was thought of the effect of the body on the mind.
>
> Florence Nightingale, 1859

These three trends mean that body image – what we think and feel about our body – is an increasingly relevant concept in all fields of nursing. If a woman is admitted to hospital for a hysterectomy, the holistic perspective of all major nursing models dictate that we must consider the effects of surgery upon her mental and social well-being. A young man with several 'tubes' protruding from nose, vein, wound and urethra will have a different picture of his body compared with his tubeless peer. The nurse cannot ignore this. The elderly person who feels like a young person still lives in an 'old body' and is regularly reminded of this. The imaginative nurse knows that this must affect a patient's health, and acts to help the person respond effectively to the altered body.

In this textbook I have set out to share with you some of my own and others' ideas on normal and altered body image. I shall suggest ways in which the nurse may assess, diagnose, plan, implement and evaluate nursing measures designed to assist the patient with altered body image. My suggestions are but a beginning, possibly useful help with a complex problem that varies with patient and circumstance. The points in this textbook are offered to help you frame the problem, make it describable, manageable and, hopefully, solvable. One textbook cannot resolve every altered body image problem; it can however trigger your imagination so that you can provide care that is both innovative, tactful and practical.

These chapters are for all practitioners. For some, the points offered will be a useful review, even a revamp of previously held conceptions of body image problems. For others the text will be completely fresh, either because they are new to the subject, or because they do not have the terminology or tools with which to tackle a problem they felt intuitively to be there. I hope student and qualified nurses will enjoy these ideas, and that specialists in the fields of burns, traumatology and oncology nursing will all gain something from this conceptual approach.

What this book cannot be is an erudite, specialist text in the realms of psychiatric nursing. This is not only because text length would not permit it but also because the debate on many key psychiatric concepts surrounding body image still continues. To do justice to this debate I would have had to either recount the different schools of thought in some depth or else commit myself to one position. Accordingly, only notes are offered on perhaps the most well-known psychiatric body image problem, anorexia nervosa. These are intended to inform on the key concerns of the problem but in no way to supplant single subject nursing or medical texts.

How to use this book

The book is divided up into a number of developing units which may either be read chapter to chapter, or dipped into as you see fit. Each chapter has its own relevant bibliography or suggested further reading which should make a useful package for college-based use. You will find that each chapter within the unit opens with a short series of objectives which the chapter should help you to achieve, and closes with a series of self-check questions for personal or group reflection. In many instances an exercise is suggested. These are designed to expand the text, either through examples or through inviting you to apply basic concepts to new settings. Self-check questions, chapter objectives and exercises are an additional benefit and may be used as seen fit. Completion of chapter questions and exercises is not obligatory for the enjoyment of subsequent chapters, but they will assist in the appreciation of sometimes complex arguments.

If you decide to dip into the book it may be useful to read Units 1 and 2 first. These units set out the normal and the abnormal of body image and provide the fullest definitions of the terminology used throughout the rest of the book. The idea behind this suggestion is that basic terms must be agreed in order to get down to active nursing care measures later on. The terminology of the text has been kept as simple and clear as possible which is important for nurses who must live with it on a daily basis.

Unit 3 considers the nursing theory which underpins the book. I have not attempted to commit the text to any particular school of nursing theory as I believe that the major theoreticians are in broad agreement on the holistic basis of nursing care. Instead, I have tried to relate altered body image problems to a general framework of rehabilitation which may itself be seen through Roper, Roy, Orem or other's perspectives. The argument of this text is that the nurse employs whatever model is most appropriate and prudent given the rehabilitation circumstances of the patient. All nurses seek to enable the patient to sustain a satisfactory body image, or to help him regain one if it has been altered.

Unit 4 onwards considers specific instances of altered body image problems and what the nurse might do. A variety of challenges are considered, from the patients with different drainage tubes to those recovering from a cerebro-vascular accident. Unit 5 addresses the relationship between altered body image and sexuality. Body image has been accepted as an important part of human sexuality, and altered body image must be seen as a critical element in the patient's care post-hysterectomy, mastectomy or following transsexual surgery. As a group, these patients have many needs which necessitate thoughtfully tailored nursing solutions. In some cases a normal body image may be regained, in others a modified final body image will have to be accepted. These patients have perhaps the most challenging body image problems of all, akin to the longer-term problems associated with ageing. Finally, in Unit 6 the methods of evaluating the nursing intervention are considered. Such an evaluation is shared with the patient, who will evolve his or her own opinion upon their personal appearance. An unshared evaluation is an incomplete one for if the body image involves the individual's own opinion on his or her appearance, then the success of nursing care can only be judged with reference to the patient's feelings.

A note on gender terminology

Within this text, in the interests of uniformity of approach, the nurse will be referred to as she, the patient as he. The only exception to this rule will be those chapters addressing uniquely male or female problems, and those sections where the male gender of the nurse may affect body image care.

Unit 1
Normal body image

Normal body image is something that we have always possessed, but perhaps never really recognised. Instead, human beings allow themselves only glimpses of how they feel about their body, the way it looks, acts and moves. Sometimes these glimpses come as sudden shocks, when someone comments on how vain or unfashionable we are! We are quickly reminded that our body image ideas are not necessarily the same as those of people around us. Body image is pushed into the limelight, albeit briefly, and perhaps without the formal title.

Unit 1 starts from the obvious position — what is a normal body image and how is it formed and maintained? Nurses must become more aware of the norm, for the patient who abruptly faces altered body image may not have had time to reflect on such matters. Wherever possible it should be the nurse's aim to restore a normal body image. However, it will be seen that this is not a simple matter because the normal body image is an ever-changing, amorphous part of the patient's life, be he six or sixty.

1   Normal body image

Study of this chapter will enable you to:

1 Offer a simple definition of *normal body image.*
2 Define what the author means by *body reality*, *body ideal* and *body presentation.*
3 List genetic and nurturant factors which contribute to the formation of a normal body image.
4 Describe why body image is not a constant phenomenon.
5 Describe recent social influences which might be said to affect an individual's body ideal.
6 Offer examples of how culture affects body image.
7 Describe briefly the terms *primary* and *secondary socialisation.*
8 Define what is meant by *self-image* and what part body image might play in its formation.

Most nurses have probably referred to 'body image' at some time in their professional lives, possibly in discussing the care of a burned patient or someone who has undergone radical surgery. We all have a vague notion of what altered body image is and have based it upon a concept of normal body image which has rarely been analysed personally. This chapter will consider what a normal body image is, where it comes from and how it is developed, and attempt to explain what effect body image has upon our self-image. The chapter poses the argument that an understanding of the normal body image is critical if the changes and problems associated with altered body image are to be appreciated.

At the simplest level body image is how we feel and think about our body and body appearance. Schilder (1935) defined body image as

> The picture of our body which we form in our mind, that is to say the way in which our body appears to ourselves.

Other writers have built upon this classic definition, emphasising that such feelings and attitudes are neither static nor simplistic (Kolb, 1975; Secord and Jourard, 1953). They collectively come to form a 'body concept' which

3

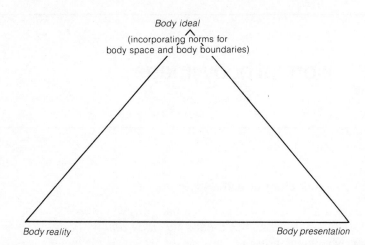

Fig. 1.1   A body image model. Model precepts: 1. Throughout life human beings
attempt to sustain balance between the three components of the body image
triangle. 2. When one body image component changes, accommodation for this is
made through the other two components, as well as the changed component.
3. Body image is constantly changing, in health as well as through illness or injury.
4. Personal body image is therefore rarely totally satisfactory – we chase a dream.

may become important for an adequate social life. Some writers have
approached the subject from a psycho-analytical viewpoint, namely that
body image is an internalised learnt representation of the body (Sandler
and Rosenblatt, 1962). It may be associated with feelings of pride, guilt,
disgust or hatred. Different theorists have emphasised different aspects of
the body image. This book will use a definition of body image which refers
to three essential components – body image is the way in which we perceive and feel about our body (body reality), how it responds to our com-
mand (body presentation) and includes an internal standard by which both
are judged (body ideal) (see Figure 1.1).

Body reality

Body reality refers to our body as it really is – tall, short, fat, thin, spotty,
sallow, coarse. It is the physical raw material first created through our
genes and thereafter moulded by nurturant influences throughout life.
Body reality is not how we would like our body to look, nor whether we
find it pleasant or disagreeable. It is the body as seen and measured as
objectively as humanly possible. Where comparisons of body reality are
made, they are made with norms for human kind, or more accurately, the
race of which the individual is a member. A 5ft 8in. tall pygmy would be

considered tall for his race but only average perhaps for caucasian people. Ideally, such a measurement of body reality relates body makeup, proportions, configuration to the wider group of which the individual is a member and does not include a value judgement.

Here is an example. Paul Lloyd is a little over six feet tall and weighs 186 pounds. He has blonde hair and blue eyes, with a mole on his left cheek and right forearm. He is aged thirty-seven and there are easily distinguishable wrinkle lines around his eyes. He has a beard growth but no moustache. Aspects of Paul Lloyd's body reality have just been described, making no comment on his height or weight, what the wrinkle lines signify, or whether Paul's body is attractive or unattractive. It is simply the most objective description of his body normally manageable.

Body reality is not a constant state however. In health our bodies are constantly changing, renewing tissue and even whole organs over a period of time. Every 120 days we replace our red blood cells in a continuous cycle designed to meet oxygenation and transportation needs. On sunlit days, shafts of light may reveal a veritable soup of floating dust in the room, some of which is composed of our worn out skin cells. We shed some of our dead tissue onto collars and blouses and call it dandruff, never stopping to consider that this is an illustration of our body in constant change.

Over longer periods of time the body develops, both in response to the imprinted genetic codes and to the environment in which we live. As a young baby our fluid balance is more precarious – we are some 70 to 75 per cent water. As we grow older, that percentage drops to nearer 60 per cent water, and this affects the texture and tone of our tissues particularly the skin. Ageing is seen by many to be synonymous with being old but we have been ageing by replacing tissues from the moment of conception. In the early years of life this involves marked changes in the proportions of various parts of our bodies. A baby has a large head in relation to the rest of the body and young animals seem to have relatively large eyes in proportion to their heads. Change may be constant or through bursts of activity, 'growing spurts' which can radically alter body size and proportions in a few short months.

Such changes to body reality can be quite momentous. The development of gender-specific characteristics during puberty has been a source of magic and wonder for centuries. Developing breasts, changing contours of the body, the growth of pubic and facial hair are all fundamental changes to body reality which have a profound effect upon our feelings and our sense of person.

Not all such changes to body reality stem from genetic codes within us. The way we earn a living, house ourselves and care for our skin can all alter the body reality. A man who works at hard manual labour will form hard skin on his hands. The office worker who does a short spell of

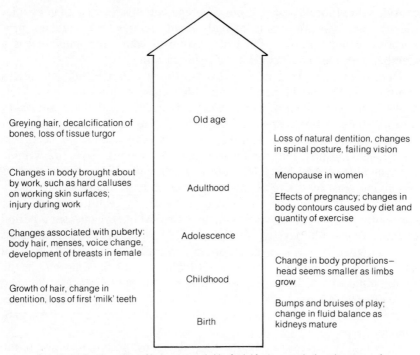

Greying hair, decalcification of bones, loss of tissue turgor

Old age

Loss of natural dentition, changes in spinal posture, failing vision

Changes in body brought about by work, such as hard calluses on working skin surfaces; injury during work

Adulthood

Menopause in women

Effects of pregnancy; changes in body contours caused by diet and quantity of exercise

Changes associated with puberty: body hair, menses, voice change, development of breasts in female

Adolescence

Childhood

Change in body proportions— head seems smaller as limbs grow

Growth of hair, change in dentition, loss of first 'milk' teeth

Bumps and bruises of play; change in fluid balance as kidneys mature

Birth

Genetic coding for colour of hair, eyes and skin; facial features and other signatures of parentage; possibly even disposition to later pathology

Fig. 1.2   Adjustments to body reality.

digging in the garden will form blisters. Both pairs of hands are undeniably examples of change in the body reality (see Figure 1.2).

Body ideal

Body reality is measured constantly against an ideal of what we think the body should look like and how it should act. This ideal is carried in our head and may be applied not only to our own body reality, but that of others near and dear to us. Body ideal is a complex and changing part of us, which we seldom prefer to confront consciously. It has several facets or norms which make it important for nursing consideration (see Figure 1.3).

Body ideal includes a norm of body contours, body size and relative proportion. This is reinforced constantly when we encounter the sizings for off-the-peg clothes and public transport seating. A similar personal norm for body space and boundaries is also part of the body ideal. We not

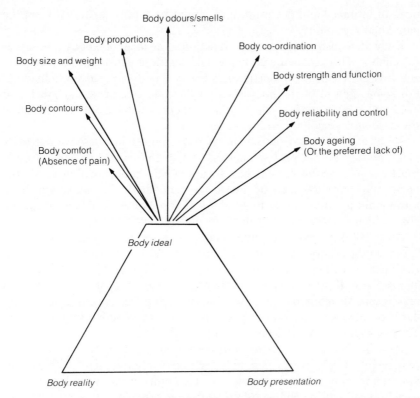

Fig. 1.3   Body ideal personal norms.

only seek to control the body we live within, but also to extend that control to an area of space around us. This home territory becomes our ideal body space and we feel emotionally safe when we can dictate who or what will enter that body space. Its control becomes critical for our sense of safety and independence. The body boundary refers to that point where body reality touches on the outside environment. Of course we cannot see or easily sense all of this, but we do form an ideal of where the boundary should be. Some patients, for instance those on mechanical ventilators, have difficulty defining their usual body boundaries. The machine tubing can come to be seen as part of the body – the machine on extension of personal body space.

People develop different ideal amounts of body space often guided by cultural norms. Mediterranean people appear to be happy with a comparatively limited space, the individual's friends and relatives freely entering the space to touch and communicate with the person. Northern European people may prefer to establish a more substantial body space holding stricter rules for entering that space. Many of these norms relate to notions of intimacy and decorum, and cannot be totally separated from the individual's sexuality.

Body ideal also relates to body function – the ideal of a body that serves us reliably. This is called a body ideal of health or active physical function and it is not clear how realistic this ideal will be for any given individual. For some, failure of the body reality will come as a profound shock and insult to a body perfect ideal, while others will have set less stringent standards for personal body function.

As already stated, others will take an interest in our personal body ideal. Nurses take a professional interest in the patient's ideals of body function. Where the patient has an unrealistic body function ideal, the nurse may have to guide or advise the individual. The nurse will have formulated a patient body function ideal and expressed this as a nursing goal, which may be either realistic or unrealistic!

Body ideal involves the individual – consciously or otherwise – measuring body reality and body presentation against a norm or standard. Each person will have their own norms or standards and these may change almost daily. If the standard is unrealistic, unhappiness or even depression may result. In many instances we do not have a free choice in such standards because society and our peers may set a more universal body ideal. These societal norms can be very difficult to resist.

Personal body ideals are often rooted in many of the nurturant factors that have already been seen to affect body reality such as education, upbringing and culture. Sociologists term this primary and secondary socialisation. During childhood we learn the normal way of arranging hair, cleaning skin, adorning faces and arranging limbs in company. Such primary socialisation is geared to the society in which we live.

To identify the earliest point at which children start to develop a body ideal, it is probably necessary to go back to pre-toddler stage children. Head argued that our earliest notions about our bodies are formed on the basis of exploring the raw material, body reality. Head was a neurologist, who believed that from a very early stage the brain was capable of sensing all sorts of data about body weight, shape, size and form. These would be incorporated to form what he termed 'the body precept' (Head, 1920). While it is difficult to prove this in any meaningful way it is known that babies even *in utero* suck their thumbs and explore their limbs, thus starting to gain some rudimentary sense of body boundaries.

It is not until the baby is born and can start to compare his or her body with others however, that the development of a body ideal becomes realistically possible. As a young child, even this may take many months to start developing. Schilder studied the phenomenon of phantom limb pains in a large number of amputee patients from a variety of backgrounds and at different ages. The feeling of a limb 'still being there' was well established in adolescents and adults, but was rarely, if ever, present in very young children. Given that phantom limb experiences are an expression of a disrupted body ideal (and not just the severing of nerve processes) it would seem that such an ideal is not completely formed in very young children.

Childhood is a time during which a rich assortment of material is gathered for the body ideal. Play enables the child to explore body strengths and weaknesses. Through play, a child may mimic the behaviour seen in the adult world. While 'cowboys and Indians' might be out of vogue as a game, there are still many other heroes to emulate. Such heroes set standards of appearance or action, which the child comes to think of as desirable. Initially, parents and teachers and older brothers and sisters are very influential. The pre-school child learns about 'correct' body appearance from mothers and fathers who offer (albeit subconsciously at times) sex-stereotyped appearances for emulation. It is often argued, at least in lay circles, that a boy needs a 'dad to look up to'. Single parent families are thought to be disadvantaged because the child is without a key reference figure during formative years.

While in early primary socialisation it is the parents that are important, later it will be the wider culture that has the most profound effect upon the child's body ideal. Fathers and mothers dress, act and groom themselves in a culturally determined way. Dressing in a turban, shirt and tie or even hair curlers can all be seen as part of culture as well as what a parent typically does. The child's developing body will then incorporate the valued standards of the wider group. If high cheekbones are considered beautiful, then this is registered as the ideal for the child's own body. The luxuriant dreadlock hair of a Rastafarian man, becomes prized as what 'should be' for the Rastafarian boy's own body.

The body ideal is not a static idea in our head. It develops alongside our body and is referenced against ever changing models or standards. From middle childhood, through adolescence to young adulthood the body ideal suffers a bewildering number of transformations. Not only do changes in the body reality have to be accommodated, but also account taken of new mass media models for the body ideal. We talk about a youth or a pop culture, with heroes who are presented through film, video or printed page. Where the image projected by the hero is very pervasive a cult following may develop. During the 1960s thousands of young people sported Beatle haircuts, and more recently punk hairstyles have been in fashion. Both are examples of individuals adjusting their body reality to match a body ideal which has been influenced through peer pressure or the mass media.

The period of adolescence has been seen as a search for an identity, a time of insecurity, of wanting to belong, yet to be highly individual. Erikson characterised this period as one of crisis which highlighted the decisions that individuals had to make (Erikson, 1968). Part of that search for an identity has concerned the body ideal, which to the adolescent seems constantly in need of updating. If it did not change then it might 'decay', become associated with a vaguely recognised body ideal found in 'old people'. Such change in the body ideal has been both stimulated and fuelled by changes in fashion and social behaviour. Whereas in a pre-mass media, parochial society, the body ideal was likely to be developed through local cultural norms, in modern societies it could be adjusted through what was fashionable. Film idols, pop artists, even television soap opera actresses and actors might stimulate change in dress, hairstyle or behaviour. The commercial fashion industry would then seek to facilitate the change of our individual body appearances, enabling us to buy the latest styles. This process of an external world offering possibilities for change in our body ideal characterises secondary socialisation too. The young, middle aged and elderly adult is regularly (if not so frenetically) invited to develop new standards of body appearance, based on what is 'sophisticated', 'classy', 'superior', 'dignified', 'fun' or 'young'.

Modern western societies have developed norms of body appearance and function which are strongly based upon a youth ideal. The implication is that to be happy you must look and feel young – successful people are young and beautiful people. Accordingly, if such ideals are influential (and the advertisement agencies have financial reason to believe they are) we will be faced with a body ideal that is receding in years just as body reality is advancing in years! This is the modern dilemma which has led to colour hair rinses, plastic surgery and the adoption of clothes and jewellery which many would associate with younger age groups.

Body presentation

Body presentation has already been mentioned in the previous section, through allusions to fashion. However, body presentation is not simply the way we dress and adorn our bodies. It is not just the way in which a manikin is dressed and groomed, but it is the way it might move and pose its limbs were it to come to life. This goes back to Schilder's work on 'body concept'. We are able consciously to review not only how our body looks, but how it functions as an expression of our will, our intentions and our feelings. Consider the following scene – a nurse is assisting a patient with a wash. The patient is in bed and can only use one hand and the nurse is helping by rinsing and resoaping the flannel. Her personal body image is already informed by body reality and body ideal (perhaps influenced by professional training) and now it will be influenced by body presentation. Despite being professionally dressed, her posture and dexterity with the bowl of water is sadly lacking. She slips and spills half the soapy water over the patient's bed clothes. The nurse's personal body image is adversely affected because nurses are supposed to be dextrous and to have a 'light soothing touch'.

The way in which we sense our body is not solely affected by how it is constructed and the ideal of how it should look. It is affected by the way our body performs in a variety of social and intimate circumstances. We may look very confident and sophisticated in our evening wear but when on the dance floor can we avoid stepping on partners or other dancers' toes? When counselling a patient, do our gestures look as though they corroborate the sentiments of our speech? Do the gestures look clumsy, intrusive or false? The divide between a body action that confirms our intended communication and one that brings it into question or ridicule is very slight indeed. This is the basis of much human comedy – a body presentation that is neither congruous with 'what we are trying to say' nor where we are saying it. Consider the scene when some unfortunate woman falls into an innocent man's arms just as the woman's husband walks into the room. Neither of the entangled individuals necessarily had a body image based upon 'the lover'. Yet body presentation does not allow them to explain easily their predicament and certainly compromises their body reality.

In summary then, body image is a fairly complex and sometimes abstract way in which we picture our bodies. Three components are necessary for the formation and maintenance of a normal body image. These are:

1. *Body reality* – The way in which our body is constructed, namely the way it really is. This is affected by both nature and nurture factors.
2. *Body ideal* – How we think we should look. We hold a personal body ideal which may also affect how we think other people 'should' look. At a professional level the nurse's body ideal may be informed by health standards. Body ideal is constantly changing and susceptible to a variety of influences.
3. *Body presentation* – How we present our body appearance (dress, pose, action) to the social world. We are able to control body presentation within certain limits, and to reflect actively on how body presentation was received by others.

Body image is, because of these variables, a very vulnerable part of our make-up. It hurts to be told that we are 'gangly', 'have no dress sense' or 'act clumsily'. Our body image depends not only upon our own body (our 'territory') but also upon fellow human beings, their appearance, attitudes and responses to us in the social world.

Self-image

Different people hold different views on what constitutes 'the self'. Just what it is, where it comes from, and how it should be expressed, are questions for perennial debate. This book deals with it more simplistically. G.H. Mead, a notable sociologist, argued that the self is composed of two interrelated parts which he rather confusingly called 'me' and 'I'. One aspect of self was the product of our personality – a unique blend of traits, attitudes and orientations which distinguished us from everyone else. The other aspect of self was the social self – created and moulded by the very processes of primary and secondary socialisation already discussed (Mead, 1934). Our notion of self-image probably stems from both of these aspects of self. We should like to believe that our self-image is congruous with, and is an expression of, our personality. Yet we also guess that our self-image is strongly affected by what other people think of us. Self-image then, is our own assessment of our social worth. It is composed of ideas of whether we are 'true unto ourselves' and whether others think we are worthwhile people. Self-image is important for our confidence our motivation and our sense of achievement.

Now the question arises, what part does body image play in all this? It is probably central to the creation of a self-image that is built upon our valuing the opinions and respect of others. The clearest way to explain this relationship is by reference to an illustration. Chapter 2 expands on the 'beauty is good' theme, but it is introduced here as a framework to help understand the relevance of body image to self-image formation and adjustment (see Figure 1.4). Assume that nurse Brown has developed a satisfactory body image of herself. She is young, her body is neither frail nor overweight, her skin is clear with no unsightly blemishes. Her uniform fits her properly and she is able to display important badges of status on her dress. Her movements in performing nursing duties are smooth and economical. All of these things accord closely with what nurse Brown thinks she should be like (body ideal). Nurse Brown has a successful body image.

What do nurse Brown's colleagues and clients think of her? In meeting her the patient notes that she looks smart and uses her skills to very good effect, feeling flattered that such a smart and efficient person should show him so much attention. In fact, he cannot help but smile at her and compliment her on her nursing care. Nurse Brown's colleagues also see that she creates a good image of the ward. She seems to encourage the patients to express their concerns and develop their confidence in the ward staff. Working with her is reasonably stress free because she 'looks as though she could cope'. One or two other nurses might be jealous of her, but do not express this openly as they suspect they will be accused of envy. Given that nurse Brown receives enough affirmative messages about her appearance and performance she may come to believe these comments are justified, feeling that she is worth a pat on the back. Through the mechanism of social acclaim, a good body image has tended to be instrumental in creating a good self-image.

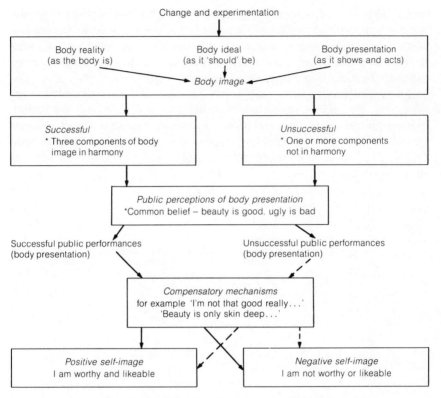

Fig. 1.4   The influence of body image on self-image.

Of course it may not be this straightforward. Nurse Brown may hold a variety of opinions which lead her to consider herself an unworthy, rather unpleasant person. When this occurs, the acclaim she receives is balanced against her private review of past behaviour, before she arrives at a current self-image. A further example might illustrate the negative side of self-image.

Nurse Green is obese and suffers from a long-standing acne problem. Her uniform does not fit very well, being tight around the waist, thus restricting her movements. Her care at the bedside looks less than polished. The patients say that she is jolly (they suspect that all fat people are probably jolly), but they do not compliment her on her work, only on her sense of humour. Nurse Green wanted to be like nurse Brown, but instead she has only a poor body image. There have been few ways in which she could disguise her excess weight. She would prefer not to be fat and has noticed how gross her movements seem to be. For her, the lack of praise and a shortfall of admirers, all confirm her feeling that she is not worth being with. Nurse Green is rapidly developing a negative self-image. She tries to compensate for this by being humorous, but this is only a partial answer. She believes that you have to be slim to be successful. In this second example, Nurse Green is poorly equipped to defend and develop a successful self-image. She may in the end turn to 'comfort eating' as an alternative, and perpetuate many of her difficulties!

These illustrations show that society acts as a mirror by which we judge ourselves. We care desperately what other people think of us. In a society that emphasises body presentation as a guide to social worth, we are forced to take our personal body image seriously. Failure to achieve a satisfactory image may affect our self-respect and with that, a number of life opportunities.

Conclusion

The chapter has outlined some of the components which comprise a normal body image and how important these are for the self. It explored how body image develops and what factors are important for that development. Normal body image is difficult to sustain because all three of the variables – body reality, body ideal and body presentation – are changing constantly. Trying to match up all three is a life-long challenge which we only succeed in transiently, or to a modified degree. If such a challenge is a life-long test for the healthy individual it can well be imagined what problems might be in store for the unhealthy, the disabled or the injured.

Review questions

1 In Chapter 1 body image has been closely defined using three component aspects. To what extent do you think average people are self-conscious about their body image? If they are not always, are there times when body image will be more noticeable, more important to them?

2 Can you identify any personal childhood influences which strongly affected your current body image?

3 Chapter 1 stated that culture and socialisation are strong influences upon the formation of normal body images. Do you think these influences can account for examples of bigotry or prejudice found in modern society?

4 To what extent are we able to resist outside influences which may affect our body ideal? If we reject current fashion for instance, are there any costs that we must be prepared to pay?

5 The personal body image of the nurse is not only important to her, but to the patient she cares for. Can you offer arguments to either support or disagree with this statement?

6 It may seem that we are manipulated by society regarding our body images. Do you think we in turn seek to affect the body image of others? If so, how?

7 To what extent does nurse education imbue within the student a professionally acceptable body image? (Remember, this may be achieved through a formal syllabus or a hidden professional socialisation!)

Suggested exercises

Exercise 1
Individually draw up a pen picture of your own body ideal and then choose a friend or colleague with whom to share a brief analysis of your findings. Try to decide what influences are most important for your body ideal and decide whether this ideal is used in turn to assess other people's body presentation. Consider your colleague's pen picture next. Although it would be best to choose a friend for this exercise with whom you are comfortable, it is not meant to become hypercritical.

Exercise 2
Cut out lots of pictures each of which emphasises at least one person (preferably colour) from a range of magazines and journals. On the back of each picture note the journal title and the article subject or advertisement which the picture accompanied. Then, with a group of friends take each picture in turn and answer the following questions, individually at first, then through discussion:

1. What sort of image is this person projecting through his or her body presentation? (eg confident, aloof, shy, vulnerable, sensuous)
2. What particular aspects of body presentation are used to create this image?
3. To what extent do you think that your interpretation of this person's image is affected by the setting in which he or she is portrayed?

Having shared your impressions with each other, if you have similar impressions about the person shown, can you agree how such a successful message has been achieved? If you differ, why do you think this is? Finally, discuss whether the image of the person in the picture is being manipulated in any way, either to sell you a product or to make you feel more receptive towards that person. Check the back of the picture for clues once you have made up your minds.

References

Erikson E., *Identity, Youth and Crisis*, Norton, New York, 1968.

Head H., *Studies in Neurology*, Oxford Press, London, 1920.

Kolb C., 'Disturbances of Body Image' in Arieti S. (ed.) *American Handbook of Psychiatry*, 4, pp 810–31, Basic Books, New York, 1975.

Mead G.H., *Mind, Self and Society*, University of Chicago Press, Chicago, 1934.

Nightingale F., *Notes On Nursing: What it is and what it is not*, Duckworth, London, 1859 (reprinted 1970).

Sandler J. and Rosenblatt B., 'The Concept of the Representational World', *Psychoanalytic Study of the Child*, 17, pp 128–45, 1962.

Schilder P., *The Image and Appearance of the Human Body*, Kegan Paul, London, 1935.

Secord P. and Jourard S., 'The Appraisal of Body Cathexis and the Self', *Journal of Consulting Psychology*, 17, pp 343–7, 1953.

Further reading

Adams G. and Crossman S., *Physical Attractiveness. A Cultural Imperative*, Libra Roslyn Heights, New York, 1978.

Dion K., Berscheid E. and Walster E., 'What Is Beautiful Is Good', *Journal of Personality and Social Psychology*, 24, p 285.

Fisher S. and Cleveland S., *Body Image and Personality*, Van Nostrand, Princetown, NJ, 1958.

Lacey J.H. and Birtchnell S.A., 'Body Image and Its Disturbances' (a review article), *Journal of Psychosomatic Research*, 30(6), pp 623–31, 1986.

Price B., 'First Impressions: Paradigms for patient assessment', *Journal of Advanced Nursing*, 12, pp 699–705, 1987.

Riddoch G., 'Phantom Limb and Body Shape', *Brain*, 64, pp 197–222, 1941.

2 Body image in a social world

Study of this chapter will enable you to:

1 Describe what is meant by the 'beauty is good' stereotype.
2 Outline Berscheid and Walster's four assumptions underpinning this stereotype.
3 Suggest why it is beneficial to be an 'attractive child'.
4 Discuss the part body image may play in courtship and marriage.
5 Outline the advantages and disadvantages of being attractive:
   (a) in the workplace
   (b) in the defendant's dock of the courtroom
6 Contribute to a discussion on the possible impact of body image on mental and physical well-being.

Abstract definitions of body image and self-image are of little value unless they are related to the real world. Therefore, this chapter will be building on illustrations from the previous chapter and considering the ways in which body image operates in particular social settings. This chapter will attempt to show that body image is not only developed within a social world, but that it is then used within the social world to secure life opportunities as they arise. Our needs for love, companionship, employment, success and education are realised through social relationships. Such relationships depend upon a degree of mutual trust, and in the early stages of a relationship at least trust is built upon a first impression of another person's body presentation.

We should perhaps like to think that we build our social relationships using an astute assessment of other people's characters, their finer qualities. In fact research tends to indicate that people are influenced by body presentation more than they would ever care to admit to. We operate using an unconscious stereotype, which Dion *et al* describe as 'what is beautiful is good'. This ascribes a wide range of social and personal qualities to those who either manage their body presentation well, or who have a culturally agreed attractive body reality (Dion *et al*, 1972).

Berscheid and Walster have outlined four assumptions that underpin this stereotype. First, we expect different behaviour in others, according to their degree of attractiveness. Secondly, we behave towards others differently according to how attractive they are. Thirdly, such interaction will have important implications for our respective social development. Fourthly, if an attractive person has been rewarded with positive behaviour from us, he or she will find it easier to behave in a socially desirable way in the future. If Berscheid and Walster are correct (and this seems possible), we should expect to find the 'beauty is good' stereotype operating in a wide range of social arenas (Berscheid and Walster, 1974).

Growing up

It is a truism that children can be terribly cruel. A boy with a 'broken' nose or a girl with prominent teeth might both attest to how quickly their peers single out such abnormalities for ridicule. Self-effacing jokes or a brace on the teeth may modify the criticism but the importance of having an attractive body reality cannot be denied. A variety of researchers have found that it is not only important to be attractive in peers' eyes but also in parents' and teachers' eyes too (Dion, 1973; Dion and Berscheid, 1974).

Adams and La Voie, examining parental expectations of their children, found that unattractive children were thought to be less likely to develop good interpersonal skills (Adams and La Voie, 1975). Dion found that badly behaved attractive looking children were dealt with more leniently by their mothers, while unattractive children were suspected of starting to show antisocial traits (Dion, 1972). This interplay of child and parental behaviour was highlighted by Osofsky and O'Connell. They argued that child socialisation was never one way from parent to child, but that the child's behaviour would strongly affect the way the parents acted too (Osofsky and O'Connell, 1972). Other research (MacGregor et al, 1953) pointed out that mothers expected their daughters to be attractive and would react negatively if they were not. Boys it seems did not have to meet such exacting standards, it being more important for them to show qualities of an independent mind.

When the child leaves home for school the body image issue remains important. In junior school, despite efforts to minimise bias, the attractive child continues to be rated more favourably by teachers (Clifford and Walster, 1973; Adams and Cohen, 1976). The child's behaviour and class background may limit such bias, but the favourable rating remains significant at a time when the child is starting to value opinions other than those of his or her parents. In older age groups Singer found tentative evidence to show that college lecturers might also be swayed in their marking by an attractive face (Singer, 1964).

It would seem then, that from an early age children are exposed to a 'beauty is good' stereotype. If this is true and Berscheid and Walster's assumptions are correct, we may expect that a number of children would not gain the most from their education and might develop negative feelings about their self-worth. In fact the picture is not quite so simple. While Dion found that women were more willing in experiments to ascribe blame to naughty unattractive children, she also found that the same group of women would punish attractive girls more than attractive boys (Dion, 1974). Thus, female beauty carried a responsibility of correct behaviour. A God given gift of attractiveness had at times to be supported by exceptional manners or good behaviour. When Dion tried a similar experiment involving men, the child's attractiveness did not appear to be significant in punishment decisions. The male group of subjects penalised the children by using a range of other criteria.

Love and marriage

Body image is especially important for choosing and keeping a mate. Folk wisdom has it that beauty is in the eye of the beholder, that beauty is only skin deep and that we may date by sexual attraction but marry according to wider personal quality criteria. Research tends not to support this very well. From early adolescence the development of conventionally admired sexual attributes appears important to men and women alike. Surprisingly, we do tend to agree on what is a beautiful body and what is an ugly one. Huston, Curran and Cavior et al all confirm the existence of a physical attractiveness stereotype in dating and marriage (Cavior et al, 1974; Curran, 1973; Huston, 1973). In western culture this emphasises slimness, smooth skin texture, and bust, waist and hip measurements. Such a stereotype appears to be important not only through courtship, but during marriage as well (Mathes, 1975).

Conventions about attractive body size and contour have tended to affect women more than men. Goin has described the importance of the breast as a symbol of sensuality, femininity and nurturance (Goin, 1982). Edgerton et al, Hooper and Knorr, and Sihm et al have all reported the importance of the breast to women who sought augmentation mammoplasty in their middle years (Edgerton et al, 1981; Hooper and Knorr, 1972; Sihm et al, 1978). Typically, such women were married, tended to suffer with shyness, sexual or marital difficulties, and periods of depression. A breast enhancing operation was seen as a way to put more matters to right than just the woman's figure. Smaller numbers of younger women also found the symbolic meaning of the breast to be problematic. They sought breast reduction in order to avoid lewd comments or approaches (Hollyman et al, 1986).

If physical attractiveness is seen as an advantage in the dating stakes, it can also be a disadvantage when found in excess. Dabbs and Stokes found that exceptionally attractive women might not at first receive invitations because they were perceived as out of the suitor's league (Dabbs and Stokes, 1975). Presumably individuals review their own body presentation in the light of that of the intended date. If the two are roughly equal then a confident approach may be made. This may then lead to beautiful people marrying other beautiful people, with all that might imply for social equality and social opportunities.

The work place

Many of the same opportunities to impress through attractiveness might be afforded through job interviews and the workplace. Here, however, the picture is a little more blurred. It would be necessary to separate out quite complex variables of power, employer–employee gender and types of workplace before being able to predict about attractiveness *per se*. Landy and Sigall studied male college tutors who were asked to read an essay prepared by attractive or unattractive female students. While this study does not address the workplace directly, it does take up the point about measuring someone else's work which is a daily aspect of business. Good essays (independently assessed) were rated as good by the male tutors, irrespective of whether they had originated from the photographed attractive or unattractive females. Poor essays from attractive students were rated much more highly than those from unattractive students. These researchers concluded that beauty could carry through an indifferent piece of work and that the struggling unattractive student might be doubly handicapped (Landy and Sigall, 1974).

Snyder *et al* found that the belief that an unseen person was attractive could encourage an intercom caller to talk enthusiastically. This in turn would encourage an unattractive call recipient to make an improved response. Selected males were offered a photograph of an attractive woman and told that she would be receiving their call. Videotapes recorded the behaviour of the unattractive females who in fact shared the call in another room. Their responses were then compared to those responses offered by women receiving calls from men who had been led to believe they were talking to an unattractive woman. Snyder found that there was an enthusiastic contribution on the part of the unattractive women and that this was due to the male callers' animated conversation (Snyder *et al*, 1977). This sort of research may have important implications, not only for understanding office relations, but for our ability to promote adjustment of body presentation in general.

Justice

Perhaps the most disturbing research relates to the area of crime and justice. The decisions of judge and jury are supposed to be impartial, founded on the circumstances of the case and guided by the edicts of law. Several researchers have noted that an attractive defendant might expect a less than objective judgment. Sigall and Ostrove suggested that where attractive defendants have been seen to use their good looks to exploit others, they received harsher judgments in a simulated court setting (Sigall and Ostrove, 1973). Dermer and Thiel found that when an attractive defendant was judged by a jury of unattractive persons, jealousy might play a role and the defendant be given a harsher appraisal (Dermer and Thiel, 1975). Against this, a number of researchers found that attractive defendants might receive more generous judgments if their attractiveness did not seem implicated in the crime (Monahan, 1941; Morse *et al*, 1974).

Conclusion

From these studies it is clear that body image has a profound effect upon our social lives. Our ability to achieve personal goals and to sustain a comfortable social niche may be limited by body reality or body presentation. 'First impressions count' runs the saying, and such impressions are often visual or tactile ones. Second and subsequent impressions may still be strongly affected by body image considerations.

The relationship between physical attractiveness and life opportunities is not totally positive. There is adequate research to indicate that an attractive body presentation will often afford the individual benefits in a variety of settings. Against this it seems that exceptional beauty brings with it some costs and responsibilities, especially for women.

Given that we look to fellow humans for approval and trust, it is worrying to note how often the research implies that a poor body image results in a poor self-image. Resultant mental and physical health problems are the domain of the nurse. Understanding many such health problems might require an appreciation of the subject here, the body image in a social world.

Review questions

1 In this chapter it has been argued that attractive individuals receive greater social opportunities. An individual may be seen as attractive

due to his or her physique (body reality) and/or a graceful manner and dress (body presentation). Is one of these more important?

2 To what extent do you think individuals use their body image consciously to achieve social goals? Are we manipulators, using our body presentation to direct social interaction?

3 If the 'beauty is good' stereotype does in fact guide social opinion, what does this imply for individuals suddenly scarred or disabled?

4 Review your own childhood. Thinking back to school groups, would you agree that some members were seen as attractive and others as unattractive? What was the effect of attractiveness upon group cohesion and morale?

5 How did you assess your attractiveness during adolescence? Did you do anything to 'improve' this?

Suggested exercise

It has been pointed out that a physical attractiveness stereotype exists and that this in turn is culturally determined. Try out a small-scale enquiry to explore this for yourself. Collect together colour head and shoulder pictures of ten individuals. The individuals featured should all be of the same sex and not members of your group or known associates. All individuals chosen should be either smiling or stern faced. A smile can affect appraisal of the image, so every individual image should be chosen to follow a general pattern. Old large size college or school photographs may serve for this exercise as most individuals will be dressed similarly.

Now cut out the relevant 'faces' and glue them to a sheet, labelling each face with a letter. Ask a sample of twenty other nurses from similar cultural background to examine the picture parade. Invite them to choose in order the three most attractive faces and then the three least attractive faces.

Take these findings into a discussion group and report on whether there was a strong agreement on the most attractive and unattractive faces. Try to determine reasons why your findings either supported or challenged the physical attractiveness stereotype argument.

References

Adams G. and Cohen R., 'Characteristics of Children and Teacher Expectancy: An extension to the child's social and family life', *Journal of Educational Research*, 69, pp 124–31, 1976.

Adams G. and La Voie J., 'Parental Expectations of Educational and Personal–social Performance and Child Rearing Patterns As A Function of Attractiveness, Sex and Conduct of the Child', *Child Study Journal*, 5, pp 125–42, 1975.

Berscheid E. and Walster E., 'Physical Attractiveness', in Berkowitz *Advances in Experimental Social Psychology*, Vol. 6. Academic Press, New York, 1974.

Cavior N., Jacobs A. and Jacobs M., The Stability and Correlation of Physical Attractiveness and Sex Appeal Ratings, Unpublished manuscript, West Virginia University, Morgantown, 1974.

Clifford M. and Walster E., 'The Effect of Physical Attractiveness On Teacher Expectations', *Sociology of Education*, 46, pp 248–58, 1973.

Curran J., 'Correlates of Physical Attractiveness and Interpersonal Attraction In The Dating Situation', *Social Behaviour and Personality*, 1, pp 153–7, 1973.

Dabbs J. and Stokes N., 'Beauty Is Power: The use of space on the sidewalk', *Sociometry*, 38, pp 551–7, 1975.

Dermer M. and Thiel D., 'When Beauty May Fail', *Journal of Personality and Social Psychology*, 31, pp 1168–76, 1975.

Dion K., 'Physical Attractiveness and Evaluation of Children's Transgressions', *Journal of Personality and Social Psychology*, 24, pp 207–13, 1972.

Dion K. 'Young Children's Stereotyping of Facial Attractiveness' *Developmental Psychology*, 9, pp 183–8, 1973.

Dion K., 'Children's Physical Attractiveness and Sex as Determinants of Adult Punitiveness', *Developmental Psychology*, 10, pp 772–8, 1974.

Dion K. and Berscheid E., 'Physical Attractiveness and Peer Perception Among Children', *Sociometry*, 37, pp 1–12, 1974.

Dion K., Berscheid E. and Walster E., 'What is Beautiful is Good', *Journal of Personality and Social Psychology*, 24(3), pp 285–90, 1972.

Edgerton M., Jacobsen W. and Meyer E., 'Augmentation Mammaplasty: Further surgical and psychiatric evaluation', *Plastic and Reconstructive Surgery*, 27, p 279, 1981.

Goin M., 'Psychological Reactions to Surgery of the Breast', *Clinics in Plastic Surgery*, 9, pp 347–54, 1982.

Hollyman J., Lacey J., Whitfield P. and Wilson J., 'Surgery For The Psyche: A longitudinal study of women undergoing reduction mammaplasty', *British Journal of Plastic Surgery*, 39, pp 222–4, 1986.

Hooper, J. and Knorr N., 'Psychology of the Flat Chested Woman', in *Matter Symposium on Aesthetic Surgery of the Face, Eyelids and Breast*, C.V. Mosby, St Louis, 1972.

Huston T., 'Ambiguity of Acceptance, Social Desirability, and Dating Choice', *Journal of Experimental Social Psychology*, 9, pp 32–42, 1973.

Landy D. and Sigall H., 'Beauty is Talent. Task Evaluation as a Function of the Performers Physical Attractiveness', *Journal of Personality and Social Psychology*, 29, pp 299–304, 1974.

MacGregor F. *et al*, *Facial Deformities and Plastic Surgery*, Charles C. Thomas, Springfield, Illinois, 1953.

Mathes E., 'The Effects of Physical Attractiveness and Anxiety on Heterosexual Attraction Over a Series of Five Encounters', *Journal of Marriage and the Family*, 37, pp 769–74, 1975.

Monahan F., *Women in Crime*, Washburn, New York, 1941.

Morse S., Reis H. and Wolff E., 'The "Eye of the Beholder" Determinants of Physical Attractiveness: Judgements in the US and South Africa', *Journal of Personality*, 42, pp 528–42, 1974.

Osofsky J. and O'Connell E., 'Parent–Child Interaction: Daughters' effects upon mothers and fathers' behaviour', *Developmental Psychology*, 7, pp 157–68, 1972.

Sigall H. and Ostrove N., 'Effects of Physical Attractiveness of the Defendant and Nature of the Crime on Juridic Judgement', in *Proceedings of the 81st Annual Convention of the American Psychological Association*, 8, p 267, 1973.

Sihm F., Jag M. and Peras M., 'Psychological Assessment Before and After Augmentation Mammaplasty', *Scandinavian Journal of Plastic and Reconstructive Surgery*, 12, pp 295–8, 1978.

Singer J., 'The Use of Manipulative Strategies. Machiavellianism and Attractiveness', *Sociometry*, 24, pp 128–50, 1964.

Snyder M., Tanke E. and Berscheid E., 'Social Perception and Interpersonal Behaviour: On the self fulfilling nature of social stereotypes', *Journal of Personality and Social Psychology*, 35, p 656, 1977.

3   Ageing – aspects of body image

Study of this chapter will enable you to:

1 Identify the life events which might affect an adequate body image in the elderly.
2 Discuss briefly why old age is a period of considerable change in body image.
3 Outline the changes occurring in body reality.
4 Account for why it may be difficult for the elderly to develop a satisfactory body ideal.
5 List body attachments which may disrupt body image in the elderly.
6 Discuss why the elderly have difficulty in expressing sexuality.
7 Outline the ways in which the elderly use camouflage to assist body presentation.
8 Review critically the stereotypes commonly offered about the elderly.

Growing old gracefully is probably one of the most widely held goals of men and women alike. It requires many human qualities – a sense of humour, the humility to accept a tiring body and the wisdom that just as we had to evolve a new body image in youth, so we must adapt again now in old age. Because ageing affects human biology, thought and social activity, it follows that it must also affect body image. During fifteen or even twenty years of retirement the elderly try to support a frail body reality, to create a satisfying body ideal and to practise body presentation which will bring the reality and the ideal a little closer together.

Being old is not just a chronological event. It has a symbolic meaning within society. Just as we create stereotypes of attractiveness and sexuality in youth, so now in senior years, the elderly have to deal with stereotypes about old age. Some are attractive, the 'Darby and Joan' stereotype is a case in point – contented, companionable couples sharing reminiscenses and a cosy if constrained life style. Other positive stereotypes recall the wisdom of old age – the wise and experienced village or tribal elder.

25

Unfortunately, in many western societies, the negative stereotype prevails. While society continues to applaud a youth and beauty culture, the image of old age will continue to be one of decay and decrepitude.

Achieving a satisfactory body image, being at peace with body and appearance, is important. A happy person is a long living person (Dunbar and Dunbar, 1954). Getting body image 'right' may offset other disappointments. The life events of old age tend to emphasise a withdrawal from active, economically productive life. Retirement (Wright, 1960) can signify a loss of value in one's life, but it need not. Elderly people may find that they no longer retain leadership positions, even if they are not forced to retire *per se* (Rose and Peterson, 1965). They become aware of the progressive loss of peers and friends and then, most telling of all, the loss of a spouse (Esberger, 1978). Under these circumstances the maintenance of an adequate body image can be very difficult, but paradoxically it can prove a resource to independent living. Communities may welcome the well groomed and well presented older person into the fold, while the ill kept and untidy may be assigned little respect and only an institutionalised life.

Changes in body reality

The rate of change in the elderly body is very variable, depending in part upon genetics, gender and previous lifestyle. It is a good maxim that well used body tissues are well preserved body tissues. Nevertheless, from the fourth and fifth decade, and in some respects even before then, there is a steady decline in the structure and function of body systems (see Table 3.1). The skin becomes wrinkled and loose, the quantity of subcutaneous tissue which supported the skin decreases. Pigmentation of the skin occurs making the individual appear 'blotchy' to a grandchild, and blood vessels may rupture resulting in the 'jolly' red nose. The hair thins and greys, a process affecting body hair as well as the scalp, and in the male, balding may occur.

In the musculo-skeletal system the elderly notice muscle atrophy, so that mobility and dexterity is limited. Joint deterioration through osteoarthrosis, and calcium loss from bone, exacerbate the problem. Demineralisation of bones, particularly the spinal vertebrae and long bones affect women following the menopause. A 'dowager hump' appears as a result of loss of vertebral integrity and the increasing curvature of the spine, making the elderly person two or three inches shorter than in adult life.

Other body changes affect elimination capabilities. An enlarged prostate in the male and loss of pelvic floor muscle control in the female can promote incontinence and with it, infection, frequency and urgency of

Table 3.1 Changes in body reality

Body system	Change	Implications
Skin	Loss of subcutaneous tissue, decreased production of sebum. Thinning hair, turning grey/white. Pigmentation changes in skin.	Lost tissue turgor, wrinkles. Dry skin and nails, cracking. Balding (symbol of lost virility, youth?).
Musculo-skeletal	Muscle tissue substituted with fat. Muscle atrophy. Demineralisation of bone. Shrinkage and distortion of spinal vertebrae, joint deterioration.	Lost height, stoop of old age. Loss of limb 'bulk' compared with trunk. Impaired balance and posture/locomotion.
Cardio-pulmonary	Endocardium thickened, deterioration in heart valves. Reduced stroke volume under stress. Atherosclerotic changes in blood vessels, decreased respiratory compliance and vital capacity of lungs. Reduced cough reflex.	Limited exercise tolerance. Poor peripheral circulation leading to cyanosis and tissue degeneration. Dyspnoea, panting, inhibited communication.
Elimination systems	Decreased renal function – glomerular filtration rate and clearance of metabolic wastes. Lower genito-urinary system – muscle weakness (pelvic floor) and obstructions such as prostate enlargement. Altered patterns of bowel activity. Lost digestive enzymes.	Lethargy, limited exercise tolerance. Unpredictable patterns of elimination, lost continence. Constipation. Weight loss/gain.
Special senses	Deterioration in taste bud sensitivity. Eye lens loses facility to focus easily, decreased peripheral vision and adaptation to dark. Lost hearing – cochlea and auditory nerve damage.	Need for artificial appendages such as eyeglasses, hearing aid, walking stick. Poor speech discrimination Need to ask for repeated messages.
Reproductive system	Minimal changes in overall sexual potential. Decreased vaginal secretions, increased refractory period for men. Slower penile erection, female may experience vaginal spasm.	Potential signal for the ending of sexual activity and identity.

micturition. Chronic incontinence causes excoriation of perineal skin and damages underwear, trousers or slacks. Peristalsis in the gastro-intestinal tract may not be so radically affected by ageing. Still, dietary indiscretion, reduced mobility and laxative abuse may precipitate constipation. In both cases, urinary and faecal patterns of elimination become less predictable, with attendant anxiety for the individual.

Cardio-pulmonary deterioration limits the exercise tolerance of the elderly. A decrease in the vital capacity of the lungs and reduced chest wall compliance, limit the ways in which we can express our feelings and aspirations. Failing vision, taste and hearing (degeneration of cochlea and auditory nerve) all reduce the stimuli to which the elderly can respond. Compensation measures, the wearing of eyeglasses and hearing aids (no matter how miniature) all affect the appearance of elderly body reality. At meal times, the addition of large quantities of table salt to meals and sugar to beverages is a noticeable trend and one that in the longer term undermines health.

Deteriorating endocrine and reproductive function is epitomised in the female menopause and the slowing of sexual responses in both sexes. Gray notes that the adrenal glands compensate for the loss of female hormones for some time after loss of ovulation, but that the changes are inevitable (Gray, 1967). Guyton has pointed out that the menopause, and the resultant reduction in vaginal lubrication is also very much a psychological event (Guyton, 1971). Male menopauses may also be expected, often in the early or middle fifties. Total sexual response may be remarkably unchanged, but it is the speed and maintenance of response which may prove more problematic. Penile erection may take longer, the frequency of coital urge reduce. Coitus may still however prove pleasurable and a bond between a couple.

Changes in body ideal

The search for an adequate body ideal in old age may be interpreted as one of Erikson's life tasks (Erikson, 1963). Can the individual accept his or her life, appearance and person as having been worthwhile, or does the individual sink into despair? A well adjusted individual can look in the mirror without horror, and upon reviewing life say honestly, 'I wouldn't do it differently if I had my life over again. I did it my way'! At this level the individual uses personal reminiscences to model a body ideal – the product of worthwhile life experiences. At another, he or she turns to the outside world and seeks models which may stand for the dignity and grace that it is felt are the essence of twilight years.

The problem of plotting the elderly's body ideal, or body image in general has exercised a number of researchers (Gilbert and Hall, 1962;

Lakin, 1956; Plutchik *et al*, 1971; Schiff, 1976). The elderly have been asked to fill in questionnaires about body aches and pains, what insurance value they would place on various body attributes, to draw whole figure drawings of human beings and to complete standard index tests. It is not always clear that the results of this research are a true indication of what the elderly would like to look like. The results may reflect a deterioration in mental or psychomotor function. Even social mores on drawing style (think of the Egyptian pyramid drawings) may affect the elderly's figure drawing (Janelli, 1986).

Despite this, some findings seem to be worth noting. McClosky found that elderly people might avoid the use of a hearing aid because it formed an unacceptable extension of their body boundary (McClosky, 1976). Horowitz had already shown that part of our body image is made up of a body space, a territory around our body which we consider 'home ground' (Horowitz, 1966). Filling that space with attachments such as a hearing aid might cause the elderly to feel their boundaries had extended, or been breached, and that they were now less compact and in control.

Lakin found that the institutionalised elderly often drew small human figures. He ascribed this to self-devaluation on the part of the individuals. In 1960 Lakin extended the work and found that non-institutionalised elderly people drew taller and more adequately centred figure drawings. It was argued that it was not age itself which determined body image, but life status. An independent setting and good social relationships would enable the elderly to form an adequate body ideal, a more satisfying body image (Lakin, 1960).

Part of the body ideal of the elderly relates to sexuality. The ideal may be one of continued sexual activity and attraction, at a time when social mores promote a stereotype of elderly asexuality. Despite the work of Kinsey *et al* and Masters and Johnson (Kinsey *et al*, 1948, 1953; Masters and Johnson, 1966), there has been a pervasive idea that sexual activity is for the young (Pfeiffer and Davis, 1972; Kaas 1978). Embarassment at holding an ideal of sexual activity can lead to the elderly trying either to suppress their feelings, or else adjusting body presentation so as not to be an elderly person anymore. The phenomenon of elderly people dressing in clothes and using jewellery associated with younger, more sexually active age groups is reasonably common. Just how difficult an equation this all can be for the elderly depends upon the sex of the individual. Fisher argued that men and women have very different experiences of ageing. Men and women value their body attributes in different ways; for example, men seeing their legs as a means of locomotion, women seeing theirs also as sexual attributes. Because the woman is more body conscious and is used to adjusting body presentation, it could be asserted that she is better equipped to strive for suitable new body ideals in old age. Failing body function may affect the male body image more (Fisher, 1964).

Body presentation – coping strategies

At a time when body reality is deteriorating and a new body ideal is slow to become established, it is not surprising that body presentation is difficult for the elderly. A lack of fluidity and grace in movement, a tremor, poorly controlled micturition and now ill-fitting clothes can all contribute to a very poor body presentation. Previous surgery, the fitting of dentures or other prostheses will not have helped. Esberger has pointed out how all of these issues appear as a threat to the elderly (Esberger, 1978). In a milieu that is very image conscious, equating beauty with social worth, it is very easy for the elderly to develop coping strategies which present a less pleasant face to the world.

One strategy has been to develop hypochondriasis, creating a ready made rationale for deteriorating appearance. If a range of medicines are consumed each may excuse in part the limitations of the elderly body presentation. Alternatively, the elderly may refuse to examine critically their own body presentation. Mirrors may be banned, visits to the doctor avoided, as the latter is itself a social mirror on their ability to maintain independence. If the elderly person does wear spectacles these may be left at home when going out, sometimes to disastrous effect. Butler and Lewis note that many elderly spend a lot of time 'body monitoring', adjusting activities to compensate for body functions which are failing (Butler and Lewis, 1973). This may include pacing housework, travel or dressing, so as to sustain the best possible body presentation when important people are

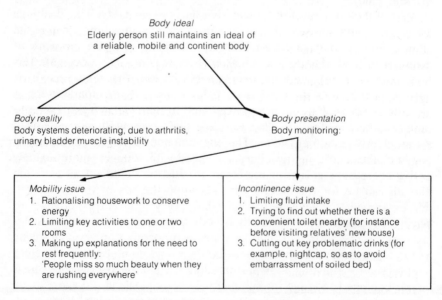

Fig. 3.1   Body monitoring – a body presentation strategy amongst the elderly.

met. This is significant considering the work of the general practitioner, district nurse or health visitor (see Figure 3.1.).

Where finances and mobility allow, a considerable amount of camouflaging may be undertaken. Elderly ladies may choose to use hair colourings and rinses, makeup and wigs to sustain a reasonably glamorous presentation. Such measures can be extremely successful when skin tone is taken properly into account. More radically still, cosmetic surgery may be employed to 'lift' a face or remove a wrinkle. Choice in clothes now emphasises a softer figure line and is labelled the classic look. Elderly men may turn to hair colourings too. The choice of a stylish walking stick, pipe or gold filled teeth are all examples of active camouflage technique.

In the field of sexuality, the elderly may still choose attractive clothing, but now the emphasis may be upon underwear. Loss of vaginal secretions may be augmented by a lubricating gel. The elderly man professes that it is quality of love making, rather than quantity that counts. Reference may be made to 'rushed sex' in youth but now it is as it should be, slow and considerate. For Masters and Johnson this shared interpretation of the sexual act is paramount if couples are to sustain a healthy sex life in old age (Masters and Johnson, 1982).

Conclusion

In the opening remarks of this book it was argued that body image is a dynamic concept, tied to the changing life events of the individual. Such change does not end with the onset of old age. Indeed, if we were to look for periods of extensive change in body image we could well pick out adolescence and old age as two 'hot spots'. The elderly may reasonably be assumed to have a body image which is unique to each individual. The body image is determined by life circumstances rather than the process of ageing *per se*. Given this however, change in body reality and body ideal are still problematic to most elderly people. Arriving at an adequate body presentation will depend upon the individual's physical and monetary resources, and upon society's acceptance of the elderly as valuable members of society. Given recent trends, the latter of these points may be very difficult to achieve.

Review questions

1 The menopause has been described as a psychological as well as a physical event. To what extent do you expect the menopause to affect your own body image?

2 The stereotypical view of the elderly as asexual is widely held. Imagine

that you were asked by an elderly woman, 'how might I continue to enjoy comfortable sex?'. How would this affect your ideas about her body image?

3 Trying to assess the elderly person's body image through asking him to draw a human body is problematic. Describe why this is so.

4 What effects do a walking stick, zimmer frame and incontinence pants have upon an elderly person's body presentation? (You should be able to answer this in terms of the person's body space).

5 Why is 'body monitoring' in the elderly significant when the community nurse makes an assessment of the elderly person's ability to cope at home?

6 To what extent are the elderly poor disadvantaged in maintaining an adequate body presentation?

Suggested exercises

Exercise 1
As a group, watch a selected television serial episode, or a film featuring at least one elderly person. Ask one sub-group of students to note changes or deficits in body reality and the second sub-group to observe body presentation of the elderly person. After viewing, ask each group to discuss their findings for 15 minutes, before providing a short summary to the whole class. Having discovered the person's body reality and body presentation, discuss the body ideal you think the elderly person was employing. The feedback discussion phase of this exercise should take 60 minutes altogether – 30 minutes' summary, plus 30 minutes' discussion.)

Exercise 2
Ask the group members to collect pictures, catalogue photographs or real life examples of appendages (for example, spectacles, hearing aids, walking sticks) which the elderly might use. Review each item in turn (perhaps asking each group to examine a different item), considering their impact upon the elderly person's body image especially body presentation. Consider how such items could be made more aesthetically pleasing. This exercise should take about 60 minutes, depending on group size.

References

Butler R. and Lewis M., *Ageing and Mental Health*, C.V. Mosby, St Louis, 1973.
Dunbar F. and Dunbar F., 'A Study of Centenarians', quoted in Soloman J.C., *A Synthesis of Human Behaviour*, Grune & Stratton, New York, p 237, 1954.

Erikson E., *Childhood and Society*, 2nd edn, W.W. Norton & Co., New York, 1963.

Esberger K., 'Body Image', *Journal of Gerontological Nursing*, 4(4), pp 35–8, 1978.

Fisher S., 'Sex Differences in Body Perception', *Psychological Monographs*, 78, pp 1–22, 1964.

Gilbert J. and Hall M., 'Changes With Age in Human Figure Drawings', *Journal of Gerontology*, 17, pp 397–404, 1962.

Gray M., *The Normal Woman*, C. Scribners' Sons, New York, 1967.

Guyton A., *Basic Human Physiology*, WB Saunders, Philadelphia, 1971.

Horowitz M., 'Body Image', *Archives of General Psychiatry*, 14, pp 213–20, 1966.

Janelli L., 'Body Image in Older Adults: A review of the literature', *Rehabilitation Nursing*, 11(4), pp 6–8, 1986.

Kaas M., 'Sexual Expression of the Elderly in Nursing Homes', *Gerontologist*, 18(4), pp 372–8, 1978.

Kinsey A., Pomeroy W. and Martin C., *Sexual Behaviour in the Human Male*, WB Saunders, Philadelphia, 1948.

Kinsey A., Pomeroy W. and Martin C., *Sexual Behaviour in the Human Female*, WB Saunders, Philadelphia, 1953.

Lakin M., 'Formal Characteristics of Human Figure Drawings by Institutionalized Aged and by Normal Children', *Journal of Consulting Psychology*, 20, pp 471–4, 1956.

Lakin M., 'Formal Characteristics of Human Figure Drawings by Institutionalised and Noninstitutionalised Aged', *Journal of Gerontology*, 15, pp 76–8, 1960.

Masters W. and Johnson V., *Human and Sexual Response*, Little, Brown & Co., Boston, 1966.

Masters W. and Johnson V., 'Sex and the Ageing Process', *Medical Aspects of Human Sexuality*, 16(6), pp 40–57, 1982.

McClosky J., 'The Most in Body Image Theory in Nursing Practice', *Nursing*, 76(76), pp 68–72, 1976.

Pfeiffer E. and Davis G., 'Determinants of Sexual Behaviour in Middle and Old Age', *Journal of American Geriatrics Society*, 20, pp 151–8, 1972.

Plutchik R., Weiner M. and Conte H., 'Studies of Body Image 1: Body worries and body discomforts', *Journal of Gerontology*, 26, pp 344–50, 1971.

Plutchik R., Conte H. and Weiner M., 'Studies of Body Image 2: Dollar values of body parts', *Journal of Gerontology*, 28, pp 89–91, 1972.

Rose A. and Peterson W., *Older People and their Social World*, FA Davis, Philadelphia, 1965.

Schiff N., 'A Study of the Differences in the Draw a Person Test of Normal Elderly Females and Normal Adult Females', Ann Arbor, MI Xerox University, Microfilms (Dissertation), 1976.

Wright B., *Physical Disability – A psychological approach*, Harper & Row, New York, 1960.

Unit 2
Altered body image

To a limited degree, all injuries, illnesses and treatments may be said to involve some alteration to body image. The alteration may be slight and temporary, and the patient may not even notice the change in body image. In other instances body image changes may be major, the damage evident for all to see. This unit will be exploring the wide range of circumstances under which altered body image may come about, how the patient may respond, and what significance this may have for the patient's future life. In looking at Goffman's work on stigma, it will be apparent that the journey back to a normal body image is limited not only by the nature of the body image injury and the patient's coping strategies, but by others' reaction to the damaged body. Unit 2 outlines further concepts which can be applied to a wide variety of patient problems and needs.

4   Origins of altered body image

Study of this chapter will enable you to:

1 Define in simple terms what altered body image is.
2 Give examples of external environmental threats to normal body image.
3 Give examples of internal environmental threats to normal body image.
4 Describe the ways in which medical therapy may cause an altered body image problem.
5 Discuss briefly (using Table 4.1), what is meant by an 'open' and a 'hidden' altered body image problem.
6 Review your daily pattern of living, identifying threats to your own body image.

In life it is necessary not only to adapt to changing patterns of normal body image, but also to altered body image. Here, altered body image is defined as any significant alteration to body image occurring outside the realms of expected human development. Accordingly, pregnancy and ageing are aspects of normal body image, whereas trauma, pathological and degenerative change are examples of situations bringing about altered body image. Altered body image is also a very personal matter. What may prove a body image problem for one individual, may be quite insignificant to another. Defining altered body image may therefore depend upon our experiences of, and adaptability within, normal body image. The more flexible we are, the better we are at maintaining body presentation and less likely to perceive problems in body image terms.

Altered body image may originate either from the external or the internal environment (see Figure 4.1). Some problems occur as a result of the two environments interacting, for example coal dust leading to chronic bronchitis and limited exercise tolerance in a miner. The external environment has changed remarkably in the face of industrialisation and pollution. Altered body image problems are in part an illustration of our failure to control successfully, or adapt to, the environment we live in.

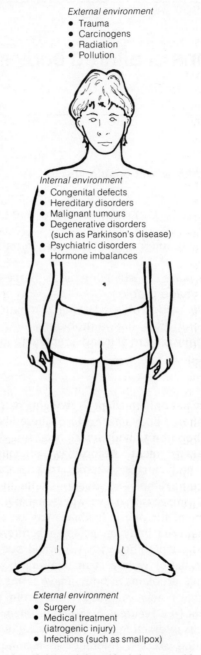

External environment
- Trauma
- Carcinogens
- Radiation
- Pollution

Internal environment
- Congenital defects
- Hereditary disorders
- Malignant tumours
- Degenerative disorders
  (such as Parkinson's disease)
- Psychiatric disorders
- Hormone imbalances

External environment
- Surgery
- Medical treatment
  (iatrogenic injury)
- Infections (such as smallpox)

Fig. 4.1   Origins of altered body image problems.

The external environment

Human beings expose themselves daily to risks which may radically damage body reality, the ability to sustain a pleasing body ideal and body presentation. For example, on an average weekday morning Mr Brown makes breakfast. To produce this meal it is necessary to use electricity, with all the attendant risks of kitchen accidents and burns. If Mr or Mrs Brown electrocute themselves there is an increasing chance that they will survive, even though the burn may be relatively major (Bowden *et al*, 1980). Improved survivial statistics do not remove the legacy of damage, to the face, limbs and torso. The burns, resultant keloid tissue formation and subsequent grafting or contracture releasing operations all contribute their share of trauma to body reality, ideal and presentation.

Having avoided first traumas, Mr and Mrs Brown drive to work. There has been a dramatic increase in road traffic accidents throughout the western world (Trust, 1987). Young *et al* discovered that motor vehicle accidents formed a significant cause of spinal cord injuries and that the majority of spinal cord victims would be male, with some half of these being young, aged 25 or younger (Young *et al*, 1982). The use of seat belts may have reduced the incidence of chest and facial injuries brought about by impact with steering wheel and windscreen, but these may be replaced by whiplash injuries to the cervical spine. A facial trauma may be replaced by a quadra or paraplegia problem.

The workplace may be equally risky for the Browns. Mr Brown may either suffer a direct trauma such as a fall, or mutilation from machinery, or he may suffer a more gradual damage resulting from pollution, for example the result of asbestos dust. Work on industrial or building sites is especially dangerous, leading to spinal and musculo-skeletal trauma (Richmond and Metcalf, 1986). The growth of health and safety legislation, safety drills and procedures, environmental health control has gone some way to limiting the problem. Occupational health nurses have also played their part. Nevertheless, the workplace is still intrinsically a dangerous place.

Even if the Browns come to no harm during the working day, there are still risks ahead during a social evening out. Sports injuries, trauma associated with the excesses of alcohol and other drugs are all possible problems that may await this imaginary couple.

Another group of individuals will suffer altered body image as a result of surgery or other medical treatment (Gruendemann, 1975; Raab 1986). At the most simple level, even the addition of a naso-gastric tube or an intravenous infusion may significantly disrupt a patient's body image. The naso-gastric tube disrupts the symmetry of the face. The intravenous infusion limits (most frequently) the arm, a limb which is critical to good body presentation.Wright and Wright, and Marcus have pointed to the large numbers of patients seeking cosmetic surgery (Marcus, 1986; Wright and Wright, 1975). Here, as in trauma, numbers are on the increase. As technology, such as fibreoptic tubes, has improved the opportunities for discrete or fine surgery, so the demand has grown. Patients may suffer scarring not only through the correction of body function failure (for example, a cholescystectomy), but also through the efforts of cosmetically assisting body presentation (Roy, 1986). The list of cosmetic operations available grows ever longer. We may have our face made to look younger, cleft lips repaired, breasts augmented or reduced in size. Excess can be trimmed from our contours, hair transplanted and the shape of our eyes made to look caucasian. While the goal of such surgery is to improve, there is always the possibility of some residual damage, no matter how unintentional. More major iatrogenic damage is not uncommon, the wrong limb having been amputated in some cases, large and often ugly scars occurring as the result of unfortunate slips, poorly controlled healing and infection, or pure negligence.

Other radical changes in body image are brought about by cancer therapy. The treatment for cancer relies predominantly upon surgery, radiotherapy and chemotherapy (Wagner and Gorely, 1979). All these treatments bring with them considerable threat to body image. Trust notes that 50,000 cases of head and neck cancer occur annually in the UK (Trust, 1987). This form of cancer requires mutilating surgery and often adjuvant radiotherapy or chemotherapy if the best prognosis is to be arrived at. Addison eloquently describes the problems of patients who are required to wear facial prostheses following surgery for head cancers (Addison, 1978). Anderson, and Goin and Goin, amongst many others, have catalogued the impact of mastectomy upon the female patient (Anderson, 1988; Goin and Goin, 1981). The problems of alopecia, weight loss, skin or oral ulceration, erythema and radiotherapy treatment markings on the skin may be as much a threat to body image as the tumour itself. The fact that the treatment is transitory does not necessarily mean that the effects are equally so.

The internal environment

The internal environment may also be the setting for alteration in body image. A passing mention has already been given to cleft lip as an altered body image, but this represents just one example of a number of congenital or hereditary problems which can occur. Obvious examples (see Table 4.1) might include spina bifida and cerebral palsy. While the former has a more obvious effect upon body reality, both make body presentation

Table 4.1 Origins of altered body image

Congenital Hereditary	Trauma	Surgery Iatrogenic	Malignant	Degenerative	Psychiatric Psychological
Open					
Down's syndrome	Facial burns	Enucleation of the eye	Cancer of mouth/mandible	Parkinson's disease	Anorexia nervosa
Cleft palate/lip	Facial fractures	Unsightly wound/poor healing (poor asepsis)	Osteosarcoma (pathological fractures)	Cerebro-vascular accident	Schizophrenia
Talipes equinovarus	Deviated nasal septum	Grafts and pedicles	Cancer of larynx (tracheostome)	Multiple sclerosis	Obsessional disorders
Spina bifida	Traumatic limb amputations		Brain tumor (altered behaviour)	Arthritis	
Hidden					
Diabetes mellitus	Burns to body	Caesarian section (bikini scar)	Cancer of uterus (hysterectomy)	Urinary continence?	Anorexia bulimia?
Hypospaedes	Syphilitic chancre	Limited mastectomy (implant)	Papilloma bladder	Coital facility	Anorexia nervosa?
Polycystic kidneys	Body area scarring (child abuse)	Orchidectomy	Bowel cancer (successful adaptation to stoma)	Accuity of hearing (conduction deafness)	Phobias

a very difficult problem. Some congenital body image problems may result from drug treatment taken by the pregnant woman. The stunted limb formation associated with thalidomide is a case in point.

Other changes within the internal environment present different altered body image problems. Malignant tumours may themselves disrupt body reality, above and beyond the effects associated with anti-cancer therapy (Gloeckner, 1984). Swollen lymphoma infiltrated glands, the bluish lesions of Kaposi's sarcoma and a fungating cancer of the breast would all serve as examples.Body image change however, does not have to be malignant. The degenerative conditions are equally threatening. Parkinson's disease, a cerebro-vascular accident, or incompetent urinary sphincters can all radically undermine a successful body image. What may make this disruption worse is the variable speed with which the altered body image occurs. Ginther discusses the anguish that multiple sclerosis sufferers experience as a result (Ginther, 1978). The pattern and pace of deteriorating function, and therefore body presentation, is extremely uncertain. Even the process of being diagnosed might prove to be a lengthy affair.

Some internal environment altered body image problems are matters concerning the mind. The experience of one's body cannot be taken for granted. When the patient is admitted to hospital, nursed in an intensive care unit, placed on a ventilator, his experience of his body, his sense of self, is strongly affected (Platzer, 1987a,b). A schizophrenic may develop a very negative body image and this may occasion violent acts of self mutilation. Anorexia nervosa is not so much a disorder of appetite, but of body perception (Canaday, 1981; Crisp and Kalucy, 1974). Even obsessional states or phobias, for example cleanliness, may intimately involve or affect aspects of body image.

Without rushing to cynicism, there seems every opportunity for altered body image to occur as a problem at some point in a lifespan.Some of the alteration will have been planned, some unanticipated. Some of the resultant body image will be obvious because of a damaged body reality or presentation (open), some will not be so readily apparent (hidden). While the nurse will anticipate that individuals constantly adjust their normal body image, she cannot expect that adaptation to altered body image will be achieved so readily. The speed of alteration may be rapid (Piotrowski, 1982) or hesitant (Ginther, 1978). This should sensitise us to the need to assist the patient with adaptation, not only because each patient is an individual, but also because each altered body image circumstance is likely to be quite unique. It is the origins of the altered body image which may often dictate the patient's response to the problem. Understanding these origins should help the nurse to understand the patient's resultant adaptation, or maladaptation.

Review questions

1 Chapter 4 offers a basic division between 'open' and 'hidden' altered body image problems. Can you think of any conditions which may be said to cause both open and hidden problems, perhaps changing between the two according to circumstance or disease progression? You could consider epilepsy, for instance.
2 A distinction is also drawn between normal and altered body image. How realistic is this when considering the degenerative problems of say, Parkinson's disease in an elderly man? Is the altered body image of his condition qualitatively that different from the normal body image changes associated with ageing?
3 Threats to normal body image may affect one or other aspect more than others, for example, cerebral palsy affects body presentation profoundly. Can you suggest other conditions affecting one aspect of body image in particular?
4 How does the concept of altered body image affect the way we present health and safety education? Consider the use of shock facial scars in poster campaigns against 'drinking and driving'.

Suggested exercises

Exercise 1
Over the period of one week collect together examples of altered body image being used in health or safety education. This may mean either videotaping a television advertisement or making notes about it. Alternatively, it may involve collecting posters or pamphlets from various health care agencies. Look over your materials and come back to the group ready to consider the question 'how effective is the use of altered body images (eg facial scarring) in health and safety campaigns?' Allow 30 to 40 minutes for discussion.

Exercise 2
In a group choose ten varied examples of altered body image, writing these up on the chalkboard or overhead projector acetate. Then, invite the group members to imagine that tomorrow they will suffer one or more of these altered body image problems. Ask everyone to write down the three problems they would *least* like to face. Then invite the members to pair off to tell the other person why they made their choices. Finally in full group session, try to establish:

1. Which were the most feared problems to face.

2. Why this was. Were there any clear patterns, such as a majority of open altered body image problems?
3. The ways in which group members had made their choices.

Suggested time allowances are as follows:

(a) for drawing up the ten-problem list, 15 minutes
(b) for choosing the three most feared problems, 5 minutes
(c) for sharing of lists, in pairs, 10 minutes
(d) for the group discussion, 30 minutes

References

Addison C., 'Social Implications of Sudden Facial Disfigurement', *Social Work Today*, 9(41), pp 18–20, 1978.

Anderson J., 'Coming to Terms with Mastectomy', *Nursing Times*, 84(4), pp 41–4, 1988.

Bowden M.L., Feller I., Tholen D., Davidson T.N. and James M.H., 'Self Esteem of Severely Burned Patients', *Archives of Physical Medicine and Rehabilitation*, 61, pp 449–52, 1980.

Canaday M.E., 'Anorexia Nervosa: Distorted body image', *Issues in Health Care of Women*, 3, pp 281–6, 1981.

Crisp A.H. and Kalucy R.S., 'Aspects of the Perceptual Disorder in Anorexia Nervosa', *British Journal of Medical Psychology*, 47, pp 349–61, 1974.

Ginther J., *But You Look So Well!* Nelson-Hall, Chicago, 1978.

Gloeckner M.R., 'Perceptions of Sexual Attractiveness Following Ostomy Surgery', *Research in Nursing & Health*, 7, pp 87–92, 1984.

Goin M.K. and Goin J.M., 'Midlife Reactions to Mastectomy and Subsequent Breast Reconstruction', *Archives of General Psychiatry*, 38, pp 225–7, 1981.

Gruendemann B., 'The Impact of Surgery on Body Image', *Nursing Clinics of North America*, 10(4), pp 635–43, 1975.

Marcus D., 'Psychological Aspects of Cosmetic Rhinoplasty', *British Journal of Plastic Surgery*, 37, pp 313–18, 1986.

Piotrowski M.M., 'Body Image After a Stroke', *Rehabilitation Nursing*, Jan/Feb, pp 11–13, 1982.

Platzer H., 'Body Image – A problem for intensive care patients (Part 1)', *Intensive Care Nursing*, 3, pp 61–6, 1987a.

Platzer, H., 'Body Image: Helping patients to cope with changes – a problem for nurses (Part 2)', *Intensive Care Nursing*, 3, pp 125–32, 1987b.

Raab D.M., 'Helping Patients Develop a Positive Post op Image', *Health Care*, Feb, pp 16–18, 1986.

Richmond T.S. and Metcalf J.A., 'Psychosocial Responses to Spinal Cord Injury', *Journal of Neuroscience Nursing*, 18(4), pp 183–7, 1986.

Roy D.J., 'Caring for the Self Esteem of the Cosmetic Patient', *Plastic Surgical Nursing*, Winter, pp 138–41, 1986.

Trust D., 'Living With Disfigurement', *Self Help*, June, pp 26–8, 1987.

Wagner L. and Gorely M., 'Body Image and Patients Experiencing Alopecia as a Result of Cancer Chemotherapy', *Cancer Nursing*, Oct, pp 365–9, 1979.

Wright M.R. and Wright W.K., 'A Psychological Study of Patients Undergoing Cosmetic Surgery', *Archives of Otolaryngology*, 101, pp 145–51, 1975.

Young J.S. *et al*, *Spinal Cord Injury Statistics: Experience in the regional spinal cord injury systems*, Good Samaritan Medical Center, Phoenix, Arizona, 1982.

5   Personal responses to altered body image

Study of this chapter will enable you to:

1 Suggest factors which may affect the individual's reaction to an altered body image.
2 Describe briefly the benefits of a social support network to a patient experiencing alteration in body image.
3 With reference to one or more models of grief response, describe typical stages of grief reaction that may be exhibited in a child or adult.
4 Outline why some patients may not interpret altered body image or disability as a problem *per se*.
5 Describe how the definition of an altered body image may be affected by the process of negotiation, between patient and others.

Just how a patient will react in the face of an altered body image depends upon a number of factors. Some of these will refer to that person's normal coping strategies, the ways in which they usually adapt to changes in normal body image (Folkman and Lazarus, 1980). Other factors will relate to the origin of the altered body image – what has brought it about, is it visible, and is it associated with guilt or shame, for example following a sexually transmitted disease? A third group of factors pertain to the significance of the altered body image for the patient's future, his or her work, social and sex life. Further, the amount and type of support the patient receives while adjusting to a new body image will also be important. A well organised and sensitive professional and social support network will assist in the patient's transition from one body image to another. (See Figure 5.1 for a summary of factors).

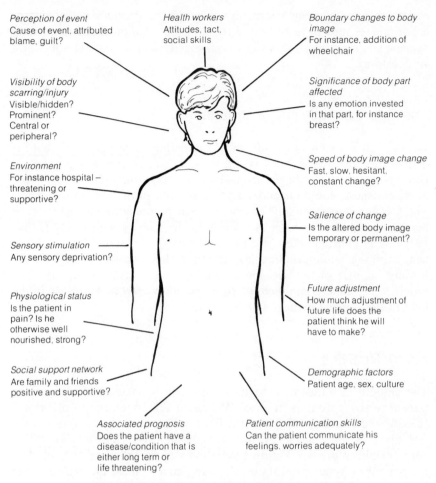

Perception of event
Cause of event, attributed
blame, guilt?

Health workers
Attitudes, tact,
social skills

*Boundary changes to body
image*
For instance, addition of
wheelchair

*Visibility of body
scarring/injury*
Visible/hidden?
Prominent?
Central or
peripheral?

*Significance of body part
affected*
Is any emotion invested
in that part, for instance
breast?

Environment
For instance hospital –
threatening or
supportive?

Speed of body image change
Fast, slow, hesitant,
constant change?

Salience of change
Is the altered body image
temporary or permanent?

Sensory stimulation
Any sensory deprivation?

Physiological status
Is the patient in
pain? Is he
otherwise well
nourished, strong?

Future adjustment
How much adjustment of
future life does the
patient think he will
have to make?

Social support network
Are family and friends
positive and supportive?

Demographic factors
Patient age, sex, culture

Associated prognosis
Does the patient have a
disease/condition that is
either long term or
life threatening?

Patient communication skills
Can the patient communicate his
feelings, worries adequately?

Fig. 5.1   Factors affecting personal responses to altered body image.

Personal coping strategies

We are all familiar with some of the more typical ways in which patients
cope with stress. Some suppress all reference to the problem, either denying its existence, or else underplaying its importance. Others try to ration-
alise their responses, rehearsing, to all who will listen, why they feel as they
do. Many try to compartmentalise the problem, suggesting that while
a problem exists, it is only really a problem in the area of dressing, or
grooming for instance. One response to an altered body image may be to
rely upon an irrational or even mythical belief (Clarke, 1975). Thus, an
unquestioning belief in the foolproof efficacy of radiotherapy may enable a

patient to deal with the treatment's side effects. Previous personal coping strategies may have to be swiftly adjusted. The practices concerning hygiene and cleanliness have to be rearranged when the patient is left with an ileostomy.

The nature of body image change

Wassner, in a review of the effects of mutilating surgery, reflects that for many of us, the human body is still viewed as a creation in the image of God, its maker. Accordingly, damage to that body, through neglect, abuse or recklessness, could engender a sense of guilt in the patient (Wassner, 1982). Some forewarning of an operation or pathological change may, or may not, enable us to react in a more dignified and practical way (Janis, 1971; Kelly, 1985; Parkes M., 1975). Belfer *et al* describe how children with cranio-facial deformities have to renew their recognition of their deformity, as part of the decision to undergo reconstructive surgery. The rationale for undergoing such a trying operation, only makes sense in the light of the original damage (Belfer *et al*, 1979).

Future lifestyles

The amount of adjustment to future lifestyle is anticipated even as the patient recovers from the trauma. Will he be able to return to work early? (Chang and Herzog, 1976). Will it limit social, marital or business relationships? In some instances, for example multiple sclerosis, this will be very difficult to predict. Future adaptation may be enhanced or limited by the patient's physiological status. A young man who has undergone lower limb amputation may be able to develop a successful body image if he has the strength and skill to use crutches properly.

Support networks

Adjustment to any life crisis appears to be enhanced when the individual has access to a wide range of help from family and friends. This may be because such a network forms an environment in which the individual can try out his or her new body image, confident that an empathetic response will be received. A number of writers have emphasised just how important nurses and other health workers are in establishing such an environment (Carroll, 1981; Darbyshire, 1986; Schawlb and Zahr, 1985; Roy, 1986; Stanley, 1977).

The 'stages of grief' response

While the range of factors affecting personal response to altered body image is extensive, most writers have still tended to characterise the response as one of grief. The grief reaction is believed to occur in response to lost body attributes or parts, to lost attractiveness, and to lost facility in ordering a satisfactory body presentation. The grief is usually seen as progressing through a number of stages although researchers disagree on what each stage involves, and in what order it appears (see Table 5.1).

Stages in the grief response

Smith *et al* studied the reaction of children to injury. This was an important study as it took into account the dynamic nature of the child's developing body image. Given that a child's body image is still developing, or perhaps not yet formed, it is reasonable to assume that a child is particularly vulnerable to the effects of altered body image. In stage 1, the global stage, the child perceives the whole body to be sick or damaged. This results in regression, a pattern of behaviour and attitudes more characteristic of a younger age group. Later, in stage 2, the child starts to differentiate the damaged from the undamaged part of the body. While this sounds straightforward, in practice, it may not be that easy when the extent of damage may not at first be apparent, or may have changed over time. In stage 3, the child compares the new body reality with what was familiar previously. Parents may be important at this stage. Finally, a successful adaptation will see the integration of body changes into a composite body image. At this point, Smith envisages the child starting a 'normal' life once more (Smith *et al*, 1977).

Belfer *et al* also refer to four stages of grief response. In their study, consideration is again focused on children, who in this instance have already been handicapped and who now face reconstruction surgery. Stage 1 in this study consists of the child and family anticipating the trauma of surgery. It involves an active decision to proceed, which reminds everyone of the existing altered body image. Later the family have concrete proof of further alteration in body image. At first, surgery or treatment may increase distortion in body image, through tissue oedema, or the presence of an intravenous infusion. Belfer's final stage, like Smith's, involves a reintegration of old and new aspects of body image (Belfer *et al*, 1979).

Kubler Ross's model of the grief response is drawn from her extensive work with the dying and their families. As with most of the other researchers, she would not argue that the stages of grief are strictly linear, that a patient cannot linger in, or return to earlier grief reactions. For this author six reactions are typically progressed through. Shock, denial of the

Table 5.1 Psychological models of personal reactions to altered body image

Researcher	Stage 1	Stage 2	Stage 3	Stage 4	Stage 5	Stage 6
Smith et al (1977)	'Global' stage (Whole body sick)	'What' stage Differentiates damaged parts	'How' stage Comparison, the new with the old	'I am' stage Child integrates new and old body image together		
Belfer et al (1979)	Anticipation Decision to undergo surgery	Operative experience. Concrete evidence of change in body image	Immediate post-op phase. Additional body image distortion	Re-integration stage building modifications into new body image		
Kubler Ross (1969)	Shock	Denial	Anger	Depression	Bargaining	Acceptance
Parkes C. (1972)	Realisation (denial of loss or change)	Alarm (anxiety, insecurity)	Searching (panic, a search for meaning of injury)	Feelings of internal loss (risk of morbid grief)	Final resolution (start of a new social identity)	
Fink (1967) Grunbaum (1985)	Shock	Denial (defensive retreat)	Acknowledgement of reality (albeit painful)	Adaptation		
Fisher (1970)	Denial of body part or change (disassociation)	Illusory restitution (phantom limb phenomenon)	Refocus of attention on healthy aspects of body	Period of crisis – reliance on unrealistic defence strategies		

(Note: Fisher reactions not strictly sequential stages)

change (in this case to body image), anger ('why me?'), depression, bargaining (with God or health workers) and finally, hopefully, acceptance (Kubler Ross, 1969). Parkes C. offers a model of grief response based upon work undertaken with mentally ill patients. Five stages are identified; realisation, alarm, searching, the sense of internal loss and final resolution. During the realisation stage, the patient often tries to deny the loss of body part or image. He may avoid looking at his stoma or burned hand, experiencing feelings of unreality, a blunting of senses. Later, this progresses to feelings of insecurity, fear and anxiety. An emotional search is then undertaken, the patient seeking to make sense of his altered appearance. Final resolution is arrived at when the patient adopts a new social identity, albeit sometimes a less attractive or a damaged one (Parkes C., 1972).

Fink and later Grunbaum both use similar terms to describe the grief response. Like Kubler Ross, they see the first reactions as shock and then denial of the changes. Later an acknowledgement of reality occurs, a painful recognition that a body part is missing, scar tissue is present and will not totally disappear. Final adaptation is suggested as stage 4, but this may take a long time to occur and may even be forestalled indefinitely (Fink, 1967; Grunbawn, 1985). Finally, Fisher considers four reactions which might occur in stages but which are arranged in this work much less rigidly. Like Parkes, Fisher sees patients denying their altered body image in the first instance. Fisher's second reaction refers specifically to the phantom limb experience – the patient recreating in mind a body attribute that is no longer present. As this fades the patient begins to refocus on his remaining healthy attributes, and through a period of stormy behaviour and crises moves to a new equilibrium (Fisher, 1970).

Limitation of the 'stages of grief' approach

At first sight, the stage of grief approach would seem to have a lot to commend it to nurses. While each researcher offers different behaviour that might be expected, there does seem to be an orderliness about the process of the patient's grief. Nursing interventions could be planned on assumptions about the integration of new aspects of the body image, or on an anticipated denial of any problem prior to final acceptance of change. Albrecht however has argued that such developmental models are not as accurate or as useful as they might at first seem. Because altered body image, disability and trauma are all conceptualised as a problem in the first instance, the fieldwork that follows will tend to see issues in terms of the gradual resolution, or lack of resolution, of problems as the patient rehabilitates (Albrecht, 1976). Oliver points out that not all patients will perceive their handicap as undesirable. Some will welcome even an altered body image, as a badge of a new patient status. The injury or disability may re-

Table 5.2 Sociological model – personal tasks after altered body image (based on Symbolic Interactionist School of Sociology)

Consideration 1
Does the trauma, pathology and resultant alteration to body image constitute a problem? Does it require explanation to anyone?

Consideration 2
If an explanation is required, this will lead to negotiation of the meaning of the new body image. What might that meaning be?

Consideration 3
Negotiation will be first and foremost with 'significant others', family, close friends or associates. Who will qualify as significant others? Secondary negotiation takes place with the public in general ('the generalised other').

---

lieve the patient of previously onerous responsibilities and stresses. There is a sense in which a wheelchair can be sanctuary as well as an extension of altered body image (Oliver, 1978).

This is reminiscent of the work of Mead and other symbolic interactionist sociologists (Mead, 1934). Perhaps what is equally important for the patient's personal response to altered body image, is the definition of that new identity. This is negotiated through interaction between the patient, his family, friends and acquaintances (see Table 5.2). Thus, the first consideration must be, does the altered body image require an explanation or negotiation at all? A deviated nasal septum, in a boxing fraternity may not. If negotiation of identity is required, then this is most important with close relatives and friends (significant others). The wider population (generalised others) is of secondary importance.

Conclusion

The foregoing material highlights the three major considerations that are important in personal responses to altered body image. The first, is the broad circumstance of the image change – the patient, his resources and the nature of change. The second concerns typical psychological responses to major body image change. These are seen against time, the patient passing through and perhaps revisiting a number of reactions which have been suggested in empirical studies. Thirdly the psychological response is mediated by social definitions of the new identity. These are negotiated through social interaction, with kin, the nurse and eventually the public at large. It is clear that the patient's responses to an alteration in body image can be complex. This need not be daunting, for here the whole gamut of patients and their variables have been considered. The nurse will deal with patients individually (see later chapters), and principles learnt here should be transferable to the better known situations of each client.

Review questions

1 One of the factors affecting personal response to altered body image is the environment in which the patient exists. What effect might the ward setting have upon the patient's response?
2 Patients may not always have an accurate idea of the life adjustments that will be necessary in the aftermath of an alteration to body image. Why do you think that this might be so in the following instances:
   (a) a patient receiving continuing chemotherapy for a malignant tumour
   (b) a patient being fitted with a temporary limb prosthesis
   (c) a patient returning home to a family which has not been involved in his pre-operative stoma education programme.
3 In what way do you think pain might affect a patient's perception of his altered body reality?
4 Mr Hughes has suffered a cerebro-vascular accident, resulting in a right hemiplegia. Despite the nurse's and physiotherapist's efforts, Mr Hughes refuses to acknowledge his paralysed right arm. What sort of grief response is he exhibiting?
5 In what way may a phantom limb assist a patient in adjusting to an altered body image?
6 How might you decide whether a patient had integrated his wheelchair into his new body image?
7 Why might you expect a patient to become angry with you following an hysterectomy?

Suggested exercise

As a rather longer term exercise, select one of the grief response models for closer study. Obtain the appropriate reference and read it through to establish clearly in your own mind, how the author is using key terms. Consult your tutor if in any doubt. Next, select a patient on your ward, or in your department, who will be undergoing some form of pre-planned, body image threatening surgery, for example a hysterectomy. Seek their permission to study their post-operative recovery. As appropriate, negotiate additional clearance with the ward manager and surgeon – it is usually ethical to acquaint fellow professionals with study interests. Having established access, plan two diaries that will be kept, one by the patient and one by you.

The patient's diary

Invite the patient to keep a daily diary that records feelings about the operation, recovery, nursing care, or anything else, for each of the post-operative days. Explain that the diary will be collected on a future date (say, post-op day 7) and that after the patient's experiences have been noted, the original diary will be returned to them. Assure them that anonymity will be maintained, the patient being given a fictitious name in the report write up. Explain to the patient that you are eager to understand the emotional experiences following surgery. Do not explain the model that you are examining, otherwise the patient may adjust the diary to suit your needs! A relatively natural set of notes are being sought.

Your diary

Complete diary entries each day on what you observe about the patient's behaviour, and hear the patient say. The diary entries should concentrate upon material which is seen and heard and there should be little or no interpretation recorded at this point. The observations should be made in the course of your nursing care, do not set out to observe as an activity apart from nursing care. Try to be unobtrusive. Continue your diary for the same period of time as the patient's. Seven days is a notional period, conditions may dictate that you shorten this period, or you may be able to extend it for rather longer.

Compare the diary entries day by day and try to answer the following questions:

1. Was there any evidence of the patient suffering grief responses as described by your model of interest?
2. Was there any evidence of the patient passing through stages of grief? If so, how many and in what order?
3. If there was evidence of a grief response, was this found largely in the patient's diary, your diary or both? What do you think is the significance of this balance or imbalance? If the patient's diary shows no obvious evidence of grief response and yours does, does this mean the patient was not willing to write about emotions, or were your observations ill founded?
4. In retrospect, does the model form a useful guide to how your patient responded to the surgery?

Write up your notes and share your findings in group seminar later. This exercise forms an excellent variation to more traditional care studies or project.

Suggested time scales for this exercise are:

(a) for reading the literature, one to two weeks
(b) for data collection, during a clinical placement, about two weeks
(c) for writing up findings including analysis, about two to three weeks
(d) for seminar presentation; typically 20 to 30 minutes with time for questions

References

Albrecht G.L. (ed.), *The Sociology of Physical Disability and Rehabilitation*, University of Pittsburgh Press, Pittsburgh, 1976.

Belfer M., Harrison A., and Murray J., 'Body Image and the Process of Reconstructive Surgery, *American Journal of Diseases of Children*, 133, pp 532–5, 1979.

Carroll R.M., 'The Impact of Mastectomy on Body Image', *Oncology Nursing Forum*, 8(4), pp 29–32, 1981.

Chang F.C. and Herzog B., 'Burn Morbidity: A follow up study of physical and psychological disability', *Annals of Surgery*, 183, pp 34–7, 1976.

Clarke M., 'Psycho-social Problems of Patients Following Radical Cancer Surgery', Proceedings *Nursing Mirror* International Conference, 'Cancer Nursing' in association with Royal Marsden Hospital, 1975.

Darbyshire P., 'Body Image – When the face doesn't fit', *Nursing Times*, 24 Sept, pp 28–30, 1986.

Fink S., 'Crisis and Motivation: A theoretical model', *Archives of Physical Medicine and Rehabilitation*, 48, pp 592–7, 1967.

Fisher S., *Body Experience in Fantasy and Behaviour*, Appleton Century Crofts, New York, 1970.

Folkman S. and Lazarus R., 'An Analysis of Coping in a Middle Aged Community Sample', *Journal of Health and Social Behaviour*, Sept, pp 219–39, 1980.

Grunbaum J., 'Helping your Patient Build a Sturdier Body Image', *RN*, Oct, pp 51–5, 1985.

Janis L., *Stress Tolerance in Surgical Patients, Stress and Frustration*, Harcourt, Brace & Jovanovich, 1971.

Kelly M.P., 'Loss and Grief Reactions as Responses to Surgery', *Journal of Advanced Nursing*, 10, pp 517–25, 1985.

Kubler Ross E., *On Death and Dying*, Tavistock Publications, London, 1969.

Mead G.H., *Mind, Self and Society*, Chicago University Press, Chicago, 1934.

Oliver M. 'Disability, Adjustment and Family Life – Some theoretical considerations', *Proceedings 2nd European Conference of Rehabilitation International, 18–21 Sept, Sevenoaks Naidex Conventions*, 1978.

Parkes C., *Bereavement: Studies of grief in adult life*, Tavistock Publications, London, 1972.

Parkes M., 'What Becomes of Redundant World Models? A contribution to the study of adaptation to change', *British Journal of Medical Psychology*, 48, pp 131–7, 1975.

Roy D., 'Caring for the Self-Esteem of the Cosmetic Patient', *Plastic Surgical Nursing*, Winter, pp 138–41, 1986.

Schawlb D. and Zahr L., 'Nursing Care of Patients with an Altered Body Image due to Multiple Sclerosis', *Nursing Forum*, 22(2), pp 72–6, 1985.
Smith E.C., Liviskie S.L., Nelson K.A. and McNemar A., 'Re-establishing a Child's Body Image', *American Journal of Nursing*, March, pp 445–7, 1977.
Stanley L., 'Does your Own Body Image Hurt Patient Care?', *RN*, Dec, pp 50–3, 1977.
Wassner A., 'The Impact of Mutilating Surgery or Trauma on Body Image', *International Nursing Review*, 29(3), pp 86–90, 1982.

Further reading

Ablon J., 'Reactions of Samoan Burn Patients and Families to Severe Burns', *Social Science and Medicine*, 7(167), 1973.
Addison C., 'Social Implications of Sudden Facial Disfigurement', *Social work Today*, 9(41), pp 18–20, 1978.
Arneson S. and Triplett J., 'How Children Cope with Disfiguring Changes in their Appearance', *American Journal of Maternal Child Nursing*, Nov/Dec, pp 366–70, 1978.
Davis F., *Passage Through Crisis: Polio victims and their families*, Bobbs-Merrill, New York, 1963.
Denning D., 'Head and Neck Cancer: Our reactions', *Cancer Nursing*, Aug, pp 269–73, 1982.
Fujita M.T., 'The Impact of Illness or Surgery on the Body Image of the Child', *Nursing Clinics of North America*, 7(4), pp 641–8, 1972.
Gillies D.A., 'Body Image Changes Following Illness and Injury', *Journal of Enterostomal Therapy*, 11, pp 186–9, 1984.
Gruendemann B., 'The Impact of Surgery on Body Image', *Nursing Clinics of North America*, 10(4), pp 635–43, 1975.
Hill C., 'Psychosocial Adjustment of Adult Burns Patients – Is it more difficult for people with visible scars?', *Occupational Therapy*, Sept, pp 281–3, 1985.
Piotrowski M., 'Body Image after a Stroke', *Rehabilitation Nursing*, Jan/Feb, pp 11–13, 1982.
Raab D., 'Helping Patients Develop a Positive Post-op Image', *Health Care*, Feb, pp 16–18, 1986.
Richards D., 'A Posthysterectomy Syndrome', *Lancet*, 2, pp 983–5, 1974.
Richardson S., 'Some Social Psychological Consequences of Handicapping', *Pediatrics*, Aug, pp 291–7, 1963.
Rosillo R., Welty M. and Graham W., 'The Patient with Maxillofacial Cancer: Psychological aspects', *Nursing Clinics of North America*, 8(155), 1973.
Stewart T. and Shields C.R., 'Grief in Chronic Illness: Assessment and management', *Archives of Physical Medicine and Rehabilitation*, 66(7), pp 447–50, 1985.
Thomas S., 'Breast Cancer: The psychosocial issues', *Cancer Nursing*, 1(1), pp 53–60, 1978.
Tierney E.A., 'Accepting Disfigurement when Death is the Alternative', *American Journal of Nursing*, 75, p 2150, 1975.
Wagner L. and Gorely M., 'Body Image and Patients Experiencing Alopecia as a Result of Cancer Chemotherapy', *Cancer Nursing*, Oct, pp 365–9, 1979.

6 Stigma – the damaged self-image

Study of this chapter will enable you to:

1 Define the term *stigma*, with reference to the work of Erving Goffman.
2 Offer examples of what is meant by:
  (a) physical stigma
  (b) moral stigma
  (c) tribal stigma.
3 Discuss why the patient with an altered body image might have to 'negotiate' his or her new social identity.
4 Describe the general tactics employed by the stigmatised, to achieve and maintain an adequate self-image.
5 Outline some of the interpersonal problems that patients may have as they return to the community.
6 List the resources that Goffman sees as being available to the stigmatised individual.
7 Outline briefly the nurse's position when addressing stigma.

In Chapter 1 it was explained that self-image is inextricably bound up with body image. A poor body image would make it more difficult for us to sustain a successful self-image. This is because self-image relies strongly upon acclaim from others. If you have an unsuccessful body image, features which are not valued by others, then society may attribute lower value to your self as well. There were many examples of this sort of value judgement in action, in Chapter 2. Body image may be negatively affected either through normal events such as ageing, or through abnormal events like trauma. It is now time to consider the longer term effects of an unsuccessful body image upon the self.

In a text which has become a sociology classic, Erving Goffman used the concept of stigma to explore how people with a damaged self-image try to manage their lives (Goffman, 1963). As Goffman points out, the term stigma originates from ancient Greece, where it was the term used to describe a visible sign that marked an individual out as a slave. A similar 'brand' was discussed in Christian circles, using the word stigmata. Stigmata are visible features, such as wounds in the hands, which cannot be ascribed to self-injury or fraud, and which are thought to signify an inner state of grace. From these examples, it is quite clear that the mark by itself signifies very little, but how the mark is interpreted makes all the difference.

Before some one bearing an abnormal appearance or feature (stigmata) can be stigmatised – that is, made to feel less than whole or welcome in that society – reference is made to the norms of the society. To take an example, a Buddhist monk in saffron robes with a shaven head, would not be considered abnormal in Burmese society, but might seem out of place in a rural British community. What is important is that no appearance *per se* is a sign of lesser social worth – it only becomes so when measured by standards or norms of appearance or behaviour which are held to be 'natural' or desirable.

Goffman described three different types of stigma. The first two are of general interest, the third is central to the material of this book (see Figure 6.1). Blemishes in moral behaviour or attitude, what might be termed 'moral stigma' may be associated with criminal or antisocial acts. Thus, a man who has once committed incest is unlikely to be forgiven easily by society, or readily trusted by his family again. He shows no outward signs of his status (unless gaoled), but he nevertheless carries his stigma through the gossip and folk wisdom that accompanies his movements in society. The second form of stigma Goffman describes as 'tribal'. This refers to the racial, religious or cultural markers of any group of people. Thus the skull cap of the Jewish people is not only an aspect of their religion and custom, but could become the visible stigmata that is used to single them out for persecution, such as happened in Nazi Germany. Tribal stigma seems to occur where a minority population, usually quite active and visible, lives within a majority population which has norms or standards which are 'threatened' by the minority group's presence. Frequently the stigma is ascribed using irrational beliefs or inaccurate information. This is the field of racism and all the misery that that has brought to the world.

'Physical stigma' addresses this book's subject areas – normal and altered body image. Stigma may be associated simply with the wrinkles of old age, an amputation, wheelchair or blindness for instance. Goffman has observed that a disability in one area (say sight) is often assumed by 'normal' people to hold sway elsewhere. Thus a blind person may find that people shout greetings at them, assuming that they are deaf too. Equally significant is the fact that people may assume that if a person has a disability, perhaps epilepsy, then all of that person's family may also suffer from it. This spreading of stigma, a contamination of all those associated with the patient or individual, may also extend to nurses. Nurses who care for the mentally ill are often thought by others to behave just a little oddly.

One nurse put it this way: '... you can always tell a mental nurse, they seem to have such a strange sense of humour. They don't trust anything you say as sincere'.

From Goffman's work, it seems evident that the negotiation of an adequate identity is very difficult following any of the following misfortunes: to be born with a handicap, to come from the wrong community, to suffer facial or moral scarring. All of these can mean a lifelong negotiation of self-worth, often when least equipped to do so. A number of tactics are employed in such negotitations (see Figure 6.1). Some are general, long term strategies. Others are employed day-to-day on an interpersonal basis.

Tactics and resources

In some instances the origin of the stigma, such as a port wine skin mark, may be eradicated. This preferable option may apply to many patients, including the burned and the congenitally injured, with varying degrees of

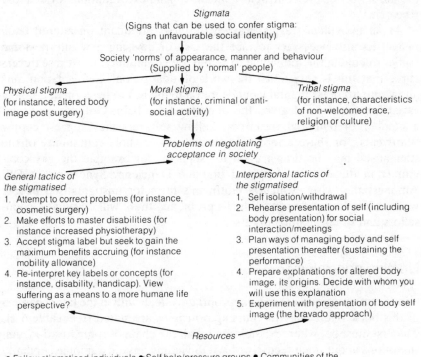

Fig. 6.1 Social identity and the stigmatised person (after the work of Erving Goffman).

success. To the limitations of surgery must often be added limitations of access of medical facilities and to money to pay for treatment. Superhuman efforts to overcome a deformity, for example walking with leg braces following spinal injury, are another option. The cost here is in terms of human motivation, pain and perhaps family relationships. Having achieved a standard of performance (body presentation), that standard may be very difficult to sustain life long. Perhaps more frequently, a limited stigma is accepted, the individual then working to either, gain benefits attached to that label such as cheap travel fares, or trying to modify the label's meaning through personal or organised re-interpretation of the stigma. An example would be the person who suffers from epilepsy. The unpredictable nature of seizures makes body presentation very difficult. Paradoxically, infrequent 'fits' means that public sympathy for the epileptic's position may be rather limited. At a personal level the epileptic individual assures acquaintances that he or she is proficient with medication and can forewarn them of what to do, should he or she suffer a seizure. Through various public groups however, this individual with others might want to emphasise the misery of seizure control as a means to gain extra funding for epilepsy research.

As an individual travels through the grief attendant on altered body image, its also necessary to face the task of devising new interpersonal tactics to enable the individual to rejoin the community. Most researchers agree that this is very much the work of 'adaptation'. Self-isolation may allow time to dress mental wounds, but a living has to be earned, a family cared for, and friends given the opportunity to help. Goffman identifies a number of potential resources. Fellow sufferers may suggest coping- 'short cuts', or share a moan. In some cases a whole community of the stigmatised may be drawn upon for support, for example the gay community in the light of Acquired Immune Deficiency Syndrome, AIDS. Amongst the 'wise', which is Goffman's term for unstigmatised people with an insight into the individual's problems, there will be nurses, counsellors and other health workers.

Nursing principles

Specific nursing goals are most appropriately dealt with in the later chapters of this book. Here only the nursing principles are stated (see Table 6.1). The first must be, where possible, to break the chain of stigmatisation. Assumptions about the infectivity of AIDS victims, insanity amongst epilepsy sufferers and their families, must be questioned through sensitive public health education. This is a difficult subject, for it is known that highlighting an issue through such a campaign can mean that it is viewed as a 'problem', and then the wrong message, a negative one, is conveyed.

Table 6.1 Dealing with stigma – nursing principles

Breaking the stigmatisation chain
1. Health education (on the meaning of disabilities, disease effects and the positive achievements possible) Target population: General public

2. Acting as a role model: setting personal examples of how to relate to people with altered body image. Stating a positive opinion in open debate

3. Directing public to accurate information sources (such as the British Diabetic Association)

4. Promoting schemes for integration of the able and the disabled or disadvantaged (for instance in education, youth or social clubs)

Promoting successful adaptation
General
1. Liaising with other health workers to facilitate access to further treatment or therapy

2. Educating patient and family about the same

3. Acquainting patient and family with benefits that they are entitled to

4. Directing patient and family to societies or associations with expertise (for example The Ileostomy Association)

5. Working with physiotherapists and occupational therapists to promote a realistic maximum independence

6. Acting as counsellor to patient as he gradually appraises his situation

Interpersonal
7. Advise patient and relatives on how to identify withdrawal, and the risks that it involves

8. Set aside time, attention and environment for patient and family to express their feelings (no matter how bitter). Recognise that to listen can be as therapeutic as to advise

9. Arrange 'rehearsal' opportunities for the patient trying out a new body image. Allow time for debrief discussion afterwards

10. Identify amounts of information, that patients may want to share with others. Consider ways of sharing that information, about the operation, the stoma, the wound, whatever

11. Introduce support counsellors and agencies

Probably some of the most effective work occurs at a more immediate, individual level. The nurse briefs friends and relatives on the needs of the patient. The patient's positive achievements and motivation are emphasised. Further treatment options such as surgery are considered in the light of the patient's needs and the doctor's advice. Importantly, it is with family, friends and work colleagues, that the patient will first 'try out' his new body image and/or self-image. Divesting these people of misconceptions should prepare the environment for a more successful patient transition.

Realistically, many patients will still suffer stigma. The nurse must anticipate this, and once the patient is well advanced through the initial grief reaction she must start to help the patient with preparing to negotiate his new body image through the outside world. This involves encouraging the patient to recognise body image change, and to express feelings about this (catharsis). It later involves anticipating social interaction and the ways in which the patient hopes to present a new appearance (body presentation). Rehearsal meetings with follow up discussion on 'how it felt' are very important in hospital. Visiting time, a trip to the hospital shop or hairdresser, may all help the patient to explore gradually his body image in a way that causes minimum damage to self-image. Limitations on the length of hospital stays often mean that this work has to be continued in the community, through district nursing services, or a day centre.

Following the transition to a new body image and new self-image, the patient has still to sustain these as independently as possible. A number of crises such as further trauma or surgery, may make this very hard work. Therefore, the notion that the nurse's work is done when the patient 'has adapted', is wrong. It is based upon a false premise. Adaptation is relative. Residual grief or regret will usually remain. While the nurse cannot promote life long dependence of the patient upon her, she must foresee that she will meet patients who need help through 'rough patches' long after they sustained their altered body image. Such help may simply involve counselling the patient, or it may involve a temporary closer support, with practical demonstrations on how to improve body presentation.

Conclusion

There is a real danger that the patient who suffers disrupted body image or self-image, may also become stigmatised. This is detrimental as it often limits the patient's routes to future happiness and confirms in the patient's mind, a poor self-opinion. Stigma is a major source of mental pain to a wide range of patients. It cannot be pretended that the individual nurse can totally alleviate the problem. However, recognising and anticipating the stigma risk, and minimising the trauma it brings to patients and their families, are very realistic nursing goals.

Review questions

1 Referring to your personal observations, and without trying to be definitive about this, how long do you think it would take for someone to become stigmatised? Can it ever be instant?

2 Do you think it is possible for the altered body image patient to accept

mentally a 'limited stigma', or is stigmatisation an all-or-nothing affair?
3 To what extent do you think a family, or a community, can insulate a person, perhaps a child, from the effects of stigma?
4 Do you feel that you have ever been stigmatised by association with any particular groups of patients? How did you recognise that this process was happening?
5 The stigmatised individual may gain solace from people with similarly altered body images, such as paraplegics. However, repeated and exclusive contact with fellow sufferers could bring problems as well as benefits. What do you think these might be?

Suggested exercises

Exercise A
Collect pamphlets and posters from one of the charities or associations promoting the cause of patients with some form of altered body image, such as arthritis sufferers. How does that organisation promote the sufferer's case in order to gain financial and medical support, limit stigma and promote the individual's dignity? Discuss your findings in seminar, allowing about 60 minutes, depending on group size.

Exercise 2
Consider the following patient's body presentation problems. Then, prepare a list of 'cues' which over time may cause that patient to become stigmatised. Here we shall define cues as any activities, signs or symptoms, or failure's in performance, which might lead to the patient's condition being widely recognised and open to valuation.

Claire French is a 29 year old school teacher. Claire has suffered from multiple sclerosis for several years now, but to date her attacks have been mild with no residual disability. Her latest attack has left her paralysed, so that she is obliged to use a wheelchair.

Some cues are obvious, such as the wheelchair. Others are perhaps more subtle, lost working days for instance. Share your list of cues in discussion. Allow 5 to 10 minutes for listing cues, and 20 to 30 minutes for discussion.

References

Goffman E., *Stigma: Notes on the management of spoiled identity*, Prentice Hall, Englewood Cliffs, New Jersey, 1963.

Unit 3
Principles of nursing intervention

The nursing process has become a well established means to deliver imaginative and effective nursing care. It is widely accepted that the nurse, in establishing a client relationship with the patient, must start from the basis of a thorough assessment of patient problems and needs. After this, appropriate prioritised care goals can be written. In order to apply this process to body image care, it is important to know how to assess body image problems or needs, and to then prepare adequate goals. It is by no means certain that matters will be as obvious or as straightforward as when delivering purely physical care.

This unit will be reviewing a few of the difficulties experienced by others who have tried to measure body image changes and deficits. It will become clear that sophisticated techniques may help to create appropriate terminology, but to date these techniques have not necessarily made nursing care more sensitive or efficient. Key body image terms will be used, such as body reality, body ideal and body presentation, to form workable concepts by which to assess patient needs and plan care goals.

7   Assessing altered body image

Study of this chapter will enable you to:

1 Describe why assessment of altered body image is important for the nurse.
2 Outline briefly some of the more common research tools used by scientists to study or measure body image.
3 Discuss the limitations of such tools, with reference to the nurse's need for a practical assessment instrument.
4 Describe the assessment areas that should concern the nurse in assessing the patient's body image disturbance.
5 Indicate why a primary nursing approach is useful in assessing patients with a major or traumatic altered body image.
6 List examples of common normal coping strategies used by people experiencing stress.
7 Define each of Cohen and McKay's categories of social support.
8 Argue why assessment of the patient should extend over many days, rather than just the admission period.
9 Discuss why the assessment of relatives and their coping strategies may also be important for the nurse.

Assessing altered body image has always been considered to be a difficult problem, by scientist and nurse researchers alike (Shontz, 1969). This has been because body image is a relatively abstract concept involving areas such as attitudes, the mind, and interpersonal values, all of which are notoriously difficult to measure. It has been difficult to establish the validity of research techniques, some of which may be measuring an individual's personality, mental health or cultural background, as much as body image or self-image *per se*. Further to this, assessment of altered body image is being used by researchers for widely different purposes. The psychologist may wish to map the body image phenomenon, linking it to the development of an individual. The sociologist is more interested in assessing the importance of body image for normal or extraordinary social interaction. Psychiatrists seek to gain clues about mental illness through altered body image states, while surgeons might simply try to understand the motivation of a patient to undergo cosmetic surgery.

The nurse by comparison addresses the issue of altered body image because it is an integral part of the patient's total well-being. A damaged body image or self-image may significantly affect the patient's rehabilitation and return to a state of independence. What the nurse wants her assessment to achieve is an adequate review of the patient's circumstances and normal body image and coping strategies. It should map the nature of the altered body image, the patient's resources and the grief reactions that might have to be considered in the plan for rehabilitation and care of the patient.

Literature review

By 1969, Shontz was able to offer a review of body image assessment techniques which spanned from the very technical to the esoteric (see Table 7.1). Since that time, the scientists' research techniques have continued to develop. The reason for such a range of techniques emerging was in part, the difficult problem of validity, but it also stemmed from the varied philosophical and discipline backgrounds of the researchers. Shontz argued that the dilemma lay in trying to reconcile the quantitative and qualitative considerations of body image. How do you measure the prac-

Table 7.1 Body image research strategies

Research strategy	Researchers
Linear methods (Shontz)	Arnhoff and Mehl, 1963; Fink, 1959; Guess, 1963; Lebovitz and Lakin, 1957; Shontz, 1963
Configurational methods (Shontz)	Cleveland, 1960; Cleveland *et al.* 1962; Rowe and Caldwell, 1963; Wechowicz and Sommer, 1960
Draw-a-picture method	Gilbert and Hall, 1962; Lakin, 1956; MacDonald, 1966; Schiff, 1976
Distorting mirrors (variation on configurational theme)	Orbach *et al*, 1966; Traub and Orbach, 1964
Topographic devices (target areas)	Fawcett and Frye, 1980; Schlacter, 1971
Questionnaires (often utilising a semantic differential scale)	Baird, 1985; Champion and Tzeng, 1982; Jourard and Secord, 1955; Plutchik *et al*, 1971; Tzeng, 1975
Repertory grid techniques	Feldman, 1975

tical effect of altered body image, and also give due recognition to the emotional disruption that accompanies it.

Some of the earlier research strategies concentrated upon measuring the accuracy of the individual's perception of body size and body part distances. Patients were invited to adjust markers to the equivalent width of their shoulders, or to adjust a movable door frame to be just big enough for them to squeeze through. These were what Shontz called linear methods. Other researchers invited patients to select model organs from a range that offered a large number of size variations. Patients had to pick out a model that represented as they perceived it, the shape and size of their own body parts or organs (Shontz, 1969). Sometimes the models were of the whole body. Rowe and Caldwell presented delinquent boys with cards that each bore one of seven different total body shapes (somatotypes). They were then invited to choose the one that they thought they most resembled (Rowe and Caldwell, 1963).

The 'draw a picture' techniques have already been alluded to in Chapter 3. These were popular in the 1960s, partly because they required comparitively little assessment equipment. The patient or respondent was invited to draw a whole body picture of themselves on paper. Importantly, they were told that it was to be a representation of themselves. In order to ensure that the individual's body image was being assessed and not his general perception of objects, their size and shapes, MacDonald and others asked the patients also to draw two other objects on the paper, such as a crayon. A distorted body, but a normal crayon picture presumably portrayed something of how the patient actually saw his own body (MacDonald, 1966). Much of this work seemed to rest upon assumptions of how we know our own body. If sight is most important, then this test in theory could be said to be valid. If however we form much of our body image through a sense of proprioception, where our limbs and trunk are relative to one another in space, then such a test might not be so accurate (Schilder, 1935). Interesting variations on the whole body theme used fairground distorting mirrors to see how much distortion the individual would tolerate as a normal representation, and topographic devices such as used by Schlacter, and Fawcett and Frye. These researchers had subjects stand upon the centre of a large vinyl target, and invited them to state how many of the concentric rings they thought they covered. Accurate comparison measurements were then made (Fawcett and Frye, 1980; Schlacter, 1971).

Other researchers have used questionnaires or interview schedules in some format or other. These have often employed a semantic differential scale, which invites respondents to make statements about their various body parts (Tzeng, 1975). Thus, someone might be invited to plot their feelings about the size of their legs (big–small, short–long, fat–thin), or the texture of their skin (soft–hard, smooth–rough). Jourard and Secord's body cathexis scale is a classic of this type. It asks the individual to state levels of satisfaction with each body part or attribute (Jourard and Secord, 1955). The body parts satisfaction approach has been used more recently in conjunction with computer analysis to form the repertory grid technique (Feldman, 1975). Statements about the body parts of others, such as mother, father, partners, are plotted alongside those of the subject. In this way statements about the individual's own body ideal and image can be considered alongside those ascribed to relatives and some tentative conclusions about anorexia nervosa and other conditions might usefully be drawn.

Several nurses have started to build upon some of these techniques, though the requirement for a practical and flexible assessment protocol, suited to varied settings, limits the use of many of them. Champion and Tzeng used semantic differential scales to study the relationship of present body image and self-image, with reference to the ideals concerning both. The authors were able to confirm the importance of body image and self-image to rehabilitation, but it was unclear just how practical such a lengthy questionnaire could be for most nursing situations (Champion and Tzeng, 1982). Baird also used a questionnaire approach, but simplified a lot of previous theoretical work to form the Baird Body Image Assessment Tool or BBIAT. This instrument was used for the assessment of immobilised orthopaedic patients, although many of its questions are applicable to wider fields of nursing. Questions put to patients covered areas such as the effect of the injury or operation upon work or financial status, social support systems, the existence or otherwise of pain, fear and attached equipment which might disrupt body image. Testing of this tool for its reliability and validity is still underway, but at least some of the questionnaire material appears promising (Baird, 1985).

Most nurses have seemed less concerned to promote an assessment instrument (feasible though this may be, if only as a body image risk assessor), concentrating instead on delineating good assessment practice. Murray makes much of interviewing, emphasising enquiry into the patient's background and values, his coping style, and the usefulness of open ended questions for gathering a balanced history (Murray, 1972). Carroll employs Aguilera's crisis intervention model (Aguilera and Messick, 1974) to outline enquiry areas. These include, the patient's perception of events, their coping mechanisms such as anger and denial, and what she calls situational supports. This approach has much in common with the one used in this volume, although Carroll makes no distinction between body reality, ideal and presentation (Carroll, 1981). Finally Gruendemann also emphasises the use of interviews, the contrast between normal and altered body image but this time following surgery. Alongside this, an equal emphasis is placed upon observation techniques. The nurse is encouraged to note the patient's body posture, positioning and 'body language'. Observations are used to corroborate the impressions formed by the nurse during interviews (Gruendemann, 1975).

Assessment areas

What then should the nurse assess about the patient who has sustained, or seems likely to sustain, a damaged body image? Four areas deserve the nurse's attention. The first three areas stem from our division of body image into body reality, body ideal and body presentation. The fourth area concerns coping strategies, including grief response and the use of social support networks.

Body reality

When the nurse first meets the patient, body reality may already be impaired. A patient entering the ward may already have a scar, limb shortening or a tracheostomy. It is important that the extent of alteration to body reality is carefully assessed as the nurse helps the patient undress, wash or settle into the ward. Basic observations may reveal yet other changes such as lost weight, dependent oedema or a subnormal body temperature. Reference to patient notes, or a brief interview should establish how much the body has been altered or damaged, and how long ago this occurred. The latter question is very important, as it is possible that a long term alteration to body reality, can become absorbed later as a part of normal body image. By assessing the physical condition of the patient the nurse may better assess the likely impact of surgery or treatment. A well nourished body may better sustain cytotoxic therapy and an intact body image or self-image. Therefore, in making a physical assessment of the patient, use this information to understand body image needs – do not compartmentalise it as a different nursing goal!

The nurse must also anticipate the alteration that is yet to affect body reality. Reference to operating lists, the consultant's briefing, treatment schedules and her own experience of seeing the effects of these will enable her to create a mental picture of the future change. Regular professional nursing updates on drugs and their effects, operations, wound drains and prostheses are necessary if an adequate assessment of altered body reality is to be made. At an early stage, it is the nurse who anticipates this altered appearance, and who may then have to interpret details for the patient. If the patient is to have surgery, the presence of operation marks is noted. This is a minor alteration to body reality, but for patient and nurse it symbolises the change that will come about later. All data concerning body reality should then be recorded on assessment sheets. The use of a simple body outline chart such as the anterior/posterior views as used in burns units is recommended. This can then form a quick reference for all the nurses caring for the patient.

Body ideal

Up until this point the nurse has used her eyes and sense of touch to collect a great deal of information. Assessing body ideal however will require that she establish a professional, trusting relationship with the patient. Interviewing patients about their body ideal may involve a check list, perhaps relating to body parts, but is much more likely to utilise information offered for other purposes. For instance, as part of settling into the ward, the nurse could compliment a patient on her dress. This often elicits a pleasant response and makes the patient feel 'at home'. It may reveal whether the patient wishes she was thinner, taller, shorter, more athletic looking. Incidental conversation, a natural accompaniment to care, is usually full of cues into body image issues. One patient says to a nurse serving his lunch, 'I wish I could look as thin as you!' This is a throw away line, but it could be used by the nurse to establish how the patient would like to look and behave.

In some instances, notably breast surgery, body ideal will be well to the fore of the patient's thoughts. The patient may take an early opportunity to tell the nurse what she hopes she will look like as a result of surgery. It is important to make a note of such hopes and to consider these in the light of what information or insight into surgery the patient is believed to have. Is the body ideal realistic, or based upon a false impression of what surgery will achieve? Assessing the patient's body ideal can never take place through one admission interview. Because body ideal is a personal matter, it must be assessed over daily nursing procedures, using a number of nurses. The nurse must almost develop antennae to pick up oblique references which confide how the patient would wish to look. This may be difficult, but it is always worthwhile and adds credence to the argument that talking with the patient is often as therapeutic as doing something practical.

Body presentation

Assessing body presentation involves the use of all of the special senses. The circumstances of the patient's illness or injury may affect matters, but the nurse should assess how the patient is dressed, how the patient mobilises and whether any particular postures or positions are adopted. Dress may give a clue to the patient's culture and status, but should also help the nurse to assess self-image, such as fashionable, serious, casual, or formal. Poorly kept clothes and a bedraggled appearance, may suggest a poor self-image, often associated with poverty. Limitations in movement, in holding a static position may be the first indication of a patient's pain and an underlying body reality problem, like a fracture.

It should not be forgotten that admission to hospital is a stressful event for many patients. Study of body presentation, such as a tense drawn up posture or the body turned away from others, may help with forming some initial impressions of the patient's feelings and self-confidence. Is self-image threatened by the new status as a patient? At the other extreme, an apparently relaxed, almost lounging demeanour, even indifference, may indicate that the patient is putting on a show of self-control. Reviewing body presentation in the light of physical assessment and the body ideal or self-ideal which the patient professes, can reveal how 'false' a performance is. The patient's pretense may collapse suddenly, and then the unprepared nurse might have to make a radical adjustment to her plan of psychological care.

It is worth remembering that body presentation is where the individual tries to match body reality to body ideal. Therefore, the nurse would be wise to bear in mind the impact of surgery or treatment upon the body reality. Will this promote a successful body presentation for the patient? Does the patient understand that he will be restricted to bed, or by ventilator, perhaps for several days? Does he know that a wound drain and intravenous infusion will be in place? It is not enough that the nurse assesses current body presentation, she must anticipate future altered body presentation too. This will enable the nursing team to put in place appropriate education and physiotherapy so that the patient's adaptation to change is facilitated.

Part of the assessment of body presentation must be addressed to the value placed upon various body 'parts'. A pianist places great emphasis upon his or her hands, not only the tools of his profession, but also a symbol of artistic sensitivity. A woman may invest considerable value in her breasts or uterus, and a man in his testicles, as essential aspects of their sexuality. Pre-operative discussion about 'how' the patient will express femininity or masculinity later may well reveal gaps in the patient's knowledge or preparation. It may never have been considered just how important body attributes were in the expression of self-image.

Coping strategies

While nurses are perhaps most familiar with collecting and assessing physical data, it is also true that they deal in psychological assessment. This need not mean that a nurse becomes enmeshed in complicated personality inventories or fits the ward interview area with a psychotherapy couch. What the nurse seeks to understand about coping strategies can usually be dealt with in everyday terminology. Often the question can be put quite straightforwardly during interview. To a question such as 'now, I expect that being in hospital has been a little strange Mr Baxter, how have you been coping with it?' the patient may say that he copes by becoming rather more quiet, mulling over observations and worries. Others may admit, often in deceptively jocular terms that they squeal 'long and loud about everything'. Relatives, if present, are usually quick to point out the patient's favourite normal technique for dealing with stress. 'She gets ratty, really bad tempered', or again, 'he tends to become very demanding and sarcastic'. It is surprising how honest and reflective patients can be concerning their coping strategies. The nurse may then explain that understanding their normal way of 'dealing with worries' will help her to anticipate and perhaps avoid some problems.

In assessing the impact of altered body image, through surgery or treatment, or through rehabilitation after trauma, the nurse must blend anticipated patient coping techniques with the common grief reaction that she expects in such circumstances (see Chapter 5). Many patients undergoing surgery are aware that a grief reaction frequently occurs. One lady, anticipating a hysterectomy confided, 'I expect I'll feel a bit weepy on day two or three'. It is worth enquiring whether the patient has anticipated mood changes during a stay in hospital. While few patients will quote the grief reaction stages off pat, many may recognise that it, 'may take a while to look at the scar'. Such an assessment may help the nurse to understand that the patient's withdrawal post-operatively is not necessarily the first signs of a major grief reaction. It may be that the patient is coping with an altered body image in a well tried and tested personal manner.

Finally under coping strategies, the social resources that the patient might draw upon should also be considered. The circle of family, relatives, work mates and friends who visit and encourage the patient are collectively, a social support network. The amount and quality of social support available to the patient may be very important in the face of major alteration to body image (Jamison et al, 1978). Cohen and McKay have outlined four categories of social support – tangible, appraisal, self-esteem and belonging (Cohen and McKay, 1984). All of these would seem important for patients considered in this book. Tangible support refers to practical aid, perhaps help with transport. Appraisal support refers to the lending of an empathetic ear, a listener who assists the patient to review events and take stock of the present situation. The patient gains self-esteem support from others who are willing to make favourable comparisons between the patient's and others appearance. A sense of belonging is achieved when the patient finds that a variety of other people are available to socialise with.

Assessing social support starts at the time of the first nursing interview and continues on throughout the time of contact with the patient. Noting the number and variety of visitors, the regularity of their visits and the apparent effects upon the patient, enables the nurse to evolve a picture of whom the patient might hope to call upon later. Often visitor or patient involves the nurse in conversation, or even future plans. This is an opportunity for the nurse to assess what the relatives or friends expect concerning the patient's future appearance or function. In cases of severe burns, or when patients have undergone mutilating cancer surgery, deputations of relatives may come to express their concern over the patient's progress toward a new appearance. Enquiries often revolve around questions like, 'do you think his scars will settle down?', 'will he be able to move about a bit more easily later?'. In trying to allay anxieties and meet relatives' needs, the nurse can also make a more accurate appraisal of how well informed the relatives are, and whether they too are coping adequately with the stress of their loved one's altered body image. This is important, for a relative may cease to be a support and may become another casualty, if nurses and doctors do not anticipate the possible family trauma associated with the patient's problems.

Assessment techniques

It is clear, given what has been said, that assessment of the altered body image patient cannot be a discrete step in a linear nursing process. Instead, assessment must start with first encounters and evolve over subsequent days until the nurse has built up a more complete picture of the patient and his circumstances. During first encounters, the nurse seeks to use an interpretive framework, one that outlines the patient's concerns and personal perspective (Price, 1987). This is difficult to achieve if nurses continue to feel that early on they must quickly propose solutions for body image problems. Time and further consultations need to pass before the nurse can hope to form a finely tailored nursing care plan.

The nurse uses her powers of observation – her eyes, ears and sense of touch – as well as interview skills to gather all the body image material. To do this successfully she must establish an empathetic relationship with the patient and kin early on. She should be honest about planned surgery or treatment, and that adapting to a new body image may take time and personal courage. She should show, possibly by reference to previous patients and herself, that she recognises that this may be frightening. She explains that she understands that different patients cope in different ways. A good patient is not necessarily an 'in control of emotions' patient.

Where patients are dealing with major or traumatic change in body image, such trust may best be built up using a primary nursing care approach. With a designated 'case load' of patients, the nurse is motivated to build her assessment of the situation, knowing that she will have control over the resultant nursing care plan. In the meantime, the patient can in turn feel that this is 'his nurse', a professional with whom he can communicate frankly. In this atmosphere, the need for extensive and formal assessment tools is reduced. The nurse is able to develop a patient profile through observations, reflections and conversations, none of which is felt to be overtly 'assessment' by the patient. While checklists of damaged body parts may be avoided, this does not mean that the nurse can afford to neglect her records of assessment. Only by recording her findings can she ethically and legally point to professionally originated nursing care. This is as true of altered body image diagnoses as any other.

Conclusion

It has been argued that the nurse's purpose in assessing body image, differs markedly from that of most scientists. She has a pressing practical concern, to assist the patient in his recovery and rehabilitation. Continuing debates over the conceptualisation, measuring and mapping of body image will be important, but in the interim, patients continue to suffer body image damage and request nurses' help. In the light of this, the nurse must rely upon field skills such as observation, interviewing, and patient history taking, until such time as specifically designed nursing assessment tools are tested and to hand. While this may soon be in sight (Baird, 1985), it seems clear that these tools will add to the assessment armoury, rather than supplant the nurse's bedside skills.

Review questions

1 Chapter 7 makes it very clear that assessing altered body image will be difficult because of the abstract nature of the problem. How do nurses currently decide that an altered body image problem exists? For instance, is a body image problem rather like pain, what the patient says it is?

2 Body image could be assessed by using a comprehensive patient questionnaire. What are the advantages and disadvantages of this approach?

3 Using the assessment areas discussed in Chapter 7, how would you set about assessing a patient's 'phantom limb' experiences?

4 Chapter 7 suggests that much assessment may be achieved using simple powers of observation. Can you suggest why observation should be fully utilised, before the nurse interviews the patient?

5 How does the presence of friends or relatives at the bedside affect the

nurse's assessment of the patient's body image worries and needs?

6 Why is a body outline map, as commonly used to map burns, so useful for plotting changes in body reality?

7 It is suggested that the nurse should assess the patient using an interpretive approach. How easy is this to achieve on a surgical ward where many of the body image problems are associated with 'standard' operations, such as hysterectomy?

Suggested exercise

This exercise involves setting up a short role played scene and evaluation of it.

Setting

Ideally this exercise should take place in the practical suite, or an appropriate classroom with 'admission desk' and chairs.

Organisation

Three character actors are required, the remainer of the group acting as an informed observer corp. The three 'actors' should be briefed several days in advance of the exercise, and asked to bring to the situation clothing in keeping with their roles. At a similar point the observers should be asked to review, in their own minds, the assessment skills that the nurse might use to identify actual or potential body image problems or needs. At the exercise, the observers are seated in a semi-circle around the role play area to promote different angles of view. The observers should consider the following questions, which are given to them on a handout:

1. What faculties, such as touch, did you see the nurse use during this first assessment of Mrs Bowen?
2. What coping strategies were being employed by the Bowen sisters?
3. How was the nurse's assessment interview used to glean information about body image problems?

Character briefings

At the actor's briefing each character is given the following details, with suggestions on how the problems or needs might be presented authentically.

Character 1: Ms Mary Bowen
Mary is the patient, a woman in her late forties who has never married. Mary has rheumatoid arthritis in both her hands and the spine and will be showing some stiffness in her hands (perhaps she cannot take her coat off). A slight stoop should be used and she should complain of pain in her spine. She does not carry anything and describes to the nurse at an early stage just how hot, tired and uncomfortable she feels. She is dressed in smart casual clothes, but the zip, buttons or catches of some part of her apparel are left undone.

Character 2: Ms Grace Bowen (Mary's sister)
Grace is the only support to Mary and they live together some way out in the country. Grace is a concerned and intensely busy woman, who brings a big bag of things for Mary to use in hospital. Grace fusses over her sister somewhat, often anticipating the nurses questions, or answering on her sister's behalf.

Character 3: Nurse Lewis
Nurse Lewis is the admitting nurse, and has been warned that a lady with acute rheumatoid arthritis is to be admitted. She is equipped with the usual paperwork and other accoutrements, like a stethescope. Nurse Lewis is patient and empathetic. She must interview the two sisters and make a first interview assessment.

Role play and review

The observers should now be briefed that the woman being admitted suffers from an acute exacerbation of rheumatoid arthritis. The role play can then commence. After the role play has ended, it should be emphasised to all present that this is a simulation. The artificial setting and circumstances means that the following discussion cannot really reflect on the nurse actors' real clinical skills. With that proviso however, the observers should be invited to offer their points concerning the questions that have been put to them. The actors should also have a chance to reflect upon the issues – they have after all experienced the process and may now offer insights on how assessment of body image might be improved. Thank all concerned, especially the actors who have perhaps played the bravest of parts.

Suggested time sequence

(a) for briefing to actors and observers, do so two to three days prior to exercise.

(b) for role play period, allow about 20 to 30 minutes (depending on actors' comfort and normal admission protocols)
(c) for discussion period, allow about one hour. A great deal of useful ideas may emerge from a good role play.

References

Aguilera D. and Messick J., *Crisis Intervention*, C.V. Mosby, St Louis, 1974.

Baird S.E., 'Development of a Nursing Assessment Tool to Diagnose Altered Body Image in Immobilized Patients', *Orthopaedic Nursing*, 4(1), pp 47–54, 1985.

Carroll R., 'The Impact of Mastectomy on Body Image', *Oncology Nursing Forum*, 8(4), pp 29–32, 1981.

Champion V. and Tzeng O., 'Assessment of Relationship Between Self Concept and Body Image Using Multivariate Techniques', *Issues In Mental Health Nursing*, 4, pp 299–315, 1982.

Cohen S. and McKay G., 'Interpersonal Relationships as Buffers of the Impact of Psychological Stress on Health', in Baum A., Singer J. and Taylor S. (eds), *Handbook of Psychology and Health*, Erlbaum, Hillsdale, NJ, 1984.

Fawcett J. and Frye S., 'An Exploratory Study of Body Image Dimensionality', *Nursing Research*, 29(5), pp 324–7, 1980.

Feldman M.M., 'The Body Image and Object Relations: exploration of a method utilising repertory grid techniques', *British Journal of Medical Psychology*, 48, pp 317–32, 1975.

Gruendemann B., 'The Impact of Surgery on Body Image', *Nursing Clinics of North America*, 10(4), pp 635–43, 1975.

Jamison K.I., Wellisch D. and Pasnall R., 'Psychological Aspects of Mastectomy 1: The woman's perspective', *American Journal of Psychiatry*, 135(4), pp 432–6, 1978.

Jourard S. and Secord P.F., 'Body-cathexis and the Ideal Female Figure', *Journal of Abnormal Social Psychology*, 50, pp 243–6, 1955.

MacDonald K., *Size Judgements and Reactions to Interpersonal Frustration*, Masters thesis, University of Kansas, 1966.

Murray R.L., 'Principles of Nursing Intervention for the Adult Patient With Body Image Changes', *Nursing Clinics of North America*, 7(4), pp 697–707, 1972.

Price B., 'First Impressions: Paradigms for patient assessment', *Journal of Advanced Nursing*, 12, pp 699–705, 1987.

Rowe A.S. and Caldwell W.E., 'The Somatic Apperception Test', *Journal of General Psychiatry*, 68, pp 59–69, 1963.

Schilder P., *The Image and Appearance of the Human Body*, International Universities Press, New York, 1935 (reprint 1950).

Schlacter L., *The Relation Between Anxiety, Perceived Body and Personal Space and Actual Body Space Among Young Female Adults*, New York University, unpublished PhD dissertation, 1971.

Shontz F.C., 'Body Part Size Judgement in Contrasting Intellectual Groups', *Journal of Nervous and Mental Disease*, 136, pp 368–73, 1963.

Shontz, F.C., *Perceptual and Cognitive Aspects of Body Experience*, Academic Press, New York, 1969.

Tzeng O., 'Differentiation of Affective and Denotative Meaning Systems and their Influence in Personality Ratings', *Journal of Personality and Social Psychology*, 32, pp 978–88, 1975.

Further reading

Arnhoff F.N. and Mehl M., 'Body Image Deterioration in Paraplegia', *Journal of Nervous and Mental Disease*, 137, pp 88–92, 1963.

Cleveland S.E., 'Judgements of Body Size in a Schizophrenic and a Control Group', *Psychological Reports*, 7, p 304, 1960.

Cleveland S.E., Fisher S., Reitman E. and Rothaus P., 'Perception of Body Size in Schizophrenia', *Archives of General Psychiatry*, 7, pp 277–85, 1962.

Fink S.L., *Body Image Disturbances in Chronically Ill Persons*, unpublished PhD dissertation, Western Reserve University, 1959.

Gilbert J. and Hall M., 'Changes with Age in Human Figure Drawings', *Journal of Gerontology*, 17, pp 397–404, 1962.

Guess P.D., *Body Image Disturbances of Brain Damaged Persons*, Masters thesis (unpublished), University of Kansas, 1963.

Lakin M., 'Formal Characteristics of Human Figure Drawings by Institutionalised Aged and by Normal Children', *Journal of Consulting Psychology*, 20, pp 471–4, 1956.

Lakin M., 'Formal Characteristics of Human Figure Drawings by Institutionalised and Non-institutionalised Aged', *Journal of Gerontology*, 15, pp 76–8, 1960.

Lebovitz B.Z. and Lakin M., 'Body Image and Paralytic Poliomyelitis: An experimental approach', *Journal of Nervous and Mental Disease*, 125, pp 518–23, 1957.

Orbach J., Traub A.C. and Olson R., 'Psychophysical Studies of Body Image 2: Normative data on the adjustable body-distorting Mirror', *Archives of General Psychiatry*, 14, pp 41–7, 1966.

Plutchik R., Weiner B. and Conte H., 'Studies of Body Image 1: Body worries and body discomforts', *Journal of Gerontology*, 27, pp 344–50, 1971.

Plutchik R., Conte H. and Weiner B. 'Studies of Body Image 2: Dollar values of body parts', *Journal of Gerontology*, 28, pp 89–91, 1972.

Schiff N., 'A Study of the Differences in the Draw a Person Test of Normal Elderly Females and Normal Adult Females', Ann Arbor, MI Xerox University, microfilm (dissertation), 1976.

Traub A.C., and Orbach J., 'Psychophysical Studies of Body Image 1: The adjustable body distorting mirror', *Archives of General Psychiatry*, 11, pp 53–66, 1964.

Wechowicz T.E. and Sommer R., 'Body Image and Self Concept in Schizophrenia, An Experimental Study', *Journal of Mental Science*, 106, pp 17–39, 1960.

8 Planning a nursing intervention

Study of this chapter will enable you to:

1 State why the nurse must review her own body image and associated needs before planning care for the patient.
2 Describe what is meant by the term *rehabilitation*.
3 List typical members of the rehabilitation team and outline what is meant by the phrase, *teamwork philosophy*.
4 Describe the four principles of action which should guide care planning activities.
5 Offer examples of body reality care planning activities, noting why these are therapeutic with regard to both physical health and body image support.
6 Describe typical body ideal interventions.
7 Discuss why body presentation interventions are so important to the patient who is to be discharged from hospital.
8 Offer a range of body presentation interventions.
9 Discuss why the patient's personal coping strategies must be taken into account when planning patient education.
10 Outline why interventions aimed at the patient's social support network might be started early during the patient's stay in hospital.

Once it has been assessed that the patient is facing a body image problem, it is important to establish a realistic nursing care plan that may lead to his rehabilitation. At least two aspects of rehabilitation are highlighted in dictionary definitions of the term. The first refers to the re-establishment of a person's good name or reputation. The second refers to the restoration of an individual's health and useful or constructive activity. Both definitions are appropriate in body image care. The patient wants to re-establish a good reputation with himself and others (self-image). This can only be achieved if he is at peace with how his body looks and behaves (body image). This chapter, therefore, will discuss the planning of patient care, using the body image model introduced in Chapter 1, and a rehabilitation framework devised for the patient's circumstances.

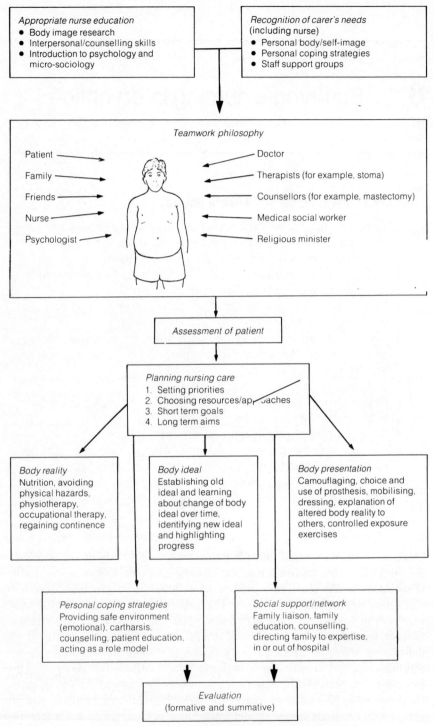

Fig. 8.1 Care planning within a rehabilitation framework.

Planning nursing care should be seen as part of a wider rehabilitation effort (see Figure 8.1). The nursing care plan will be but one expression of a teamwork that brings patient, kin and professionals together to solve body image problems. The plan must consider the unique circumstances of the patient and the ways in which the body image problems are perceived and interpreted. It is also designed to encourage the patient to take final control of his health and body image maintenance (Marten, 1978; Price, 1986). Care provision is as much about doing things with, as much as for, the patient. In order to achieve this the nurse should review her own body image and coping strategies, before advising the patient.

Preliminary needs

The preliminary needs are those of the nurse herself! Unless she is equipped to provide informed intervention, any care may be ineffective or even harmful to the patient. To that end nurse education should ideally include a review of the body image research literature. It should equip her with basic interpersonal and counselling skills, so that she understands that the way she gives care, as well as the care itself is also important. An appreciation of interpersonal psychology and sociology is also key to care planning success. Only through considering the grief response, cultural and social aspects of body image, and the development of stigma, can we anticipate the widest care needs.

Remind yourself that your own personal body image and coping strategies will also affect the situation. In the earlier sections of this book it was suggested that we not only form a body image for ourselves, but that we also project one onto those close to us. This was seen in terms of maintaining personal self-image and through trying to influence the company that we keep. Although an understandable human trait, it can affect the way the patient is nursed, and may even affect the success or otherwise of his rehabilitation. If the nurse harbours a negative personal self-image, she may not prove sympathetic to a patient with a similar problem. Stanley and Denning have both made this point very clear (Denning, 1982; Stanley, 1977). The latter author examined the problem of patients with head and neck cancer. She concluded that the nurse's reactions to deformity or surgery could be crucial for the patient's own first reactions to his appearance. A nurse who has always preferred to avoid the thought of mutilation to her own face, may find it difficult to support a patient with just this problem. Darbyshire and before him, Kelly and May, reviewed many of these adverse reactions by hospital staff. It seemed clear that the patient suffering from an altered body image may also face a communications barrier with professionals that are still busy dealing with their own feelings about deformity (Darbyshire, 1986; Kelly and May, 1982).

An important second step to care planning therefore, is a personal review of feelings concerning deformity. To facilitate this, support groups for nurses who work in areas of high stress, such as burns units, should be set up. In this setting the nurse can explore how she feels about her own body and body image problems in general. A clinical psychologist or experienced counsellor should be invited to help in the identification of personal coping strategies. Such discussion is designed to help the nurse 'know her self', so that she might then understand her reactions and present a more supportive service to the patient. Feeling anger or disgust at facial deformity may not be a bar to successful patient care. Failing to recognise and respond professionally to these feelings in her self might be.

Teamwork philosophy

Identifying body image problems, plotting care goals, cannot be achieved without discussion with other rehabilitation team members. Initial plans are often modified after a progress discussion with the patient, stoma therapist or medical social worker for instance. Therefore, the notion of writing care plans in tablets of stone on admission day must be abandoned. Planning must be seen as process rather than paper record and this is facilitated by the use of computer based care plans. In this arrangement records can be adjusted and updated on an almost hourly basis.

The rationale of rehabilitation teamwork is that each member brings something unique to the problem in hand. The patient, his experience of the problem and his preferred ways of coping. The relatives, background details on social support available and ways of motivating the patient. Doctors and paramedical therapists, technical knowledge and skills appropriate to the problem. The nurse acts as primary assessor of patient and progress and is constantly in contact with him. She is frequently the patient's advocate during care discussions. She may act as teacher, guide and assistant to the patient in the matter of physical care. The product of this shared effort is presumed to be more worthwhile than individual solutions. Indeed, without recourse to each of the team members, it is likely that the patient will make only a partial or inadequate rehabilitation.

Because the patient's needs are changing throughout the rehabilitation period, and because different team members are more or less central to meeting these needs, leadership of the team must change. In the early days the nurse may take charge, as it is she who develops an initial appraisal of the patient's reactions to body image change. Later, following surgery, the doctor or stoma therapist may hold centre stage. After a major injury, such as a scald, this may be a protracted process. Eventually however, the control of rehabilitation must rest with the patient and relatives. It is only in terms of his life, work, social circumstances and needs that final progress can be measured. This often occurs long after the hospital stay is over (Platzer, 1987). Final acceptance of the new body image and successful management of the same, may take years to achieve. In hospital, the nurse may have been cheered by the gratitude of 'her' dependent patient, but she should seek to make him independent as promptly and as safely as possible.

Principles of action

Four principles should guide the nurse as she prepares the patient care plan (see Figure 8.2). The first is setting priorities. Different aspects of care will need attention, and some aspects will be more urgent than others. It is usually most important to deal with matters of body reality first. A patient who has a tracheostomy in place may die if suction is not completed regularly. Such suction reminds the patient of his dependence upon the nurse and reinforces a negative, 'less than whole' body image. Nevertheless, education about the functional need for suction may have to precede advice about tracheostomy dressings (body presentation) for safety reasons. By choosing priorities of care in the light of patient safety, expressed need, surgery and future management, the nurse shows that she anticipates change and is confident that the patient can be guided through it. Priorities may involve anticipating a body image problem. For instance, it is better to advise the patient about alopecia before large amounts of hair drop out.

The second and third principles are interlinked. Short term care goals are used to achieve longer term aims. A patient is assisted to manage his stoma in privacy, before he is asked to deal with it in more public circumstances. A patient is helped to choose a breast prosthesis, before she is encouraged to venture forth into social gatherings. This seemingly obvious principle has not always been acted upon by nurses or other carers. Judging how many long term aims can realistically be achieved during the patient's hospital stay, the nurse may be influenced by the need to 'get things done before discharge', rather than establish sound grounds for later progress. Asking a patient to proceed to bigger challenges, without some success at earlier goals, is likely to produce failure or trauma. The patient's confidence is built through smaller 'enabling goals' being achieved. Most patients prefer to use the stepping stones across the river, rather than the pole vault.

Lastly it is equally important in assisting the patient to choose the right resources and team members. Not only should nurses consider what resources to call upon, but also when to make that call. Inviting the counsellor to the ward too early or too late will not help the patient. It is useful to note which nurses establish a good rapport with the patient and rela-

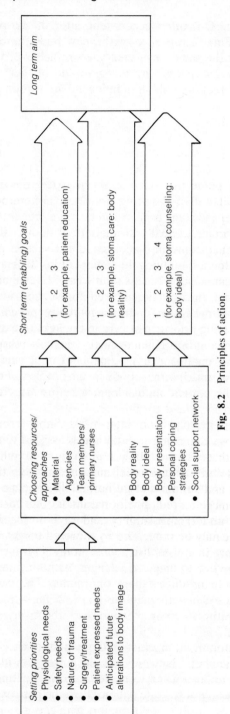

Fig. 8.2 Principles of action.

Long term aim

Short term (enabling) goals

1 2 3
(for example, patient education)

1 2 3
(for example, stoma care: body reality)

1 2 3 4
(for example, stoma counselling: body ideal)

Choosing resources/approaches
• Material
• Agencies
• Team members/primary nurses

• Body reality
• Body ideal
• Body presentation
• Personal coping strategies
• Social support network

Setting priorities
• Physiological needs
• Safety needs
• Nature of trauma
• Surgery/treatment
• Patient expressed needs
• Anticipated future alterations to body image

tives. These staff members may then be encouraged to act as primary nurses, channelling care and support to the patient from the rest of the team. Care delivered through a trusting relationship should be that much better received.

Body reality interventions

The nursing care plan that is drawn up concerning body reality is hard to distinguish from care planned for the patient's general physical care. Clearly, if the patient's body and its functions are looked after, then it should be easier to sustain a body image which relies upon this body. Care may be planned to prevent damage or deterioration to the body. It may be designed to limit the trauma caused to the body, for example post-surgery, or to improve body structure or performance. On the care plan these interventions may be listed as responses to malnutrition, surgical shock or dehydration. Even the simplest physical care measure (direct or indirect) contributes to the patient's body image and self-image needs.

Care designed to avoid the hazards of immobility may be used to illustrate this point. The patient who is 'bed bound' is likely to experience a significant change in body image. Lying on his back his perspective of communications with the nurse is changed. His body is 'flat on its back', something normally associated with the dead, the dying or the highly vulnerable. The nurse is upright and in control. Musculo-skeletal and circulatory deterioration may lead to 'foot drop', deep vein thrombosis, muscle wastage and decubitus ulcers (Buergin, 1987). All of these complications are likely to prove damaging to body ideal. The patient does not want sores, or a foot that will not allow him to walk upright. Passive physiotherapy exercises and pressure relief measures all help the patient to avoid such problems and sustain a more normal body image.

Care planned to promote a good nutritional intake also sustains body image needs. Patients undergoing surgery and several other types of treatment experience a catabolic state. The body breaks down more tissue than is built up, resulting in weight loss, a fall in fat reserves (changing body contours) and sometimes, poor tissue integrity. Body weight is an important facet of body image. Most people know what they weigh, how much they should weigh and how they feel about the difference! By adjusting nutritional intake, promoting tissue repair and growth, nurses cannot fail to have a positive effect upon body image.

Here is another illustration. The nurse who plans an aseptic change of a dressing, not only achieves a low wound infection rate, but also sends a body image message to the patient. Avoiding suture line infections makes for a neater scar line, which will later fade and seem inconsequential on the summer beach.

Body ideal interventions

The nurse cannot overestimate the importance of body ideal to the patient. So alongside practical physical care, the nurse chats with the patient, trying to identify his preferred body ideal, and whether he still feels this to be realistic. A key nursing goal is to help the patient to realise that all body ideals are transitory, and relative to human development. The body ideal, while cherished, will change with time and this process continues even when the body image has been damaged. It may be helpful to recall previous normal body ideals, the nurse sharing some of her own. A body ideal from childhood might retrospectively seem ridiculous and it is now possible to smile about it. Once, however, it was prized, like the one the patient worries about now. Therefore, the plan should be to respect the patient's grief, but to reward any recognition shown that the body ideal is a changing and an often resilient part of body image.

Inviting the patient to share in discussions about heroes, 'images of how I should be', is especially useful with children. Such discussions may highlight areas where care may help the patient to bring the elements of his body image closer together. An athletic body ideal may still be possible from the wheelchair, if instead of leg power, the patient emphasises arm power, through archery or wheelchair basketball. The revelation that the nurse and other patients hold different body ideals may assist the patient to understand that because his own ideal is not achieved, this does not mean he is devalued in other people's eyes. So a care plan may introduce this plurality of body ideals on the ward, for both patients and staff. Discussion is a useful way of helping the patient to learn about such variety.

Body presentation interventions

Perhaps the most fertile field for care planning is found here. Comparatively short hospital stays can make detailed body ideal care difficult to achieve. Many body reality changes, such as infection, are not completely within the nurse's control. Success in body presentation care planning is critical, for if the patient is ill prepared for returning to the world outside more crippling body image damage may yet be inflicted by ill considered opinion or public reaction. In this area, more than any other, nursing care is likely to affect the success or failure of rehabilitation. Short hospital stays, 'high tech' treatment and staff shortages may get in the way, but the patient must be helped to face the world beyond the ward and the family's protective cocoon.

The nurse is trying to facilitate a body presentation over which the

patient has maximum behavioural and decisional control (Averill, 1973).
The nurse helps the patient to achieve this over perhaps months or years,
handing support work over to community nurses once the patient is discharged from hospital. Even if the patient cannot fully control his body
and its movements, as with cerebral palsy, he must have the decisional
control over how to account for the altered presentation. To deny the
patient this would be to deny his dignity as a human being.

A common nursing goal is the successful camouflaging of deformity or
disability. The term camouflage is applied here to both the visual appearance of body parts, and their movement or function. We can camouflage
a facial scar with the use of skilful makeup and a patchy hair loss with
a wig or attractive hat. An abnormal limb movement, perhaps the result
of muscle spasm, may be camouflaged by carefully restraining the limb, or
emphasising another part of the body movement, possibly by building up
an improved walking gait. Camouflage is often thought of as the means
to hide something nasty or sinister. Nurses should see it as the means to
help patients thrive and progress, as a protective device in a sometimes
predatory world.

In one sense a prosthesis, such as an artificial limb or a false eye, is also
a camouflaging device. Planning to use a prosthesis, the nurse must liaise
with the surgical fitter and sometimes acquaint patients with alternatives
not immediately available through the local health care system. A dis-
traught patient may accept any quick solution and later discover that while
the prosthesis works it is hardly aesthetic to look at. To this end care may
be planned to not only help the patient learn to use the prosthesis effectively, but also to acquaint him with further improvements in prostheses
as these become available. Prostheses therefore aid care in at least two
major respects. Firstly, they rapidly improve the total body shape of the
patient, especially if correctly structured, coloured and textured, for
example a false limb. Secondly, they assist in the development of more
normal movement, itself an integral aspect of body presentation.

Other interventions concern practicalities of dressing and mobilising.
Learning how to choose clothes to hide a neck scar, or to minimise the
appearance of a spinal deformity is very important. In a real sense, the
clothes worn when coming out of hospital are every bit as important as
the debutante's ball gown. Gait is also a major clue to body image problems. It is the gait of the cerebral palsy child and the cerebro-vascular
accident patient that often labels them with their disability. Both appearance and gait are improved by physiotherapy exercises. Physiotherapy
concentrated on walking, turning, sitting and standing not only improve
muscle function but also assists in the creation of a new acceptable body
image.

Ordering the progress of such interventions requires special planning.

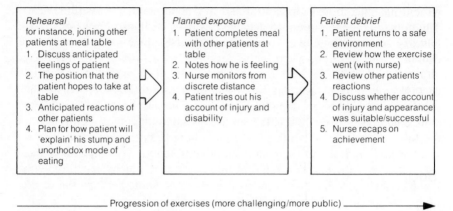

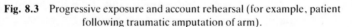
Progression of exercises (more challenging/more public)

Fig. 8.3   Progressive exposure and account rehearsal (for example, patient following traumatic amputation of arm).

Where the problem is major, affecting both appearance and movement, the plan may emphasise a progressive exposure to new environments and people. Having tested out the presentation in private, for instance a walk with a zimmer frame, the nurse asks the patient to anticipate how the same exercise would be done in public. The patient then moves onto practising walking on the ward and then later further afield. After each adventure the nurse debriefs the patient, emphasising the progress made (see Figure 8.3 for a further example).

Personal coping strategies

While it is not always possible to predict a grief response accurately, provision should be made for patient's who behave aggressively or seem upset and withdrawn. The nurse should have established already how the patient normally copes with stress and this should be used as a guide to the reactions that may occur later. Part of the plan may be to set aside a private room, or space, where the patient can express bitterness or despair. This should be away from the more public ward areas and be equipped with chairs and facilities for making drinks. Here, a primary nurse may assist the patient in expressing anger, with an assurance that letting off steam is a means of making progress.

Care planning for patient education is most strongly affected by the patient's personal coping strategies. Well timed education may minimise the traumas of altered body image, but poorly timed material will seem insensitive at the very least. Oermann *et al* argued that education should be 'sensory' in nature (Oermann *et al*, 1983). Being able to anticipate how something would feel, look, smell or hurt, enables patients to cope with the problem much more successfully. Being able to anticipate when and where something would happen, for instance the removal of a wound drain, also helped. As a general rule, educating patients before operation is preferable. Providing the patient with a supportive environment in which to explore feelings should improve later rehabilitation (Johnston and Carpenter, 1980; Sime, 1976).

Social support network

If the nurse turns to the psychologist for help with planning an improved patient coping response, she turns to the family and medical social worker to assist the patient here. Having assessed the attitudes, interest and support of kin, it may become evident that the patient will not receive much assistance upon discharge from hospital. Where kin networks are weak, which may be the case for a variety of reasons, the care plan must address the need to arrange interim support measures. Halfway hostels or housing may provide a temporary haven where the patient can explore a new body image, even if it is in an artificial setting. This measure has been especially important amongst mentally ill patients.

Other care plan goals might be to educate the family about the patient's problems, so that prejudice is forestalled and a more objective opinion formed. Any such education must start from the premise that the family are part of the rehabilitation team. Criticising the relatives for not supporting their sick family member precludes them from feeling like equal partners in care. The family may also be suffering from aspects of the altered body image. Family resources may be slight, and a contribution greater than what relatives can afford, either in time, money or emotions should not be expected. Under these circumstances resources must be sought for the family, possibly from an outside hospital support agency.

Conclusion

Planning care for the patient cannot be seen as a single action in a linear nursing process. Rather, it is a process that evolves through contact with the patient and other rehabilitation team members. Care planned to assist the patient with body image problems cannot always be separated from care aimed at other problems. For some patients however, body image concerns may be foremost, and resolution of the same may have the most profound and long lasting effect upon the patient's later life.

Review questions

1 It could be argued that while the nurse is not always suited to leading the rehabilitation team, she is best suited to co-ordinating its efforts. Can you argue for or against this statement?

2 Can you identify further members of the rehabilitation team that might be added to Figure 8.1, for example the speech therapist?

3 To what extent do you think your nurse education has equipped you to deal with body image problems (either personal or patient's)?

4 Try to recount an example that you have known, where short term goals really did promote the achievement of long term aims.

5 Try to describe how oral hygiene may also affect body image (as well as appetite and oral infection rates).

6 Should the nurse quickly try to divest the patient of hopes and aspirations concerning a previous body ideal?

7 How might camouflage and dress be used to deal with a urinary catheter and leg bag?

8 Why might a file of voluntary, charitable and government support agencies be a useful acquisition for the hospital ward?

Suggested exercises

Exercise 1
Using a directory or telephone guide, draw up a list of societies or support groups that you feel might have something to offer the altered body image patient or his relatives. Discuss these with other group members before writing to such agencies asking for literature on local group or counsellor services. Build a ward file, indexed and arranged alphabetically, which may be of assistance to your patients.

Exercise 2
Consider the following patient and her circumstances. Then through group discussion try to decide who should become rehabilitation team members, and which body image interventions will require your earliest attention.

Sharon is a 6 year old girl who has scalded the side of her face and right shoulder as a result of a kitchen accident. She has been admitted to the burns unit and is now, 5 days later, recovering slowly. Her mother Karen has been at the hospital since her admission.

Allow 20 minutes for discussion and then 40 minutes for feedback to the rest of the class.

Exercise 3
On paper, note down memories of an injury, wound or deformity, that made it difficult for you to nurse a patient confidently. Try to specify how

you felt about the deformity and how you felt it affected your nursing care. Share your ideas with a close friend or counsellor. Try to establish how you might have coped better with the patient's disfigurement.

References

Averill J.R., 'Personal Control over Aversive Stimuli and its Relationship to Stress', *Psychological Bulletin*, 80, pp 286–303, 1973.

Buergin P., 'Interventions for the Person with Degenerative Disorders of the Musculo Skeletal System', pp 1019–24 in Phipps W., Long B. and Woods N. (eds), *Medical Surgical Nursing: Concepts and clinical practice*, C.V. Mosby, St Louis, 1987.

Darbyshire P., 'When the Face Doesn't Fit', *Nursing Times*, 24 Sept, pp 28–9, 1986.

Denning D., 'Head and Neck Cancer: Our reactions', *Cancer Nursing*, Aug, pp 269–73, 1982.

Johnston M. and Carpenter L., 'Relationship Between Pre-operative Anxiety and Post-operative State', *Psychological Medicine*, 10, pp 361–7, 1980.

Kelly M. and May D., 'Good Patients and Bad Patients: A review of the literature and a theoretical critique', *Journal of Advanced Nursing*, 7(2), pp 147–56, 1982.

Marten L., 'Self-care Nursing Model for Patients Experiencing Radical Change in Body Image', *Journal of Obstetric, Gynecological and Neonatal Nursing*, 7(6), pp 9–13, 1978.

Oermann M. *et al*, 'After a Tracheostomy: Patients describe their sensations', *Cancer Nursing*, 6(5), pp 18–23, 1983.

Platzer H., 'Body Image 2: Helping patients to cope with changes – a problem for nurses', *Intensive Care Nursing*, 3, pp 125–32, 1987.

Price B., 'Giving the Patient Control: A model of rehabilitation', *Nursing Times*, 82(20), pp 28–30, 1986.

Stanley L., 'Does Your Own Body Image Hurt Patient Care?', *RN*, 40(12), pp 52–3, 1977.

Sime M., 'Relationship of Pre-operative Fear, Type of Coping and Information Received about Surgery, to Recovery from Surgery', *Journal of Personality and Social Psychology*, 34, pp 716–24, 1976.

Unit 4
Alterations in body image

Having established the principles of assessing and planning for patient altered body image problems, it is important to look at a range of clinical areas where care may be put into practice. No volume on body image nursing can be exhaustive, but this unit will consider some of the more common challenges that arise.

Patients undergoing 'routine surgery' are frequently assumed to have no altered body image problems, but this is a fallacy. A short term catheter or naso-gastric tube is capable of causing a disproportionate amount of body image trauma. Other patients, with apparently hidden alterations to body reality may experience both acute and ongoing traumas, such as the stoma patient. Hidden altered body image needs are still very tangible for the patient, and create an ambiguity in how to deal with social acquaintances.

Unit 4 considers a vast range of disease and trauma, all of which can bring about altered body image. It is important to remember that the extent of body image trauma may not correspond with the degree of body damage. Each patient requires an individual assessment and care plan, the nurse drawing upon the common concerns outlined here.

9 The surgical patient

Study of this chapter will enable you to:

1 Outline why the nurse may not prove sensitive to the body image worries of the patient undergoing elective surgery.
2 Describe how traditional pre-operative preparations may affect the patient's body image.
3 Argue why body image concerns may have to be considered alongside those for patient safety.
4 Describe the effect that pain may have upon body image.
5 Discuss the relationship between control over pre- and post-operative events, and body ideal.
6 Outline the means by which the nurse may avoid degrading the patient during his admission to the ward.
7 List the post-operative attachments that may disrupt patient body image.
8 Suggest measures designed to minimise the disruptive effects of naso-gastric or other post-operative tubes.

Most people will undergo some form of surgical procedure at some time in their life, and the risk of this increases with age. Of course, the procedure may be very minor, such as the suturing of a wound at a clinic or a dental extraction while in hospital. It may, however, be more substantial, for instance a cholecystectomy or a varicose veins operation. All of these measures will involve some degree of alteration to the patient's body image. The alteration may be temporary, but this may not be apparent to the patient when contemplating the surgery. Almost certainly, nurses will have underestimated the altered body image effect of such surgery. This is a shortfall in care and a lost opportunity to demonstrate to the patient what professional nursing care encompasses.

Familiarity with 'standard operations' can breed contempt. Because a nurse knows what the scars will look like and that these will later fade, it does not follow that the patient knows this. Even if he did know, he cannot be forced to be confident about it! For the patient this is 'his operation' with all the hopes and fears that attend the idea. Patients have been busy in their own lives, for instance plumbing, teaching, driving – it was the nurses who saw the successful results of past operations, not they. Therefore, there is an excellent case to be made for considering the body image implications of even routine surgery.

Body reality and surgery

Alterations to body reality start well in advance of the first cut of the surgeon's scalpel. Many of the alterations are surrounded by controversy, with research findings that question traditional practices accumulating. The use of extensive pre-operative shaving is a case in point. The rationale of this was to minimise the risks of wound infection. In fact a substantial amount of research now indicates that shaving increases the incidence of wound infection (Seropian and Reynolds, 1971). Micro-cuts caused by razors can house pathogens which are accidentally transferred into the wound. Shaving the patient would seem to be contraindicated and many hospitals now support the use of depilatory creams or the abandonment of depilation altogether. This is important for body image. In earlier chapters it was stated that body hair, particularly, of the head, was important in sustaining a pleasing body image. Removal of such hair, particularly when this leaves a clearly defined hairless boundary, does affect the patient's body image. Even if this is hidden from normal view, the regrowth of hair is likely to be an itchy reminder that the body is not as it was before. With both infection and body image concerns in mind, nurses should be working with medical colleagues to question the pre-operative shaving practice. There are probably asepsis, body image, comfort, time and cost benefits to be gained by all.

Planned operation sites are marked on the skin by the operating surgeon. In busy hospitals this is an important patient safety measure. In this instance, the nurse is wise to preserve such an important mark, explaining to the patient why it is there. Nevertheless it must be recognised that this is a mark which invades the patient's privacy. People do not normally expect strangers to come and draw on them. In the light of this, the size of such operation marks should be discussed with the surgeon. It is not wished to undermine safety, but neither should the patient have to suffer a gratuitously large or colourful mark. If the mark has to be large, or perhaps widely disseminated, such as with vein surgery, then the nurse might assist the patient to use clothing to cover the area. The longer style of dressing gown has much to commend it in this respect. Covering up such marks may go some way to avoiding the often jocular remarks from others about 'scribbles over your legs', which on occasion can cause offence.

For safety reasons it is also necessary to make the patient 'nil by mouth' prior to surgery. The word 'starved' is avoided here, although some patients who wait a long time for their operation may find this word apt. Denying food to the stomach does change the body experience. The patient complains of feeling 'hollow' or he notices some 'heartburn'. The nurse must therefore also question the length of time that patients are kept nil by mouth pre-operatively. Research has once again indicated that patients are denied food for too long a period (Hamilton-Smith, 1972). The risk of aspirating a previous meal while under anaesthetic should not

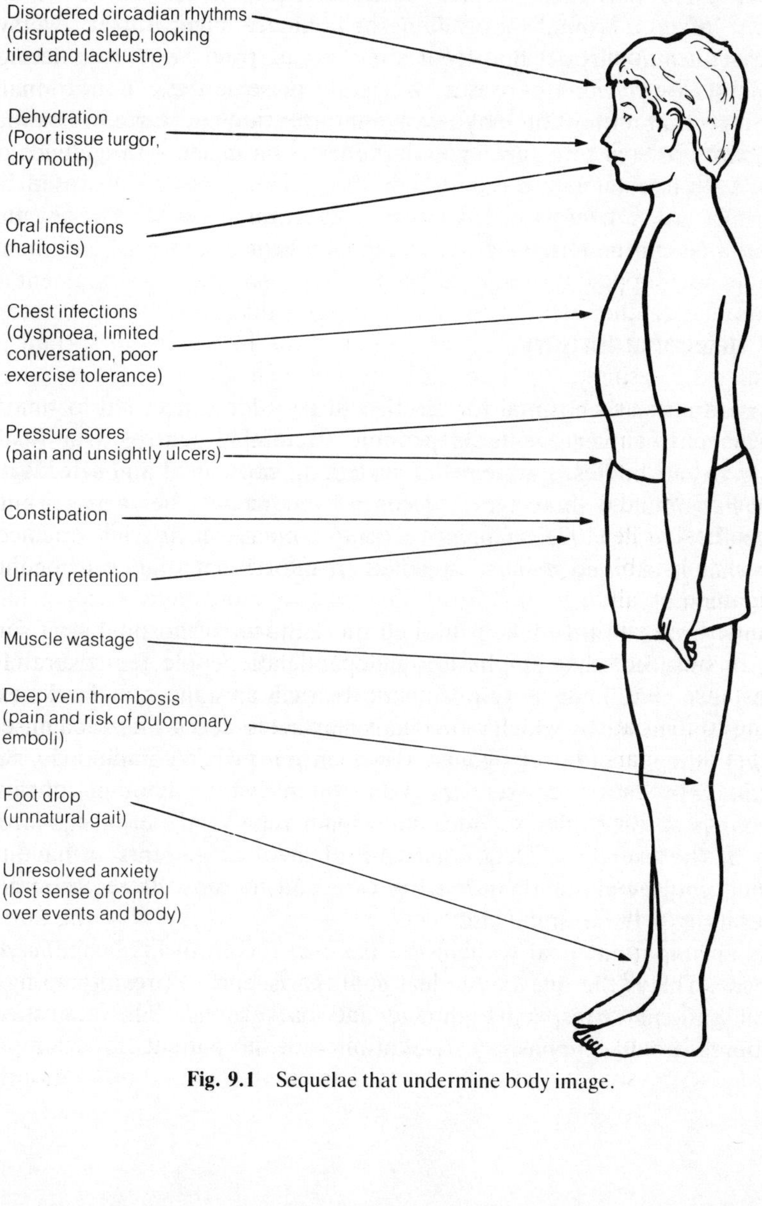

Disordered circadian rhythms
(disrupted sleep, looking
tired and lacklustre)

Dehydration
(Poor tissue turgor,
dry mouth)

Oral infections
(halitosis)

Chest infections
(dyspnoea, limited
conversation, poor
exercise tolerance)

Pressure sores
(pain and unsightly ulcers)

Constipation

Urinary retention

Muscle wastage

Deep vein thrombosis
(pain and risk of pulomonary
emboli)

Foot drop
(unnatural gait)

Unresolved anxiety
(lost sense of control
over events and body)

Fig. 9.1 Sequelae that undermine body image.

promote twelve hour nil by mouth periods pre-operatively. Only exceptional anaesthetic risks would seem to necessitate this sort of time span.

Pain control, either by drugs or other means, is also important for body image. A few common experiences will serve to illustrate the point. Firstly, the more pain there is present within a body part, the larger that part seems to become. You will perhaps recall how large your mouth felt if you have suffered from a dental abscess. Secondly, the more pain present there, the more time the patient is likely to spend attending to that area. He rubs or pats a sore limb. He looks at it more, and repositions it frequently. This may cause further damage to the area, for instance when a patient infects a wound by prodding or poking a finger into it. At the very least, it may distract him from attending to other body area needs, for example for hygiene purposes. We might propose the equation: pain equals attention. Attention may involve interference and further damage or infection. This is turn further undermines body image – the patient is at once both fascinated and repulsed by the damaged tissue. The moral is straightforward – comfort needs must be attended to early to avoid the sequelae that can undermine body image (see Figure 9.1).

Body ideal and surgery

Patients admitted to hospital for elective surgery are concerned to retain as much control over events as possible. Retaining control over what happens to our bodies is a means of sustaining body ideal and self-ideal. Averill has outlined three types of control – cognitive, behavioural and decisional (Averill, 1973). Cognitive control means having all the facts about what is planned or has happened. If the patient's ignorant of the facts he cannot be in total control, and what is more, may become unpleasantly aware of this deficit through the attitudes of hospital staff. To sustain a self-ideal that emphasises independence people feel that they must be seen to be knowledgeable about their circumstances. Behavioural control is the means by which individuals may act to deal with problems or needs. Holding a cold pack against a swollen joint while completing your own static physiotherapy exercises is an example of behavioural control. The cold pack probably provides some pain relief and permits greater efforts at the exercises. Decisional control involves patients in making informed choices about their nursing care and therapy. It requires the co-operation of the hospital staff.

It is an important goal to help the patient to control his hospital experiences. This is the one body ideal goal that seems to prevail amongst surgical patients, irrespective of age and background. The admission procedures should emphasise consultation with the patient, for example when does he normally retire and how does he prefer to deal with discomfort? It should permit the patient to retain the symbols of control wherever and whenever possible. Try to let the patient wear his own day clothes rather than instantly assigning him pyjamas. Encourage him to think of his bed space as a personal space, which is encroached upon later only with due courtesy by the nurse. Note the patient's preferences and try to show that these have been taken into account. What we are trying to avoid is any sign of a 'degradation ceremony'. Goffman used this term to explain how patients lost status through admission procedures (see Figure 9.2) (Goffman, 1961).

During the stay, there will be times when of necessity the patient cannot be in control. While under the effects of pre-medication, or recovering from anaesthesia, nursing staff must act as the patient's guardian. The nurse should encourage the patient to anticipate this, but through patient education and example, assure him that she will attend to his needs in a respectful manner. She will address him in terms that he has chosen and always wait for his reply before trying other means to rouse him. She will anticipate that it is embarrassing to be clothed only in a theatre gown and to lie supine. Body ideal emphasises an upright posture, with the opportunities that this affords for conversation on equal terms.

Individual arrives at hospital, wearing or carrying the symbols of his social status (often high), for instance, a suit, neatly pressed shirt and tie, a briefcase with his papers

In addition, some aspects of this body presentation will be unique expressions of this person's personality (such as a preference for a buttonhole carnation, and a habit of lounging in an armchair, across the arms)

Patient encounters nurse who may unwittingly undermine, both the symbols of patient's previous social status, and his opportunity to express idiosyncracies of his nature. This through:
1. Inviting him to dress in standard nightwear
2. To submit to a series of admission checks, in an order that has become standard for all patients
3. To submit to a battery of questions that are 'standard' and 'just for the record'
4. To adopt a child like state, asking the nurse for basic details which have not been volunteered by her from the outset

The patient has taken up the patient role, and in the process been strongly reminded that he is one of a group, in an institution, who has individual needs and worries, but who has been encased in a uniform, and made to feel most unindividual

Fig. 9.2 Degradation ceremonies.

Body presentation – before and after surgery

There are a number of practicalities involved in assisting the surgical patient with body presentation. These are largely associated with the attachments we make to him such as wound drains, naso-gastric tubes, catheters and intravenous infusions. The principle points about such 'tubes' are these:

1. They should remain *in situ* only for as long as they are necessary.
2. They should be attached and positioned so as not to cause pain or disruption to body appearance or movement.
3. Where necessary, they should be camouflaged or concealed.

Tubes and other attachments have to be accommodated within the patient's body space. However, they may be seen by others as extensions of his body, to the point in some areas where it can be confusing as to whether machines are attached to the patient or the patient becomes an extension of the machine!

Naso-gastric tubes are particularly problematic as they occupy a facial position. The following points should help. Always provide nasal toilet before and after the tube has been inserted. Encrustations on the tube or a sore nose are both sources of patient anxiety. Toilet may be achieved using a saline solution and lubricating gel or petroleum jelly used to cover the sore edges of the nostril. Check the tube at the point it emerges from the nose to see if is it pulled at too tight an angle. The tube should be secured to the nose with a minimum of adhesive tape or a small proprietary holder. Always ask the patient if he has any tape allergies first and always replace old and grubby tape promptly. Perspiration may easily loosen the tape. It is also important to select the correct length of naso-gastric tube. If it is too long, yards of tubing can seem to envelope the patient's head. If it is too short, it appears that the patient has grown a trunk. Measure the tube length from nose to ear and from there to the lower point of the sternum. Allow an additional length to either position the tube end discretely over the ear, or to be pinned down onto the pyjama lapel. The tube should not be prominent enough to create a line across the patient's field of view, so allow a loop to keep it snug to the cheek contours.

Intravenous infusions should always be positioned in the patient's non-dominant arm, unless there are contrary medical considerations. Freedom for the 'writing hand' helps to sustain more normal function and an independent looking body presentation. Try to ensure that the tubing is secured with a bandage that is sufficient to hold splint and/or tubing in place on the arm. Do not use excessively large splints, longer than the length from finger tip to just above the elbow, or swathes of bandage which can unravel alarmingly. Always ensure that the empty infusion bags and surplus infusion lines are removed from the stand. While some patients do need to have multiple infusions running, this is not the norm. Patients left surrounded by run through equipment can begin to look like proprietors of second hand stalls. Having attached an intravenous line to the patient, reposition his possessions for him. He must be able to reach personal effects, call buzzers and locker, without bed acrobatics. The patient left out of touch with his possessions is left with a disorganised body space. If he attempts to rectify this himself, he may be left with infusion fluid everywhere and the need to resite the 'drip'.

Wound drains and urinary catheters must also be positioned for comfort and discretion. It is important to secure these using suitable non-allergenic tapes which do not leave an excoriated skin area after removal. Failing this, safety pinning the tube to bed clothing or pyjamas may be preferable if the patient is confident about controlling movement. Short wound drains, for example corrugated, are not usually problematic, unless their length causes the wound dressing to bulge. The problem resolves as the drain is shortened. Long wound drains, such as Redivac, prove a little more challenging. Bottle and tubing are ideally secured to the bed, or if the patient is mobile, are carried on a belt underneath the nightdress or dressing gown.

There are good reasons to remove urinary catheters as soon as possible, and to avoid their use completely unless absolutely necessary. Catheterisation leads to urinary tract infections, no matter how sophisticated the catheter. Correct selection of catheter, for instance for patient size and intended length of use, is one key to avoiding a disrupted body image. Repeated catheterisation has a demoralising effect upon the patient. Once the catheter is *in situ* it should be secured against the patient's thigh and the attached drainage bag supported (see Figure 9.3). While the patient is in bed this may be along the bed edge, but beware folding cot sides. While the patient is mobile a support belt or leg bag may be employed. While short term catheterised patients have been invited to carry their 'shopping' bag around in a wire cradle, this is hardly adequate as a body presentation method. Support beneath dressing gown is likely to prove far more satisfactory. One elderly lady, who rarely needed her urine testing or inspecting, knitted her bag a woollen cover. This could easily be removed for inspection or emptying the contents. The final result was 'far more feminine' she said!

General coping strategies

A number of more general coping strategies may be used to deal with body image problems post-surgery. One of these will be the adjustment of clothing, bed area, grooming and the use of appropriate toiletries. At an early post-operative point the nurse provides the patient with a wash and removes the operation gown and superfluous dressings or packs. Removal

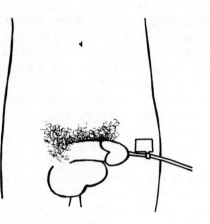

Catheter secured to right or left of
penis, thus avoiding pressure on the penile
scrotal angle

Catheter secured more medially
in female patient. This
prevents pressure of catheter
against external genitalia

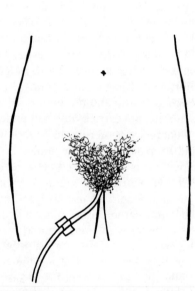

Fig. 9.3 Catheter positions.

of these items not only makes the patient more comfortable but also symbolises a return of limited patient control. Where possible the clothes are the patient's own, often bought especially to make them feel brighter after the operation. Regaining dentures, spectacles, contact lenses, a hearing aid all become part of this picture of returning normality. The patient hopes to groom himself, and to have a shave before visitors come to see him.

All of this may take place a little while after anaesthesia, especially if the patient experiences pain or restriction of limbs. It is worth briefing patient and relatives about this before the operation. In this way, visiting may be delayed until the next post-operative day, or the patient may receive their relatives at a later time, after freshening up. While we all anticipate feeling a little 'groggy' post-operation, many people still believe that they must look their best to receive visitors. This should be born in mind as now the patient welcomes visitors to an area that is partly prepared by the nurse.

Conclusion

At the start of the largest unit within this book, it has been important to recognise the very real body image needs of patients undergoing comparatively routine surgery. Subsequent chapters will deal with quite specific disorders and body image nursing problems. Here, a more general set of circumstances have been reviewed, and it has been noted how easily body image can be affected by the surgical process. From the time of admission to the time of discharge, surgical patients seek to retain control over their body, and through that an undamaged body image. The nurse is a major resource in achieving this goal. Her help will involve practical assistance, camouflaging or positioning the various surgical appendages. At other times it is as fundamental as helping with grooming, or assisting the patient to anticipate the temporary loss of control associated with anaesthesia. Many of the points made here remain true for patients with more complex body image problems. None of them can be separated from a close attention to detail that has been rather euphemistically called 'basic' nursing care.

Review questions

1 Patients may have to wait some time before they are admitted for elective surgery. Do you think the waiting time facilitates or hinders the patient's preparation for the likely altered body image?

2 This chapter proposes that many pre-operative practices, founded upon tradition rather than research, should be changed. Why do you think such practices have held sway for so long?

3 What might be the body image benefits of abandoning pre-operative shaves?

4 Try to offer further examples of the different types of control (cognitive, behavioural and decisional) described by Averill.

5 How might modern methods of anaesthesia be used to facilitate greater patient control during operative procedures? (Hint: think of spinal or local anaesthesia.)

6 In the light of points made about body presentation here, what recommendations would you propose concerning dressings and how they are secured?

7 Why is the facial position of naso-gastric tubes so important in body image terms?

8 In reviewing this chapter, would you agree that measures designed to

support body image are also likely to meet other nursing care goals? (This may not be as obvious as it seems!)

Suggested exercises

Exercise 1
Visit a surgical ward and interview the nursing staff about pre-operative depilatory measures. Establish how the hair is removed and what this involves for the patient. Enquire what comments the patients tend to make about the use of shaving or depilatory creams. Compare your notes with colleagues and then answer this question: could the shaving of a patient be seen as one of Goffman's degradation ceremonies, even if only unwittingly?

Exercise 2
Using a sheet of gingerbread outline men (see below) invite a sample of ten nurses to shade the areas of the body that they would expect to be shaved for each of the following operations:

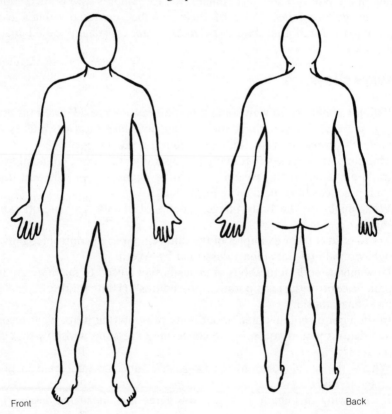

Front   Back

1. Putti Platt Repair (right shoulder)
2. Appendectomy (elective)
3. Trendelenberg and stripping of varicose veins (left leg)

Then, using an acetate sheet with a further equally sized gingerbread man, invite the nurses to shade in the areas of the body which they think are most important for the maintenance of normal body image (you may make your figures gingerbread ladies if you wish). Overlay this 'map' over each of the above operation gingerbread men. Try to establish which body areas were thought to be most likely to cause body image concern (where the shaded areas overlap). Compare your notes with colleagues. (Note: the outline figures opposite may be traced and reproduced.)

A suggested time schedule is as follows:

(a) for data collection, the period of one clinical placement
(b) for analysis and review of findings, one half day workshop back in school or college of nursing

References

Averill J.R., 'Personal Control over Aversive Stimuli and its Relationship to Stress', *Psychological Bulletin*, 80, pp 286–303, 1973.
Goffman E., *Stigma: Notes on the management of spoiled identity*, Prentice Hall, Englewood Cliffs, New Jersey, 1961.
Hamilton-Smith S., *Nil by Mouth*, Royal College of Nursing, London, 1972.
Seropian R. and Reynolds B., 'Wound Infections After Pre-operative Depilatory Versus Razor Preparation', *American Journal of Surgery*, 121, pp 251–4, 1971.

Further reading

Winfield V., 'Too Close a Shave?', *Nursing Times*, 5 March, pp 64–8, 1986.

10 The patient with a stoma

Study of this chapter will enable you to:

1 Outline the different types of stoma a patient may have.
2 List some of the common concerns expressed by patients (through the literature).
3 Indicate the common problems that may necessitate the formation of a stoma.
4 Discuss why careful siting of the stoma is important for the patient's body image.
5 Indicate how pre-operative nutrition and the wearing of a stoma appliance can contribute to post-operative recovery.
6 Describe how skin care contributes to an acceptable body image.
7 Discuss the effects of altered elimination patterns on an ostomist's body ideal (especially with reference to hygiene and sexuality).
8 Outline the principles of counselling that might be employed with an ostomist.
9 Suggest measures involving stoma appliances and dress, designed to enhance body presentation.
10 Discuss the importance of a good handover of patient support from the hospital nurse to relatives and community nurses.

At a conservative estimate in 1988, there were over 52,000 ostomates in the United Kingdom (Dyer, 1988). Other authors would place the figure much higher. Devlin estimated that there were 10,000 ileostomists and 100,000 colostomists (Devlin, 1982). Across the Atlantic over 100,000 stomas are being formed every year (Woods, 1975). Perhaps what is most disturbing about these statistics is that it is not known exactly how many people are dealing with one form of stoma or other, and by implication, how many of them will have suffered an altered body image.

Here, a stoma is defined as any portion of bowel or ureter which has been brought to the abdominal surface to provide for elimination needs.

The effects of this upon the patient's body image are likely to be both abrupt and long lasting. As Salter has pointed out, we do not expect to witness excretion onto the abdominal surface, to see an artificial anus when we look down (Salter, 1986). We rarely expect to take more than a passing interest in the care of such an orifice. The ostomist can neither forget defaecation, nor escape from the need to tend to the stoma with care. In a compelling account of his own stoma Kelly described his grief, and problems in re-establishing an adequate body image (Kelly, 1985). Using Parkes' grief reaction model he reviewed his feelings and behaviour towards the nursing staff (Parkes, 1972). There was an overwhelming sense of dependence and of anger. In a later paper similar adjustment difficulties were found amongst a sample of fifty other ileostomists (Kelly, 1987). They faced two major uncertainties, one psychological and one appliance related. Psychological uncertainty centred upon body image disturbance, and appliance concerns upon their function and reliability, itself a body presentation problem. In many ways the patient undergoing a stoma operation, colostomy, ileostomy or urostomy, is the archetypal 'altered body image patient'.

Despite a recognised history of adaptation problems, the short hospital stay, embarrassment over stoma management and the lack of body image education for staff, still mean that many patients are ill equipped to make the best rehabilitation from surgery. Druss *et al* pointed out patient worries over appliance leakage during sexual activity and, the problem of odour (Druss *et al*, 1968). Dlin and Perlman noted how important spouse and other kin's reactions could be to the ostomist (Dlin and Perlman, 1971). Fertility concerns were uppermost in the mind of other patients (Gruner *et al*, 1977). While the patient's original health problems may affect their response to surgery, for example relief from the symptoms of Crohn's disease, patients typically took a year or more to recover feelings of sexual attractiveness (Gloeckner, 1984).

Origins and types of stoma

Three different types of stoma are identified in most texts (Elcoat, 1986). The first is the ileostomy, which is an artificial opening into the small bowel, usually the ileum. Second is the colostomy, which is an opening into the large bowel, either ascending, transverse, descending or sigmoid colon. The third is the urostomy, which is the implanting of ureters into an ileal conduit which will then itself form the stoma (see Figure 10.1). Both the ileostomy and colostomy may be either a temporary or permanent stoma, depending upon the patient's circumstances (see Table 10.1).

A wide range of traumatic, congenital and pathological problems may necessitate the formation of a stoma (Elcoat, 1988a,b). Children and adults

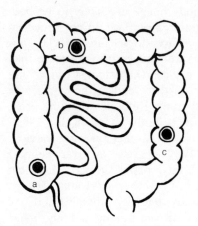

 = Stoma location

Colostomy
a. Ascending colon (right abdomen)
b. Transverse colon (upper abdomen)
c. Sigmoid colon (lower left abdomen)

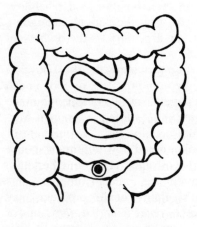

Ileostomy
Stoma usually in lower right abdominal
quadrant

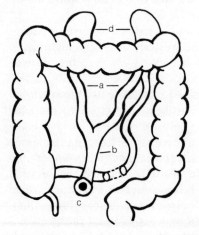

Urostomy (ileal conduit)
a. Ureters (implanted into . . .)
b. Released segment of ileum (which
    retains its own mesenteric blood supply)
c. Stoma (lower right quadrant of
    abdomen)
d. Kidneys

Fig. 10.1 Types of stoma.

Table 10.1 Abdominal stomas

Stoma	Indications (examples)	Typical drainage/product
Colostomy (temporary)	Resting bowel after surgery/trauma post-obstruction	Ascending colon: watery/semi-solid, frequent Transverse: semi-liquid or soft Sigmoid: soft to firm (liquid immediately post-surgery)
(permanent)	Cancer of bowel, Crohn's disease	see above
Ileostomy (temporary)	Trauma/obstruction	Liquid and unpleasant smelling
(permanent)	Carcinoma bowel, familial polyposis, ulcerative colitis	see above
Urostomy (ileal conduit; permanent)	Cancer urinary bladder, urinary incontinence (chronic), neurogenic bladder	Urine

involved in trauma, for instance through a road traffic accident, may require emergency bowel surgery and a temporary stoma. Other patients will have a history of altered bowel function over a prolonged period of time. Both Crohn's disease and ulcerative colitis result in abdominal pain, malabsorption of nutrients or fluids and a disruption of patterns of daily life. At first sight the prospect of swapping such misery for a stoma might seem a welcome arrangement. This is particularly so when the patient understands that he is likely to gain weight and may expect to feel generally fitter. However, not all such patients are able to remain positive about their stoma.

A third group of patients will face a stoma as part of curative or palliative measures taken against cancer. In the western world the high incidence of bowel cancer is associated with a lack of dietary fibre. Bowel resections frequently mean that the bowel must be temporarily rested before re-anastomosis is attempted. In cases of radical resection such an anastomosis is impossible. A permanent ileostomy or colostomy must be formed.

A urostomy is also frequently the result of cancer surgery. In many instances carcinoma of the urinary bladder has spread to a point where diathermy or limited excision is impossible. A total cystectomy means that the ureters must be redirected into an ileal conduit or other outlet. As with cancer of the bowel, such surgery may be palliative, enhancing patient comfort and independence without promising a cure.

Urinary diversionary surgery is sometimes performed to alleviate chronic incontinence. Such patients have a long history of discomfort and embarrassment associated with leakage of urine, sometimes even past an indwelling catheter. Neurological deficits, paralysis or weakness may mean that it is easier to deal with a stoma on the abdomen than perineal hygiene problems or catheter care.

Each type of stoma will have a different appearance and perform in a specific way (see Figure 10.2). Patients often do not realise this and may

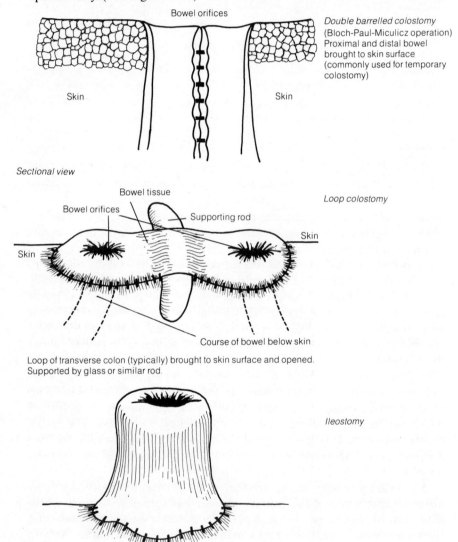

Bowel orifices

Double barrelled colostomy
(Bloch-Paul-Miculicz operation)
Proximal and distal bowel
brought to skin surface
(commonly used for temporary
colostomy)

Skin   Skin

Sectional view

Bowel tissue

Bowel orifices

Loop colostomy

Supporting rod

Skin

Skin

Course of bowel below skin

Loop of transverse colon (typically) brought to skin surface and opened.
Supported by glass or similar rod.

Ileostomy

Section (terminal) of ileum brought to skin surface and everted/sutured down
to form prominent stoma.

Fig. 10.2   Typical stoma appearance (drawings not to scale).

come to hospital with a stereotypical idea of what stomas are like. In any case, oedema and swelling of the stoma immediately post-operation, will make it very difficult to form an accurate picture of what the stoma will eventually look like. Some common points about stomas serve both to measure the health of the tissue and to assure the patient that what he sees is what the nurse and doctor expected. Stomas look pink and moist, an appearance that the patient may associate with the mucosa of his mouth. They should not look purple or black, which indicate ischaemic change or even necrosis. They will not feel like skin if touched. Nerve endings that give us the experiences we associate with touched skin are absent in the stoma, which is a surprise to many patients. After initial post-operative oedema, the colostomy will not noticeably stand up above the surface of the skin, but will be almost flush with it. The exception is a loop colostomy where a rod supporting the loop of bowel will keep it in a higher profile. In contrast to colostomies, an ileostomy or urostomy will protrude a little above the surface of the skin.The emergent portion of ileum has been folded back on itself and sutured down onto the skin surface. Some stomas may have more than one orifice. Even so, they usually constitute one entity when we consider practical care and body image disturbance.

Altered body reality

The alterations to body reality are associated with underlying disease or trauma, the surgery performed and the resultant change in elimination, for example consistency, frequency, position and force of product. The patient who suffers from an inflammatory bowel disease or cancer may already have lost body weight as well as suffer discomfort from diarrhoea or constipation respectively. In the case of the patient with cancer especially, malnutrition may already be a problem (Holmes, 1986). Inadequate nutrition is associated with poor tissue repair and a high incidence of post-operative complications (Dickerson, 1986). It will be important from a pre-admission stage to make good nutritional deficits, such as protein and trace elements, if body reality is not to be further compromised. The nurse must ensure that the patient understands that his fears about a stoma can be minimised if he achieves a good post-operative recovery. Complications are likely to inhibit the return of an acceptable body image.

The surgical alteration to body reality can also be addressed early on. Patients coming into hospital have not been accustomed to sharing in the choice of operation site, but this should be so with the prospective osto-mist (Foulkes, 1981; Hughes *et al*, 1983). The choice of stoma site is affected by the need to achieve a good seal for appliances, and by surgical technique considerations (May, 1977). The choice should also take into account the patient's normal activities such as work and sports, and the style of clothes in which they would like to dress, for instance considering the position of waistbands. An experienced nurse stoma therapist should work with the patient and surgeon to identify one or more sites which meet the patient's lifestyle needs.

While this approach obviously offers a lot in terms of patient involvement, there may be occasions where the need to raise a trouble free stoma takes precedence. An ileostomy or a colostomy may have to be supported by local groups of muscle (Todd, 1978). The choice of stoma site may also be affected by other considerations such as the patient's dexterity, neurological function and body posture, for instance if the patient is in a wheelchair. Elcoat offers a nine point guide in choosing a stoma site and these include the patient's culture and religion, hobbies, occupation and mobility (Elcoat, 1986). Choosing the stoma site therefore necessitates a full patient history and lifestyle assessment, as well as recognition of the surgical limitations.

The patient's diet is of course not only important for tissue repair. It will have an important effect upon what the stoma discharges. The Ileostomy Association suggests that eating habits need not be totally dictated by the stoma. Many dietary adjustments are advised short term, the body eventually adapting to the high roughage content of some foods. Accordingly, avoiding short term excesses of peas, beans and other fibrous vegetables as well as alcohol may limit the number of very liquid stools or flatus. The patient is also advised to avoid nuts, such as peanuts, unpeeled apples and other foods with poorly broken down fibre content. These can cause discomfort as they are evacuated through the stoma (Ileostomy Association, 1988). Individual patients discover individual dietary remedies, but it is important to maintain a good fluid intake, approximately 2 litres per day, and not to unbalance the diet for short term convenience. Patient and nurse must realise that diet control is not merely a nutritional concern, but one which will also affect body image. What comes out of the stoma may become linked with the patient's feelings about his body and its cleanliness.

The third body reality concern requiring attention is the patient's skin condition and care. Urine and faecal matter lying on the abdominal skin can cause tissue breakdown and make the sealing of stoma appliances and infection difficult problems. The skin may also be damaged by poorly applied or removed appliances. In addition to choosing a stoma site therefore, the patient should be involved in pre-operative skin care, learning to recognise the role of healthy skin and how to maintain hygiene in the light of forthcoming surgery (see Table 10.2).

Cleansing the skin with warm water, thorough drying and the use of properly fitted stoma cuffs and bags should minimise the risk of leakage and skin excoriation. Hypoallergenic adhesives are often available with appliances, so that skin reactions are now less common. In the case of

Table 10.2 Skin hygiene and protection

Problems	Nursing actions
Excoriation (Associated with faeces or urine lying on skin eg alkaline nature of ileostomy drainage)	*Preventive:* teach skin hygiene measures washing abdomen with warm water and avoiding all but mild soap. Learning to fit skin barrier pads (for example, stomahesive, Colly-Seel, karaya seal or spray on skin preparation). Cutting or fashioning accurate opening for stoma in pad/skin barrier. *Problem solving:* check for changes in stoma size and whether it retracts when patient lies down (brings stoma into different alignment with skin) Refashion gasket seal to suit changes. Review washing and drying of skin (dry skin surface necessary for good seal). Check position of belt/waistband for pressure on bag/pouch. Fit methyl cellulose skin wafer if skin broken down (absorbs exudate). Continue with a drainable appliance over top to minimise need for appliance change.
Skin allergy (Local skin may show a minor sensitivity or a full blown angry reaction. Repeated exposure to allergen will exacerbate the reaction)	*Preventive:* when trying new seals or applications patch these on area of skin away from stoma first. Same procedure with new adhesives. Take patient history of allergies. *Problem solving:* identify allergen with patient history/patch testing. Revert for time being to tried and tested appliances. Consult with manufacturers about product compounds. Consult dermatologist/stoma therapist. Explain what has happened to patient and encourage him not to scratch or interfere with the area (infection risk).
Local tissue trauma (Rough removal of appliances, especially with the use of certain adhesives may leave a raw irritated skin area)	*Preventive:* highlight benefits of good skin hygiene techniques. A healthy and dry skin makes a better seal surface. Lighter adhesive seals may be employed. Try to plan appliance changes as unrushed affairs, where the patient's 'professionalism as an ostomist' can be shown to the full. *Problem solving:* review use of seals and appliances. Observe patient's techniques. Suggest alternative lighter appliances and redemonstrate the drying of skin surface, especially over skin wrinkles or creases.

an ileostomy, the stoma should protrude enough to limit the chances of leakage when the seal is fashioned around it. Badly excoriated skin is unsightly and limits the appliances and clothes (body presentation) that may be worn. Complicating infection may limit the patient's attendance at work or school and further undermine his self-image.

Threats to body ideal

Rituals associated with the elimination of urine or faeces highlight several important points regarding body ideal. The first is that elimination of faeces is not seen directly. The process takes place out of view and in a place of privacy. Abdominal sensations warn us of the need to visit the toilet and providing we do not experience problems, defaecation is completed through brief muscular effort, and perineal hygiene through tactile control. When a man voids urine he does have sight of the process, but control is still primarily tactile in nature. The control over elimination is something we associate with adulthood, independence and cleanliness. Loss of control over elimination is associated with dependence and body deterioration.

Secondly, people tend to expect that elimination will occur below or behind them. These are areas that are often seen as 'dirty' and not associated with the positive aspects of life. The abdomen is a body area that is portrayed in literature, paintings and advertising as a 'wholesome' area. From a side view it should be firm and trim, from an anterior view appropriately curved to indicate a waist. It should only be 'blemished' by a 'belly button'.

Thirdly, despite the fact that the organ of elimination and reproduction may be one and the same thing, namely the penis/urethra, we still conceptualise them in mutually exclusive terms. It does not seem appropriate to worry about elimination at the same time as coitus, or to expect that problems with the former should have much to do with the latter. When people idealise body function the sexual and elimination functions are seen as mutually exclusive.

The patient with a stoma finds it difficult to sustain an adequate body ideal on all of these counts. Firstly, excreting onto the abdomen forces them to regularly visualise the excreta and the stoma appliances necessary to contain it. The abdomen is no longer smooth and trim, there are blemishes and a scar, as well as a stoma bag which now fills an area of the body space. Moreover, surgical interference with muscle and the autonomic nerve supply to the pelvis may mean that sexuality is affected, for instance failure of erection or ejaculation in the male. Impotence may result in one-quarter of male patients following rectal excision for cancer (Dlin and Perlman, 1971). A total cystectomy may involve the sacrifice of pelvic nerves necessary for ejaculation. Some colostomists have noticed an involuntary defaecation due to autonomic nerve activity during orgasm (Devlin and Plant, 1979).

Other disruptions to body ideal have been more akin to the experiences of amputee patients. Some ostomists have reported a 'phantom rectum', an urge to defaecate via a 'back passage' even though they recognise that the rectum has been removed (Devlin, Plant and Griffin, 1971). Usually this phenomenon fades with time, but in the early post-operative patient it is a disturbing experience.

The nurse must intervene to support the ostomist's body ideal using an assessment that starts pre-surgery wherever possible. The body ideal is supported with counselling provided by a nursing team that recognises the value of talking with, and listening to the patient. Watson found that counselling significantly improved patient self concept and esteem (Watson, 1983). Kabza argued that such counselling should extend to spouses too (Kabza, 1983).

Patient counselling should set out to help the patient to assess his own feelings about the stoma and its management. The nurse should not prescribe solutions but listen for 80 per cent of the time, so that she can reflect on solutions available later. Such solutions will usually include a reappraisal of the importance of the abdomen as an aspect of the body presentation. Patients may be helped to revalue other body attributes in compensation. A female ostomist may still have a trim figure in swimwear and a sense of sexuality need not die with her operation. When the male patient cannot achieve ejaculation this may be due to physiological or psychological trauma. In the case of the latter, counselling husband and wife together about sexuality and the stoma can mean that full function returns earlier than anticipated. It is important that the surgeon briefs the nurse on whether pelvic nerves have been cut or damaged, so that a realistic picture of the future can be considered with the patient.

Revaluing other body attributes may also be helpful with patients who find that a stoma inhibits libido. Fears about stoma action or accident during intercourse may be reduced by prior stoma irrigation/toilet, or by adopting alternative coital positions. The stoma may be covered with an attractive opaque pouch, and positions employed which limit pressure on the ostomist's abdomen. Tactile stimulation may concentrate on other body areas, so that even the patient who cannot achieve an erection may gain a satisfying sexual experience.

Identifying such personal fears will necessitate the nurse using private counselling rooms or areas. The counselling may involve an experienced visitor from one of the three ostomy associations (see Appendix A). Whichever of these paths are taken, it is likely to be a lengthy process, involving a gradual adjustment of body ideal.

Body presentation

The ostomist seeks to present an essentially normal body to the world. Admittedly, the muscular control of elimination has been lost and the area of elimination changed, but waste is still excreted as with all human beings. Against this, the 'hidden' altered body image may not be that easily controlled. Odours from bags, a poor seal and leaks, lack of adequate disposal facilities, the position of the stoma during body contact, all mean that a hidden problem will become an open problem to a limited number of intimate others.

Limiting the altered body presentation means employing appropriate stoma bags, seals, filters, anti-flatus and odour devices. More importantly it depends upon the patient using these devices competently and these appliances working well. Patient comfort cannot be achieved without patient confidence. An important dinner date, an examination or interview might all be ruined if the appliance does not work.

A number of one and two piece bags are marketed as well as, more recently, non-allergenic caps which may be worn as a snug 'stopper' within the stoma orifice (see Figure 10.3). Choosing the appropriate appliance must be a considered process, involving the advice of ostomists, a stoma therapist and the nurse. Mishaps will occur and in the early days it will be hard for the patient to bring himself to adjust appliances and correct mistakes. For this reason, the first stoma bags are normally transparent so that problems and product can be properly examined.

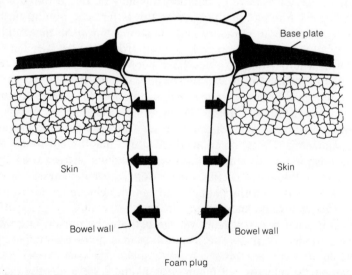

Fig. 10.3   Stoma cap (colostomy). Hypoallergenic cap fits into colostomy orifice, secured by a base support seal against the skin. Inserted foam plug expands to fill the stoma and limit or prevent the escape of faeces, and filter flatus.

Later stoma bags may not only be opaque, but incorporate an attractive cover design. Cover pouches can be either colourful or flesh toned, so that they do not show easily through a summer shirt or blouse. Two piece bags have the advantage that a base plate remains *in situ*, the bags being clipped or pressed onto a skin protecting frame. As the stoma becomes less oedematous such skin coloured base plates may minimise the visual impact of the stoma.

Flatus filled stoma bags are avoided by a flatus valve which usually incorporates charcoal to remove unpleasant odours. Such charcoal filters do, however, lose their effect over time, say 12 to 24 hours. If the patient is not confident about such 'gadgets' it may be sensible to empty the bag through the gate clip before venturing into social settings. Similarly, if a deodorant is not added to the bag, emptying the bag more regularly, though inconvenient, may boost patient confidence.

Some colostomists are able to dispense with bulky appliances, wearing a small dressing over the stoma after irrigating it (Griffiths and Shorey, 1978; Stockley, 1981). While this approach cannot be used with all patients, it does seem to solve many body presentation problems (Phillpotts *et al*, 1976; Williams and Johnson, 1980). Taught irrigation methods, using aseptic technique and an irrigation cone, a dextrous ostomist may remain free of worry for up to two days at a time. This is an obvious body presentation advantage to patients such as airline pilots or other travellers.

After stoma surgery, the patient's wardrobe will usually have to be reappraised. Tight fitting jeans or skirts may be very fashionable, but they may be unsuitable if they constrict the stoma or pinch the appliance. A bikini may be replaced with an attractive one piece swimsuit, and here the patient's spouse should be encouraged to take an active interest in the choice of colour and style. Choosing new clothes can come to be seen as a treat for a brave loved one, as much as a chore necessitated by surgery.

Most patients recognise that fashions change rapidly and that at any time a number of different waistlines will be acceptable. For male patients the problem of giving up closer fitting trousers may be more difficult. Some young male ostomists may associate fuller cut trousers with the elderly. They might be encouraged to consider even lower waistbands (hipster) and a fuller cut shirt and jacket to disguise a higher set stoma appliance. Belts may be used to gather a blouse or shirt to form a waistband at a new and comfortable level.

Up to this point the camouflage measures available have been emphasised. The patient is still, however, going to be faced with the problem of building confidence in the appearance, and accounting for the stoma should he need or wish to. At this level the nurse involves herself in helping the patient to rehearse social encounters and a range of explanations that might prove suitable for the patient's different acquaintances (see Table 10.3).

Table 10.3 Accounts of altered body image
Example: Mr Burrows has a colostomy after a history of ulcerative colitis

Approach	Social contacts	Rationale
Complete disclosure Sharing details of operation, feelings about same, current problems, anxieties.	Mrs Joyce Burrows Daughter: Jane Burrows Work colleague: Gordon Mr Douglas: village chemist	Mr Burrows was helped by the nurse to select people who would share in full disclosure because of practical need (family), moral support at work (Gordon best friend), and chemist (because he will supply appliance needs and advise).
Limited disclosure Operation alluded to, with a recognition of the altered lifestyle this has meant (such as to diet, hygiene). Details about stoma not divulged.	Other workmates Mrs Burrows family and friends Friends at local pub	While Mr Burrows may grow in confidence about accounting for his surgery he does not have to detail it to briefer acquaintances. He assesses his appliance control and believes that details are not called for here as accidents can be avoided or handled.
Scant disclosure References to hospital stay acknowledge, recovery rate indicated, also degree of independence now. No details of surgery or current stoma management.	Customers met at work Short acquaintances (for instance, local shopkeeper) More distant relatives	Here contact time with others is very limited, and privacy vastly outweighs the benefits of giving details. If acquaintances become close friends they may be moved to a higher group.

Note: Nurse does not dictate categories or acquaintances/friends that should fall into each. Instead, she helps patient to review the logic of who he sees fit to tell full details.

The process starts in hospital with shared meal times, television viewing and the reception of visitors. Pre-operatively the patient can be introduced to an established ostomist who has already dealt with a range of social circumstances. Later, the nurse can join this consultation to share ideas on dealing with the first post-operative visitors.

It is also constructive pre-operatively for the patient to wear a stoma appliance which will be used after surgery. The nurse and stoma therapist help the patient to fit the appliance, showing how a strong seal might be made. In the privacy of a side room the patient can be encouraged to try out various items of clothing to discover which look and feel best with the appliance *in situ*. At a meal time, or similar occasion, the patient can join the other patients, wearing the new appliance. After, the nurse debriefs the patient, making a note of how he felt, what problems emerged and what solutions seem possible for the future. Such rehearsing of body presentation enables the patient to learn, and to explore his feelings within a safe environment. The early practical and emotional support by the nurse may serve to establish a sound and trusting relationship post-operatively.

Similar rehearsals may be employed post-operatively. During the early days after surgery the nurse will gradually increase the patient's involvement in stoma care. These are steps in gaining control over the stoma in privacy. The patient has not been invited to try out mastery of the stoma in company – visitors have usually been only the most intimate relatives. Later rehearsals will involve the patient in fitting his own appliance, using appropriate deodoriser or filters, dressing, and describing to the nurse the anticipated reactions of other patients on the main ward. The nurse assures the patient she will be beside him during this first 'short ward walk', and that she will support the account of his stoma if he feels able to offer one. Following a limited adventure the patient and the nurse should take time out to evaluate how the patient felt, the techniques he used to cope and their success or otherwise.

Successful coping

As has been noted in earlier chapters, the patient's success in coping depends in part upon his personal strategies and social support. It is anticipated that the patient will grieve the loss of normal elimination and perhaps a sense of sexual identity. The passage through the grief reaction is not always straightforward. Some patients will be discharged angry, while others more worryingly will still seem to be denying their altered body state. Because such a process may take years to complete it is important that the nurse work with intimate relatives, so that they might understand the practicalities of stoma management and its effects upon body image. We must help the wife or husband to understand why his or her spouse is angry and feels dehumanised or dirty. We must offer them the prospect that grief can be worked through, control regained and an active life re-embarked upon. This will mean providing the family with contact numbers and addresses for the appropriate stoma society, an understanding local pharmacist to dispense equipment, and a community stoma therapist nurse who can continue to problem-solve with the family.

Because of modern hospital practices it is unlikely that all the desired care will have been completed pre-discharge. Other patients seek the beds and may be in urgent need of bowel or bladder surgery. Frustrations about not carrying care through to conclusion may usefully be answered by ensuring that we offer the community nurse very thorough notes on the patient's care.These should explicitly address body image issues, the practicalities of stoma care, the patient's feelings about his body and appliances. If the patient has been offered responses to stoma problems and helped to build confidence in an alternative body ideal and presentation, then the first steps have been useful ones.

Review questions

1 Why do you think in the short term, a patient with a long history of bowel disease, might adapt more successfully to his new stoma?
2 If the stoma surgery was performed upon a child, how might this affect the development of his or her body image?
3 Chapter 10 suggests practical ways of overcoming libido problems amongst ostomists and their spouses. To what extent do you think the nurse is equipped to offer useful help in this?
4 Ostomy associations run networks of visitors. To what degree do such visitors offer the patient a pre-planned package of help?
5 What are the advantages of stoma irrigation with regard to body presentation?
6 A patient's cultural, work or social life may all have to be taken into account when siting a stoma. Try to suggest three or four activities and the implications that these might have for a patient dealing with such stoma siting.
7 Suggest four ways in which the patient's skin, and body presentation are protected after the formation of a stoma.
8 Why do you think it is so important to debrief a patient after he has tried wearing his stoma appliance for the first time in company?

Suggested exercises

Individual
Obtain a stoma appliance and, following the manufacturer's directions, fit and wear it for one day. Keep a diary noting how you felt about this. Record whether the appliance felt comfortable, sticky and secure. Share your experiences with other students, or ostomists.

Collaborative
Using Chapter 10 and literature from the ostomy associations (see Appendix A for addresses), try to draw up a one page (A4) 'do's and don'ts'

checklist for a new ostomist. Compare your checklist with others and discuss how you made your choice of what to include on the sheet. Discuss any points about differences in terminology or layout chosen. Finally, decide how such an advice sheet should be used by the nurse.

Group

Copy the problems outlined below, and issue these as challenges to syndicates of students. In each case, the syndicate should consider how they would counsel the patient with that particular problem. Ask them to identify what additional details they would want to know about the patient. Feed back problems and counselling approaches to the whole group. In so doing, compare and contrast approaches. Suggested timings would be: for the syndicate discussion, 20 minutes; for the feedback (depending on group size), 30 minutes; and for highlighting approaches a 10 minute summary.

1. A salesman who has become a colostomist and who now feels that he must plan his work and travel so that he is always near to public toilet facilities.
2. An obese elderly lady who finds that her ileostomy appliance often leaks. Her daughter and son-in-law are soon coming to stay for a week and she is dreading what might happen.
3. A 28 year old single lady who has an ileostomy and who is now eager to accept a dancing date from a man at the office. She worries about whether or not to broach the subject of her stoma.
4. A 34 year old man who finds that his wife has started to treat him as fragile since he had a urostomy formed. He loves her very dearly, but cannot bear the way she is acting.

References

Devlin H.B., 'Stoma Therapy Review, Part 1', *Coloprotology International*, Edition 4, pp 172–6, 1982.

Devlin H.B. and Plant J.A., 'Sexual Function: An aspect of stoma care', *British Journal of Sexual Medicine*, 6, pp 33–7, 1979.

Devlin H.B., Plant J.A. and Griffin M., 'The Aftermath of Surgery for Anorectal Cancer', *British Medical Journal*, iii, p 413, 1971.

Dickerson W., 'Hospital Induced Malnutrition', *Professional Nurse*, Aug, 1986.

Dlin B.M. and Perlman A., 'Emotional Response to Ileostomy and Colostomy in Patients Over the Age of 50', *Geriatrics*, 26, pp 113–18, 1971.

Druss, R., O'Conner J., Prudden J. and Stern L., 'Psychologic Responses to Colectomy', *Archives of General Psychiatry*, 18, pp 53–9, 1968.

Dyer S., 'The Development of Stoma Care', *Professional Nurse*, April, pp 226–30, 1988.

Elcoat C., *Stoma Care Nursing*, Bailliere Tindall, London, 1986.

124   Alterations in body image

Elcoat C., 'Stoma Care – Identifying patient's problems', *Nursing Times*, 84(8), pp 67–70, 1988a.
Elcoat C., 'Stoma Care – Taking an holistic approach', *Nursing Times*, 84(9), pp 57–60, 1988b.
Foulkes B., 'The Practical Management of Bowel Stomas', in Breckman B. (ed.) *Stoma Care*, Ch.4, Beaconsfield, Beaconsfield, 1981.
Gloeckner M.R., 'Perceptions of Sexual Attractiveness Following Ostomy Surgery', *Research in Nursing and Health*, 7, pp 87–92, 1984.
Griffiths A. and Shorey J., 'Modern Colostomy Management', *Update*, Jan, pp 105–14, 1978.
Gruner O., Naas R., Fretheim B. and Gjone E., 'Marital Status and Sexual Adjustment After Colectomy', *Scandinavian Journal of Gastroenterology*, 12 February, pp 193–7, 1977.
Holmes S., 'Nutritional Needs of Surgical Patients', *Nursing Times*, 7 May, pp 30–2, 1986.
Hughes E., Cuthbertson A. and Killingbeck M., *Colorectal Surgery*, Ch.12, Churchill Livingstone, Edinburgh, 1983.
Ileostomy Association, *Ileostomies and Eating Habits*, (broadsheet) Mansfield, Notts, 1988.
Kabza L., 'Impact of Ostomy upon the Spouse', *Journal of Enterostomal Therapy*, 10, pp 54–7, 1983.
Kelly M., 'Loss and Grief Reactions as Responses to Surgery', *Journal of Advanced Nursing*, 10, pp 517–25, 1985.
Kelly M., 'Adjusting to Ileostomy', *Nursing Times*, 83(33), pp 29–31, 1987.
May H.J., *Enterostomal Therapy*, Ch.13, Raven Press, New York, 1977.
Parkes C.M. *Bereavement: Studies of grief in adult life*, Tavistock, London, 1972.
Phillpotts E., Griffiths D., Eltringham W. and Espiner H.J., 'The Continent Colostomy', *Nursing Mirror*, 20 May, pp 53–4, 1976.
Salter M., 'Self Image and Sexuality', *Primary Health Care*, March, pp 8–9, 1986.
Stockley A., 'Irrigation', Ch.11 in Breckman B. (ed.) *Stoma Care*, Beaconsfield, Beaconsfield, 1981.
Todd I., *Intestinal Stomas*, Ch.1, Heinemann, London, 1978.
Watson, P.G., 'The Effects of Short-Term Post-Operative Counselling on Cancer/ostomy Patients', *Cancer Nursing*, 6, pp 21–9, 1983.
Williams N. and Johnson D., 'Prospective Controlled Trial Comparing Colostomy Irrigation with Spontaneous Evacuation Method', *British Medical Journal*, 12 July, p 107, 1980.
Woods N.F., *Human Sexuality in Health and Illness*, C.V. Mosby, St Louis, 1975.

11 The amputee

Study of this chapter will enable you to:

1 Outline the common circumstances leading to the amputation of a limb.
2 Indicate the body image implications of having an amputation at different stages of life.
3 Suggest body reality measures designed to facilitate patient rehabilitation and the rebuilding of an acceptable body image.
4 Outline the function of phantom limb experiences for the patient, in terms of his body ideal.
5 Identify the common grief reactions found in amputee patients.
6 Discuss the role and limitations of counselling the amputee patient in the hospital setting.
7 Describe what is involved for the patient who 'negotiates his new prosthesis' in the social world.
8 Suggest ways in which the nurse might help the patient to deal with social encounters.
9 Identify ways in which groups of patients and established amputees might help the patient to establish an acceptable body presentation.

The amputee may be a 6 year old child still heavily dependent upon parents, or an adult previously athletic and wage earning, or an elderly man who has tired of coping with diabetes mellitus over decades. This selection of patients emphasises just how varied the amputee's circumstances can be. Because patients undergoing amputation come from widely differing age groups, the basic body image problems of limb loss (upper or lower) will be complicated by the developing changes attendant upon ageing (see Chapters 1 and 3). The nursing care of such patients must be tailored to meet some very individual body image needs because no two 'amputees' are alike.

There are probably three major indications for performing an amputation (see Table 11.1). Trauma is the most obvious though not necessarily

Table 11.1 Aspects of amputee altered body image, by age and aetiology

Age group	Typical aetiology	Body image notes (overview)
Children	• Malignant bone tumours (such as Ewing's sarcoma)	Body image problems complicated by cancer therapy. Frequent child and parental guilt fears associated with amputation. Phantom limb may be absent, particularly in the very young. Parental grieving for loss of limb may be very pronounced. Child often incorporates prosthesis into body image very well.
	• Trauma (for example road traffic accident)	Sudden loss of limb allows no psychological preparation. Parents may themselves also be injured. Bilateral amputations become an increasing prospect.
Adolescents	• Malignant bone tumours (such as osteosarcoma)	Rapid changes in body image through puberty – the amputation complicates this in relation to sexuality. Incorporate prostheses perhaps better than many adults (already flexible to change in body image – although feelings of sexual competence undermined). Phantom limb experiences much more common. Cancer therapy complications (see Chapter 14).
	• Trauma	See notes above concerning trauma.
Adults	• Trauma • Osteosarcoma (young adults) • Peripheral vascular disease (older adults)	Identity based upon functional performance, work, parenthood, spouse roles. Function becomes an important part of body/self-image. Lost athleticism, vigour, strength.
Elderly people	• Peripheral vascular disease • Trauma	Possible enhancement of sense of body failure. Fewer members in social support network, carers may themselves be incapacitated. Cognitive or cardio-pulmonary function may limit the use of prostheses.

the commonest. The patient reaching hospital may have a mutilated limb, or indeed one that has already been severed in a road traffic accident. Developments in microsurgery have meant that many more limbs are saved. Nevertheless, a percentage are still unsalvageable, either due to initial damage, circulatory distress or infection. Amongst children and young adults, malignant bone tumours are also a major reason for performing an amputation. In these circumstances the life threatening nature of the disease may leave little time for the patient to prepare for surgery. Adjuvent chemotherapy or radiotherapy compounds the body image trauma. Perhaps the most common reason of all for amputation is peripheral vascular disease. Patients with a long history of diabetes mellitus or arteriosclerosis may not be able to sustain adequate circulation to their legs. The onset of gangrene, or the failure of earlier vascular surgery will necessitate amputation if the patient is to recover successfully.

The level at which an amputation is performed, for instance mid thigh, will determine the degree of function left to the patient. The more of the limb left intact, the better the chances of maintaining 'normal' function and an adequate body image. Prostheses fitted to a substantial and well formed stump are likely to be mastered with greater ease (Herberts *et al*, 1986; Steinberg *et al*, 1985). Here it is assumed that all levels of amputation pose a substantial body image threat which patient and nurse must deal with together.

Body reality – creating firm foundations

By any standards a limb amputation is a major operation, especially for the very young and old. There is a very real risk of the patient dying, either through the effects of surgery or subsequent complications. Therefore, the body reality nursing interventions are critical, both to sustain life and then to establish body function that will permit the fitting and use of a prosthesis (see Table 11.2). In preparing the patient for surgery, it is essential to be sure that he understands what is to be done and what will be done to help him. This is difficult in the circumstances of a malignant tumour, but it is the basis for ethical nursing care and establishing what the body will later look and feel like. Establishing a frank and trusting relationship is important for future rehabilitation measures. The nurse can then go on to emphasise positive quality of life measures which start to compensate for the loss. Rehabilitation must add 'life to years' as well as 'years to life' (Zeiter, 1969).

Post-operative nursing care is designed to minimise the physical damage to the patient through supplementing body resources (nutrition, pain control), anticipating and preventing complications (immobility, infection) and preparing the patient for new limb function (physiotherapy, stump care). To heal the stump wound to a point where it may support body weight or prosthesis, the diet will have to contain adequate protein, zinc and other trace elements. An obese patient may have to reduce weight if the stump is to be successfully accommodated in a prosthesis and weight bearing begun (Badenhorst, 1986).

Muscle spasm may be relieved with an anti-spasmodic drug such as

Table 11.2 Useful body reality interventions for amputee patients

Intervention	Rationale
Provision of high protein, high roughage diet. Carbohydrates provided, assessed in light of patient, body weight and age.	• Promote wound healing and prosthesis fitting. • Limits risk of constipation (immobility). • Fluids reduce risk of infection (UTI). • Planned dieting enhances chance of successful use of new prosthesis (eg not overweight).
Regular assessment of the stump, circulation, skin integrity, possible haemorrhage.	• Many older patients have poor circulation (especially if diabetic). Breakdown of wound might destroy function of stump as a connection point for prosthesis.
Physiotherapy: chest, leg, stump.	• Pre-operatively important to avoid complications associated with surgery. Limbs not affected by surgery may have to take extra strain. • Controlled quadricep exercises on stump will help sustain adequate 'bulk' for prothesis fitting. May also limit muscle spasm and flexion deformity of the hip (mid-thigh amputation)
Mobilising (out of bed into chair, using crutches).	• Prosthesis fitting may take time and risks of immobility are pressing. Patient has the opportunity to explore contacts with other patients before experimenting with a new and possibly difficult to control prosthesis. • Facilitates toileting.
When resting, maintain stump in functional alignment (for example stump flat on bed, with rolled towel to stop external rotation, post-mid-thigh amputation).	• If the stump is pulled into an abnormal alignment, a flexion deformity (for instance of the hip) may occur. This interferes with posture and balance as the patient learns to use his artificial limb. • Physiotherapist will suggest posture exercises which encourage this (for instance, by lying prone)
Pain relief – posture change/(muscle spasm) analgesia.	• Pain undermines patient motivation at physiotherapy and working with prosthetic fitter. • Changing position reduces risk of pressure sores and acquaints patient with feel of body in movement.
Promoting self-care in hygiene.	• Reminds patient of the wide range of functions they still control. • Acquaints patient with the feel and appearance of stump once dressing down and sutures removed.

diazepam, or by physiotherapy. Physiotherapy also assists the patient in avoiding chest or urinary tract infections, as well as flexion deformity of the hip in the case of mid-thigh amputations. Deep breathing and expectorating exercises are vital to the patient who has been a heavy cigarette smoker. Giving up this habit is critical if further amputations are not to result through peripheral vascular problems.

A firm stump bandage and raising the foot of the bed may contribute to reducing stump oedema and later problems in fitting a prosthesis. Once risks of haemorrhage and oedema have subsided the patient is mobilised on crutches. Healthy remaining limbs receive equal physiotherapy attention, as these will be important in this mobilisation and while the patient waits for their prosthesis.

Body ideal – phantom limbs and other issues

The ways in which the amputee struggles to accommodate his body ideal and stump/prosthesis seem to vary according to the patient's age (see Table 11.3). Phantom limb does not appear to be a common problem in very young children who have not formed a complete body image (Aitkin, 1963; Kolb, 1972; Simmel, 1966). For similar reasons young children seem to adopt the prosthesis into their body image quite readily (Kyllonen, 1964). Adolescents and adults appear to experience phantom limbs more frequently. While there is still debate on the origins of the phantom phenomenon here it will be treated as an experience that results from radical change in body boundaries. A limb has been lost or shortened, and with it that body space previously controlled by it. Phantom limbs tend to shrink over time to the level of the remaining stump. In the interim the patient must come to terms with the new body boundaries.

Nurses should recognise the phantom experience and talk openly about it if the patient wishes, otherwise the patient may worry that it is an abnormal experience. Encouraging the patient to touch the stump, to judge its length against a remaining limb, and to feel the prosthesis against it will gradually serve to replace fantasy with reality. Explaining why the phantom occurs, as a normal coping mechanism, may make the patient feel more confident and able later to replace the phantom with more functional aids.

The grief reaction, particularly denial, is a very common response to amputation (Hansen and Osborn, 1971; Kikuchi, 1972; Siller, 1960). Denying the reality of stump and artificial limb enables the patient to preserve a body ideal based on full function and wholesome appearance for rather longer. Should the nurse try to confront directly such denial she is likely to meet with avoidance behaviour (Vincent and Rothenberg, 1969). Children may ask questions about when the limb will regrow (Hansen and Osborn,

Table 11.3 Finding a new body ideal – common reactions of amputee patients

Age group	Reaction	Notes
Children	● Blaming adults for lost limb	Nurses frequently receive blame, the surgeon may have been seen as life saving. Must anticipate angry patients.
	● Adopting a new idol (such as Douglas Bader, or the bionic man)	Patient revalues prosthesis as a symbol of bravery or special function.
	● Denial (refusing to look at or touch stump)	A holding position, giving the child time to create explanations of change.
	● Phantom limb	Phantom limb allows accommodation of body reality and body ideal gradually. Phantom limb often 'shrinks' to real proportions of stump. Young children may not have a phantom, as body image not complete at very young age.
Adults	● Phantom limb	A much more common experience in adolescents and adults.
	● Anxiety (about function and acceptability of new body)	Adult experiences tend to promote the idea that adults must be productive in economic terms. There is a search to find out how true this is with friends/ relatives.
	● Revaluing other functions/ values	The patient may explore whether body ideal might be based on different values (often passive, perceptual roles, rather than active interventionist roles).
	● Grief reaction	(See Chapter 5)
Elderly people	● Depression	The patient's body ideal may have been under threat through other ageing processes. There may be little or no early attempt to rebuild a body ideal. The nurse must help patient to search for new standards.
	● Revaluing experience	Elderly patients may initially seem euphoric at being freed from a painful limb. They state instead that intellectual skills, and experience are the measures by which they value themselves.

1971). In these circumstances a primary nurse or preferred relative may act as impromptu counsellor. It is to be hoped that the patient will express his fears and beliefs and that he may come to understand the limitations these impose on his progress. Reflecting on such fears and beliefs, as well as on future plans for rehabilitation may assist the patient to review their usefulness.

Elderly patients may well alternate between depression and an unrealistic euphoria (Thompson and Haran, 1984). Part of the euphoria is often based upon the sudden freedom from a chronically painful limb (better a smaller body than a pain racked one), and partly on an over optimistic appraisal of the patient's social support network. Thompson and Haran found that nearly half of a sample of elderly amputees unrealistically assessed the health of key carers to be good. They could not understand the pessimism expressed by spouses, who contemplated caring for them at home. This in itself is a form of denial.

The nurse is unlikely to resolve body ideal dilemmas completely while the patient is in hospital. Faced with patients who deliberately resolve to be heroic about their amputation, those who develop a clinging dependence and the depressive, the nurse must utilise group resources (Parkes and Napier, 1970). In units dealing with numbers of amputees, this should take the form of encounter groups. There, patients, relatives, parents and therapists may share their ideas about body features, body function and the future. Alongside a supportive team who introduce the prosthesis, there should be nurses, counsellors and more experienced amputees who help the patient to understand his feelings of anger and disgust, anxiety and euphoria (Ham et al, 1987).

There has been a tendency to see rehabilitation as an activity pursued when the therapist departments are open. The night nurse may find however that the patient chooses her shift to share feelings of being devalued and stigmatised. Counselling cannot easily be postponed until the clinical psychologist is on duty. Therefore, it is useful if the nurse can listen to the urgent concerns of the patient and record these for further discussion later. Counselling involves active listening and reflecting on the patient's words, without necessarily offering a solution. Suggesting hasty, poorly worked out answers to problems is unlikely to enhance patient self-respect, or make matters better.

Body presentation – negotiating the new image

Establishing an acceptable body presentation is important while the patient tries out his new prosthesis. It will, after all, be quite visible even with covering clothes. Further, the prosthesis may be with the patient for a very long time and necessitate a review of body space – the area around his body that he feels he has to manage in some way. Because the prosthesis is highly visible, it should be anticipated that the patient's family will also be eager to develop explanations for what sociologists might term the patient's 'deviant' appearance.

The first steps in such presentation are not wholly in the nurse's control. Patients are referred to artificial limb and appliance centres (ALACs) where a prosthesis is prepared or adapted. Fitting the prosthesis may take many weeks and the resultant artificial leg or arm may not be ideal from a body image perspective (see Table 11.4). Therefore, encourage the patient to plan relevant questions and requests before visiting the centre.

Table 11.4 Characteristics of prostheses which promote a positive body image

Suitability to body reality needs	It must be chosen to deal with the real problems in hand. A poorly chosen prosthesis may cause further damage and undermine the patient's progress. A skilled limb fitter and advisory service is a must.
Safety	The prosthesis must be safe to use. Confidence in prosthesis is necessary for body presentation.
Reliability	The prosthesis must not only be safe, but must continue to support body presentation over time and in many different circumstances.
Lightweight	A heavy prosthesis tires the patient and reminds him of negative limitations.
Comfort	The prosthesis must not damage the stump. Painful prostheses are abandoned and a new body image (say in a wheelchair) has to be considered.
Adjustability	Many patients are still growing and will want a prosthesis that enables them to deal with this. Fitments and straps must be adjustable (for example at times of toileting).
Hygiene	The prosthesis must be easily cleaned and, hopefully, serviced at home. If the materials retain an unpleasant smell, this also undermines body presentation.
Aesthetics	The materials should be attractive to look at and touch. The patient may prefer skin tone colouring, with a texture that emulates the natural limb. The prosthesis should not creak or squeak.
Back up services	Repairs to the prosthesis should be rapid, with a temporary replacement prosthesis to use in the meantime. Delay in prosthesis provision may make the limb less acceptable as prejudices, fantasies about it are built up.
Wearability	The prosthesis should not damage clothing, underwear or overclothes. Hopefully, 'bulges' will be kept to a minimum.

Emphasising realistic hoped for mobility and appearance may mean that the best possible prosthesis is received. In preparing such questions the patient can be referred to well established amputees who have already 'worked through' the presentation difficulties inherent in wearing a prosthesis.

Because the amputation is an 'open' alteration to body image the patient must negotiate the appearance of his prosthesis in an active way. The patient and his kin should be briefed about this, so that regular social encounters may be anticipated and prepared for. Here, a three stage review of social encounters is used, through which common errors and options are identified.

Stage 1 – first encounter

Patients may not realise it but their appearance causes a dilemma for the undamaged people that they meet. The prosthesis or altered gait attracts the eye, but social convention will not permit the other to remark upon it unless he or she is either a child or an intimate acquaintance. It follows then that there is a notional acceptance of the patient as 'unchanged'. The patient may either conspire in this game or he may bring his prosthesis to the attention of the other person. Playing the game of 'unchanged friend' involves certain risks for both patient and the other person. What future activities and plans may be discussed or shared when the amputee is present? Should he be invited to the football match? It may be more fruitful to share points about the prosthesis with all those that the amputee feels are ready for such revelations. Testing the water may include an amusing reference to the artificial limb, such as 'it's a real nuisance carrying an oil can everywhere'. Making a joke at the amputee's own expense may permit the other person to relax.

Stage 2 – getting to know you

Having recognised the existence of prosthesis, the nurse might now advise the patient that it is important to help others to understand what he can do with the limb and how he feels about other people's questions or interest. This means that the amputee must take the lead in developing the encounter. Now that the nurse has helped him to anticipate encounters and he has had chance to observe how uncomfortable others might be in dealing with the meeting, the way forward is to reward friends for their interest in the problems and accomplishments of being an amputee. Smiling, offering honest and balanced answers to questions, are techniques to be employed here.

Stage 3 – making firm friends

Having once built the confidence to open relationships, the patient has to be reminded that future encounters will not always run smoothly. A new friend may have to be helped to explain the amputee's appearance and the origins and function of his prosthesis. Making firm friends involves the amputee in guiding others on how to handle previously taboo discussions, and in so doing to encourage the formation of more varied social networks.

While the patient is still in hospital nursing staff should be aware that these very same stages define their encounters too. In first meetings, nurses have the advantage in that their concern with the patient's stump is 'legitimate'. The nurse might use this legitimate concern to help relatives to start looking at and touching the stump or prosthesis. Finding ways of helping the patient to prepare for stage two in an encounter entails mapping the limitations of the patient's confidence. With some patients nurses have achieved this through inviting them to list 'things I'd like to tell' and 'things I'd not like to tell' about the amputation, stump and prosthesis. Having arrived at two lists in three sections it is then possible to consider ways of leading into the preferred, less threatening disclosures. An example should make this clear.

Things I'd like to tell about my prosthesis

- 'It doesn't hurt me.'
- 'It feels supple and pleasant.'
- 'It can help me hold things, albeit clumsily.'

Possible conversation leads

- 'Wearing an artificial limb is a bit like a shoe. New ones sometimes rub, until they're broken in.' (Use of a familiar analogy.)
- 'I couldn't bear my limb when they first showed it to me. I thought it would feel hard, solid and ungiving. I found it felt a lot softer than that.' (Matter of fact approach, but empathising with anticipated reservations of others.)
- 'I've given up poker for the time being. My hand was so clumsy, I thought it was on the other players side!' (Self-mocking humour and rather clever play on the word hand! Anecdotes for many occasions.)

Valuable preparation for stage three of encounters is afforded when the nurse puts the patient in contact with other patients on the ward, or support groups. In psychiatric settings the group and environment have long been seen as possible therapeutic tools. They must also be seen in this way by the general nurse. In hospital many patients will share a common bond of altered body image. Because all have some dent in the image armour, much can be gained from empathetic fellow patients, who have been chosen to make up a social occasion. Contacts made in hospital may be carried forward to the outside world, forming a bridge for the lonely and the less confident.

Conclusion

It is not a foregone conclusion that the amputee will rehabilitate. Some patients may never give up their denial of the amputation, or only so late that the damage done to their self-image is considerable. Accommodating a prosthesis into the body image takes time, especially for the adult and the elderly. Nurses caring for the amputee face distinctly new body image challenges here. The problem is 'open', uncomfortably so. The patient's health and age related factors must be taken into account. Using the principles outlined here the nurse can make a start on helping the patient to rebuild his damaged body image. During the period of hospital care the patient might learn to ask searching and positive questions despite his feelings of anger or betrayal. If the nurse can respond with some practical techniques for social encounters, and promote the safe use of the prosthesis, then rehabilitation will have begun.

Review questions

1 Many children undergo amputation of limbs and successfully incorporate prostheses into their body image. Do you think parents are able to respond so positively? If not, what factors do you think are involved?
2 If asked the following question, 'how on earth can stump care have anything to do with formulating a positive post-operative body image', make a convincing reply to suggest that there is a connection between 'practical nursing care measures' and 'this abstract stuff about body image!'
3 In your own words, define what is meant by a 'phantom limb'.
4 Which aspects of the grief reaction are especially common amongst amputees?
5 Jane is a 6 year old amputee who has suggested to you that her leg will surely regrow, just like another tooth coming through when one falls out. What coping strategy is Jane using?
6 What are the three stages of social encounters?
7 What are the advantages of involving an established amputee in the rehabilitation of the patient?
8 List six characteristics of an ideal prosthesis (body image concern).

Suggested exercise

Draw up your own list of things 'I'd like to tell', and 'not to tell' about an imaginary artificial limb and preceding amputation. Define the nature of the operation first, for instance below knee amputation following a road traffic accident. Try to write down four or five points in each category.

Now in group, share the things that you would like to share about your limb and operation. The group leader should try to group these points under headings, such as 'appearance', 'function', 'feel', 'how it makes me feel'. If all members of the group agree, share the 'not to tell' points and place these points into categories too.

Then try to answer these questions:

1. Were there clear tendencies of what most wanted others to know about their situation?
2. Were there similar tendencies of what most did not want others to know?
3. What are the implications for nursing care, helping the patient with body presentation?

Note to group leaders – the lists of 'what I'd prefer not to tell about prosthesis or operation' need not be exposed if group members are reticent. It is important to respect the privacy of members who may find it hard to separate an imaginary circumstance from their personal feelings.

When briefing the group for this exercise, emphasise that this is an imaginary exercise and that members will be invited to share their lists only if they are happy to do so.

Timing suggestions are as follows:

(a) for drawing up lists, singly or in pairs, allow 15 minutes
(b) for discussion, allow 60 minutes, dependent upon group size and the range of points made

References

Aitkin G.T., 'Surgical Amputation in Children – AAO5 Instructional Course Lecture', *Journal of Bone and Joint Surgery*, 45, pp 1735–41, 1963.

Badenhorst J., 'A Multidisciplinary Approach to the Rehabilitation of the Amputee', *Rehabilitation in South Africa*, June, pp 34–8, 1986.

Ham R., Regan J. and Roberts V., 'Evaluation of Introducing the Team Approach to the Care of the Amputee: The Dulwich Study', *Prosthetics and Orthotics International*, 11, pp 25–30, 1987.

Hansen H. and Osborn J.G., 'Amputation in Children: Psychological adaptation' Paper presented at the *Annual Meeting of the American Psychiatric Association*, Autumn, 1971.

Herberts P. *et al.* 'Rehabilitation of Unilateral Below Elbow Amputees With Myoelectric Prostheses', *Scandinavian Journal of Rehabilitation Medicine*, 12, pp 123–8, 1986.

Kikuchi J., 'A Preadolescent Boy's Adaptation to the Traumatic Loss of Both Hands', *Maternal Child Nursing Journal*, 1, pp 19–32, 1972.

Kolb J., quoted in Ritchie J. 'Body Image Changes Following Amputation in an Adolescent Girl', *Maternal Child Nursing Journal*, 1, pp 39–46, 1972.

Kyllonen R.R., 'Body Image and Reaction to Amputation', *Connecticut Medicine*, 28, pp 19–23, 1964.

Parkes C.M. and Napier M.M., 'Psychiatric Sequelae of Amputation', *British Journal of Hospital Medicine*, Nov, pp 610–14, 1970.

Siller J., 'Psychological Commitments of Amputation in Children', *Child Development*, 31, pp 109–20, 1960.

Simmel M.L., 'Developmental Aspects of the Body Schema', *Child Development*, 37, pp 83–95, 1966.

Steinberg, F., Sunwoo I. and Roettger R., 'Prosthetic Rehabilitation of Geriatric Amputee Patients: A follow up study', *Archives of Physical Medicine Rehabilitation*, 66(Nov), pp 742–5, 1985.

Thompson D. and Haran D., 'Living with an Amputation: What it means for patients and their helpers', *International Journal of Rehabilitation Research*, 7(3), pp 283–92, 1984.

Vincent H.B. and Rothenberg M.B., 'Comprehensive Care of an 8 Year Old Boy Following Traumatic Amputation of the Glans Penis', *Paediatrics*, 44, pp 271–3, 1969.

Zeiter W.J., 'Historical Development in Physical Medicine and Rehabilitation During the Last Forty Years', *Archives of Physical Medicine and Rehabilitation*, Jan, pp 1–5, 1969.

Further reading

Humm W. and Rainey A.E., *Rehabilitation of the Lower Limb Amputee*, 3rd edn, Bailliere Tindall, 1979.

Powell M., *Orthopaedic Nursing and Rehabilitation*, 9th edn, Churchill Livingstone, Edinburgh, 1986.

12   Patients and plastic surgery

Study of this chapter will enable you to:

1 Outline the wide range of patients who may benefit from plastic and cosmetic surgery.
2 Clarify your own feelings about the ethics of cosmetic surgery, compared with other types of surgery.
3 Discuss briefly some of the emotional and social problems experienced by children born with congenital deformities.
4 With reference to research, outline the typical psychological stages that a patient will go through when preparing for and recovering from plastic surgery.
5 Suggest nursing interventions that are designed to minimise the problems experienced before and after surgery.
6 Recognise common prejudices that may undermine the nursing care of the patient undergoing plastic surgery.

There will be some nurses who have strong ethical reservations about some patients undergoing plastic or cosmetic surgery. They would wish to question the right of an individual to undergo a 'face lift' or breast augmentation, while others wait for life saving surgery or deal with chronic pain. Such an ethical reservation has a lot to commend it, especially when nursing and medical services are limited. Nevertheless, it is a reservation that focuses upon just one aspect of plastic surgery (the cosmetic domain) and upon a limited measure of human need (utilitarian). In this book it has been suggested that an altered body image really does cause the patient a lot of misery. It can significantly affect a person's life opportunities, to develop, to love, to socialise and to work. The comparison between the need for a total hip replacement and the need for a rhinoplasty may not be a simple one. It may not be possible to separate out the human distress caused by the sagging skin of old age, from that caused by a cleft lip to a growing child.

Patients seek out plastic surgery for a variety of reasons (see Figure 12.1). For some there is a need to construct replacement body parts when

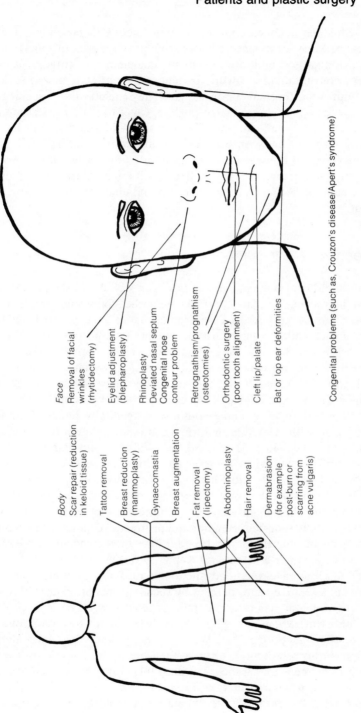

Body
Scar repair (reduction in keloid tissue)

Tattoo removal

Breast reduction (mammoplasty)

Gynaecomastia

Breast augmentation

Fat removal (lipectomy)

Abdominoplasty

Hair removal

Dermabrasion (for example post-burn or scarring from acne vulgaris)

Face
Removal of facial wrinkles (rhytidectomy)

Eyelid adjustment (blepharoplasty)

Rhinoplasty
Deviated nasal septum
Congenital nose contour problem

Retrognathism/prognathism (osteotomies)

Orthodontic surgery (poor tooth alignment)

Cleft lip/palate

Bat or lop ear deformities

Congenital problems (such as, Crouzon's disease/Apert's syndrome)

Fig. 12.1   The need for cosmetic/reconstructive surgery. Note: some trauma will necessitate cosmetic surgery to multiple body areas (for example, burns, road traffic accidents).

the individual has been left congenitally deformed. Others will be referred by burns specialists or by oncology departments – the patient's image having been traumatised by a prior accident, malignancy or surgery. Alongside these conventionally 'worthy' patients we meet patient who seek to simply improve a 'normal' body image. They include those seeking to adjust the contours of their nose or jawline, eager to erase the stereotypes that accompany a 'weak chin' or a 'bent nose'. All of the patient's have a perceived desparity between body reality and body ideal. This will have caused problems in the way they have presented themselves to the world. In a very real sense, many of them will have felt crippled, either by trauma, birth, disease or societal norms that demand that we look young and beautiful.

The need for plastic surgery

The need to adjust body appearance has been well established in medical research literature. Studying patients with the congenital problems of Crouzon's disease and Apert's syndrome, Belfer *et al* pointed out that parents of such children might withdraw emotionally from them. Others tended to attempt to defend the child by an unrealistic denial of the altered body reality. Because children rapidly form a body image which must equip them to live an adult life, this author recommends early surgery to abort the need for maladaptive defences by patient or parents (Belfer *et al*, 1979). Other authors have pointed out how congenitally damaged children might struggle with schooling or forming intimate relationships (Grantly and Clifford, 1979; Longacre, 1973; McWilliams and Paradise, 1973; Richman, 1976). Studying adolescents with cleft palate deformities, Bernstein and Kapp noted just how long such corrective surgery may go on for. Child development was undermined by parental feelings of guilt, worries that the child might choke, and unrealistic beliefs that the child would be mentally retarded. Regular and protracted contact with hospitals and clinics meant that the family found it hard to become an independent self-supporting unit (Bernstein and Kapp, 1981).

Other studies have recorded the demand for orthodontic surgery, 'need' being a relative term, defined by social norms. Stricker *et al* report a high rate of dental malocclusion amongst teenagers, 54 per cent of 12 to 17 year olds (Stricker *et al*, 1979). Malocclusion tends to be a strong influence on the perception of facial attractiveness. When the patient undergoes surgery (an osteotomy), he may then have considerable difficulties adjusting to his new appearance. Up until this point the prognathism has served as a crutch, an explanation for all his difficulties in social relationships and work. Its removal forces the patient to confront the fact that life success or failure does not solely rest upon body image, important though this may be.

It has been said that the face is the window onto the soul and certainly the face is capable of some 100,000 different expressions (Birdwhisthell, 1970). Therefore, it is not surprising that there is much interest in facial plastic surgery.Meyer and Jacobsson reviewed the factors that seemed to predict patient satisfaction with perhaps the most common facial operation, namely the rhinoplasty. Many of their findings confirmed those of other researchers (Meyer and Jacobsson, 1986). Older patients adjusted more readily post-operatively and men rather less so than women (Rees, 1978; Tardy, 1980). Patients who had clear and realistic expectations of what the operation might achieve also faired better (Graber, 1980). Most of these authors agreed that a distinction might be drawn between those patients who sought the operation for personal goals, and those who were responding to external pressures (Hay, 1970; MacGregor, 1971). Internally, self-motivated patients gained the most satisfaction from surgery. There is a clear need to understand the patient's motivation for elective surgery, before operation (Edgerton, 1975).

Nursing roles – patient problems

While each patient's needs and problems will be particular, some common concerns seem to apply to a wide range of patients preparing for plastic surgery. These are strongly associated with body ideal, and, to a lesser extent body presentation. The first problems may be uncomfortably near to home, occasioned by the expectations of the nurse. Nursing staff seem to expect that patients should be stoical and accept their lot in life (Lazarus, 1985). They are also expected to communicate clearly and well (Stockwell, 1972). There is an expectation that they will conform broadly to certain cultural facial norms (Lucker, 1980). Clearly, these patients have problems on all counts. They manifestly do not accept 'their lot', they may have uneven or unattractive facial expressions and they might never aspire to the stricter facial norms. It is important, therefore, to suspend common prejudices, to empathise with the patient and to recognise the longing for the self-esteem that might follow as a result of surgery (Baer and Lowery, 1987; Roy, 1986).

Despite the fact that this surgery is elective and often long anticipated by the patient, considerable pre-operative body image problems should still be anticipated. Belfer et al describe four stages through which the patient passes. These may form the basis for several nursing interventions (see Table 12.1). In taking the decision to undergo surgery – and there may be multiple operations over a number of years – the patient is showing

Table 12.1 Interventions during a patient career (stages after Belfer *et al* (1979) see text)

Decision to undergo surgery	Preparation for surgery	Immediately post-operation	Re-integration phase
Assisting patient to clarify hopes and aspirations	Establish trust relationship	If not already established consider writing a diary with patient (catharsis). To prove a record of change	Telephone counselling
Identifying body ideal and what influences it	Educate patient concerning pre- and post-op specifics. Be honest concerning post-op pain, swelling, bruising and any prostheses or splints	Possible use of periodic photographs for similar purpose	Set up support group
Advocating patient's enquiries to surgeon			Assist patient to explore the experience of social encounters post surgery
Facilitating patient contact with previous patients	Brief relatives on same. Emphasize the crisis point nature of post-op period and how they can help by acceptance of temporary body presentation	Use of analgesia and strategies to reduce swelling/bruising	Plan possible future measures
Outlining hospital period, the nursing care and effects of surgery		Reassure patient about the temporary nature of swelling or bruising	
Once patient clear about motives, reaffirm patient's right to tackle the problem	Empathetic listening – the patient is about to make raw once more his body image problem	Brief patient and relatives about process of re-integrating change into new body image	

considerable fortitude. He is forcibly reminded of his deformity, and must recognise its shortcomings. Because this is a painful insight into the gap between body reality and body ideal, he may ascribe the motivation for the operation to a relative, for instance 'my mother wants me to have the operation'. This poses the question of internal motivation versus external pressure. Does the patient truly seek the operation for himself? It is important that nurses help the patient explore this question pre-operatively. It is important because repeated surgery for external pressure reasons may eventually cause the patient to despise himself for not making his own decision. The patient no longer controls his body ideal, but express through surgery the body ideal ascribed to him by parents or other relatives. It is implicit that the patient should give only informed consent to surgery and nursing care. Becoming adequately informed about the 'pros' and 'cons' of an operation may necessitate a degree of self-insight.

Once surgery is underway the patient soon realises that now the discussed change is for real. Up until this point he may have fantasised about what this meant for his body ideal. Immediately, pre-operatively it is appropriate to remind the patient about the temporary or intermediate effects of the surgery. There may be short term pain and a great deal of swelling and bruising. In the immediate post-operative period, body image may be adversely distorted, so that the patient feels betrayed by the surgeon or nurse. Goin et al point out that the patient often experiences a post-operative depression on the second or third day after the operation (Goin et al, 1980). This reaction may in fact occur many weeks later. For Belfer the post-operative period is the psychological crisis point. It is important that the nurse re-emphasises the temporary nature of the swelling, that new scars will fade and flatten. It will be necessary to re-affirm that the bravery shown by the patient was worthwhile, and that the demand for surgery was reasonable (Courtiss, 1980). During this period it is worthwhile acquainting the close relatives with details of the disruption to the patient's body image. They should be encouraged to express their own faith in the value of the patient's efforts, and that he is still lovable, even though he may be covered in dressings and badly contused. It may be a mistake to put them off visiting until the patient 'looks a little better'.

Belfer's final stage involves the patient re-integrating his new appearance into his body image. Over a period of several months the patient must reorganise his body image defences and adjust his body presentation. Previous explanations of appearance may no longer be tenable. He may have to continue wearing a pressure bandage or prosthesis. Orthodontic operations may leave a brace or splints in situ. This is seen as a period of critical introspection with the patient reviewing just what surgery has meant for his body image. For most of this period the nurse is unlikely to be in close contact with the patient. It is important, therefore, that the patient is helped to anticipate this introspection before leaving hospital.

Relatives too may benefit from a discussion which recognises that their patient may appear very cynical and self-critical. It should be pointed out that the patient will most certainly be monitoring their reactions to his new body presentation (Belfer *et al*, 1979).

During the post-operative period it is often constructive to help the patient record changes in a written form. This may then be looked back on at a later date and used to recognise the progress already made. John had suffered multiple facial lacerations following a road traffic accident. The recent rhinoplasty was just one step in the rehabilitation programme. During his post-operative quieter momements John was encouraged to keep a diary on how he felt about his appearance, the surgery and his nursing care. It was agreed that his fiancee would also keep a diary and that the nurses would share observations from his nursing care plan. At visiting times notes were exchanged on perceptions of John's recovery. Through this strategy John was able to compare his own subjective disgust at his appearance, with the clear affection expressed in his fiancee's diary. The nursing notes spelt out clear improvements in facial swelling and the removal of nasal splint and packs. John kept his diary for the next few months, before he threw away what had now become a redundant crutch – his record of expressed doubts, or anger or fear.

Conclusion

There is no way in which John's story, or Belfer's model can adequately illustrate every nursing concern or patient need. Nevertheless, they do point to the need for a nursing ethos that respects the patient's legitimate concern with body image. Nursing staff are ill equipped to pre-judge the degree of pain or anguish that brings a patient to plastic surgery. Rather as in the assessment of pain, the nurse should accept that body image trauma is what the patient says it is! Such an open, non-judgemental acceptance of patient need should not however extend to committing the patient to surgery without first helping to clarify hopes and aspirations. There are limits to what surgery can realistically achieve, especially when measured against the standards of facial and body beauty shared in western society. There is always a need to recall that body ideal may be unrealistic and that over time a new body ideal may have to be accommodated.

In setting out to concentrate upon the body ideal issues, the nurse has not foresaken practical concerns. A patient who removes pressure bandages or a splint too early, as a result of despair and depression, will undoubtedly suffer a very obvious setback. By counselling the patient and relatives about typical experiences pre- and post-operatively, the coping strategies that the patient uses to combat negative impulses may be enriched. By clarifying what surgery can and cannot do, the patient may be helped to establish realistic expectations of future social encounters. The new face, bustline or body contour may assist in building a confident and sociable self – it cannot totally supplant that self.

Review questions

1 Many patients who undergo cosmetic surgery designed to combat the effects of ageing do so using private health care. To what extent do you think this affects people's opinions about the ethics of cosmetic surgery?
2 Can you account for why there is a high proportion of facial plastic surgery performed?
3 In what ways might congenital facial deformities affect the relationship between parents and child?
4 Patients may attend for surgery under pressure from their relatives. Why do you think relatives may initiate such pressure?
5 Can you suggest why older patients and women might adjust more readily to their new body image post-rhinoplasty? You might like to consider factors such as cultural expectations of the sexes and the role of life experiences in coming to know ourselves.
6 In what way does Belfer's model of patient experiences help us to anticipate patient's needs pre- and post-operatively?

Suggested exercise

The question of patient need and patient rights exercise philosophers' and nurses' minds alike. Longman's *Family Dictionary* defines 'need' as, 'a lack of something necessary, desirable or useful' or else 'a physiological or psychological requirement for the well being of an organism'. The same dictionary defines a 'right' as, a 'power, privilege, interest etc. to which one has a just claim'. In order to help you clarify your own views on cosmetic surgery try to create a short list of needs and rights met by each of the following operations and circumstances:

1. Martin, who is having a rhinoplasty to correct a 'hook nose' that he was born with. Martin is aged 21 and single.
2. Martha, who is having a breast augmentation. Martha is 37 years old and was recently divorced. She is now hoping to meet a new partner.
3. Samantha, who is having a breast reduction operation after being seen for years as a 'sex object' by fellow male students. She is 19 years old.

Once you have formulated your own list, share these with the rest of the group. Try to discover just which criteria are being used to decide what is a 'need' and what is a 'right'. Do you find that a right is seen as morally higher than a need?

Points for teachers/group leaders

This exercise is likely to throw up some strongly held views and of course there is no absolutely correct solution. It is suggested, therefore, that you set aside a three stage timing for this, as follows:

(a) for the drawing up of lists of needs and rights, allow 10 to 15 minutes.
(b) for the sharing of needs and rights perceptions, allow a minimum of 45 minutes (more for a very large group, especially if from different cultures, backgrounds).
(c) for relating perceptions to nursing/professionalism, allow 30 minutes.

References

Baer E. and Lowery B., 'Patient and Situational Factors That Affect Nursing Students Like or Dislike of Caring for Patients', *Nursing Research*, 36(5), pp 298–302, 1987.

Belfer M., Harrison A. and Murray J., 'Body Image and the Process of Reconstructive Surgery', *American Journal of Disabled Child*, 133, pp 532–5, 1979.

Bernstein N. and Kapp K., 'Adolescents with Cleft Palate: Body image and psychosocial problems', *Psychosomatics*, 22(8), pp 697–703, 1981.

Birdwhisthell R., *Kinesis and Context*, University of Pennsylvania Press, Philadelphia, 1970.

Courtiss E., 'Doctor, Am I Being Vain?', *Plastic and Reconstructive Surgery*, 65(6), p 819, 1980.

Edgerton M., 'The Plastic Surgeon's Obligations to the Emotionally Disturbed Patient', *Plastic and Reconstructive Surgery*, 55(81), 1975.

Goin M *et al*, 'A Prospective Psychological Study of 50 Female Face Lift Patients', *Plastic and Reconstructive Surgery*, 65(4), pp 436–41, 1980.

Graber L., 'Psychological Considerations of Orthodontic Treatment' in Lucker G., Ribbens K. and McNamara J. (eds) *Psychological Aspects of Facial Form*, pp 81–117, Monograph 11, University of Michigan, Ann Arbor, 1980.

Grantly H. and Clifford E., 'Cognitive Self Concept and Body Image Measures of Normal, Cleft Palate and Obese Adolescents', *Cleft Palate Journal*, 16, pp 177–82, 1979.

Hay J., 'Psychiatric Aspects of Cosmetic Nasal Operations', *British Journal of Psychiatry*, 116(530), pp 85–97, 1970.

Lazarus R.S., 'The Trivialisation of Distress', in Rosen J. and Soloman L. (eds) *Prevention in Health Psychology*, University Press of New England, Hannover, N.H., pp 279–98, 1985.

Longacre J., *Rehabilitation of the Facially Disfigured*, Charles C. Thomas, Springfield, Illinois, 1973.

Lucker G., 'Aesthetics and a Qualitative Analysis of Facial Appearance' in Lucker G., Ribbens K. and McNamara J. (eds) *Psychological Aspects of Facial Form*, pp 49–79, Monograph 11, University of Michigan, Ann Arbor, 1980.

MacGregor F., 'Selection of Cosmetic Surgery Patients', *Surgical Clinics of North*

America, 51, p. 289, 1971.

McWilliams B. and Paradise L., 'Educational Occupational and Marital Status of Cleft Palate Adults', *Cleft Palate Journal*, 10, pp 223–49, 1973.

Meyer L. and Jacobsson S., 'The Predictive Validity of Psychosocial Factors for Patient's Acceptance of Rhinoplasty', *Annals of Plastic Surgery*, 17(6), pp 513–20, 1986.

Rees T., 'Rhinoplasty in the Older Adult', *Annals of Plastic Surgery*, 1, p. 27, 1978.

Richman L., 'Behaviour and Achievement of Cleft Palate Children', *Cleft Palate Journal*, 16, pp 4–10, 1976.

Roy D., 'Caring for the Self-Esteem of the Cosmetic Patient', *Plastic Surgical Nursing*, Winter, pp 138–41, 1986.

Stockwell F., *The Unpopular Patient*, Royal College of Nursing, London, 1972.

Stricker G., Clifford E., Cohen L.K., Giddon D.B., Meskin L.H. and Evans C.A., 'Psychosocial Aspects of Craniofacial Disfigurement', *American Journal of Orthodontics*, 76(4), pp 410–22, 1979.

Tardy M., 'Rhinoplasty in Midlife', *Otolaryngologic Clinics of North America*, 13, p. 289, 1980.

13 After a cerebro-vascular accident

Study of this chapter will enable you to:

1 Suggest why the body image needs of the cerebro-vascular accident (CVA) patient are becoming increasingly more important for the nurse.

2 Argue why the elderly patient's body image needs should be addressed, despite the difficulties associated with assessing and rehabilitating the 'stroke' victim.

3 Suggest how early physical therapy and protective measures may contribute to the patient's body image rehabilitation later on.

4 Describe the importance of 'control' in the elderly patient's body image rehabilitation.

5 Explain why the patient's pre- and post-CVA body ideal may be different.

6 Describe simple measures by which patient identity and through that, body ideal, may be re-established.

7 Outline the important part that relatives play in patient rehabilitation.

8 Discuss the measures that nurses and other therapists will have to employ if an adequate body presentation is to be re-established.

9 Discuss critically your own education with regard to rehabilitation training. Outline to what extent this has equipped you to effect adequate rehabilitation of the stroke victim and his body image.

A cerebro vascular accident (CVA) may fairly be seen as a disaster, affecting victim, relatives and friends alike. The World Health Organisation describes the stroke as something characterised by a 'focal neurological deficit' due to the disturbance of cerebral blood supply (WHO, 1971). Myco tends to see it in terms of a catastrophe, affecting all areas of the person's life (Myco, 1983). This chapter will err on the side of the descriptive and subjective definitions, because the body image disturbances associated with the cerebro-vascular accident are very personal and not easily discussed in pathology terms.

Cerebro-vascular accidents are a comparatively common problem in an ageing population. Wade points out that in a typical British health district there will be 1500 people who have suffered a CVA and that half of these will be left with significant problems (Wade, 1988). Each year 400 more people will join the district list. In the USA the numbers of disabled stroke victims now easily exceeds earlier estimates of two million (Politicoff, 1970). Given that most western populations are characterised by increasing numbers of people living to the ages of 70, 80 or beyond, it must be expected that CVAs and the associated body image problems can only continue to grow.

The prognosis for the stroke victim depends upon the origins of the problem and the quality of nursing care and support received following the episode (see Table 13.1). Wade points out that one-third of patients die within the first three weeks and that 50 per cent will die within a year of their stroke (Wade, 1988). Incontinence of urine was seen as a poor prognostic sign. Nichols has been a little more optimistic, with one-third of CVA victims being anticipated to survive for three years (Nichols, 1976). Such problematic prognoses amongst elderly patients might make rehabilitation appear to be a less than fruitful medical venture. Accordingly, the attention paid to body image rehabilitation has sometimes been slight. Low expectations of patient recovery may affect the support that the nurse

Table 13.1 Origins and prognosis of cerebro-vascular accidents

Cause	Percentage of deaths (CVA) resulting
Cerebral thrombosis	62
Cerebral haemorrhage	16
Subarachnoid haemorrhage	12
Embolism and other aetiology	10
Causes of cerebral thrombosis:	Atheroma, arteritis, cerebral thrombophlebitis, haematological conditions, for example myeloma, polycythemia
Causes of cerebral haemorrhage:	Aneurysm, hypertension, tumours, trauma, angioma
Subarachnoid haemorrhage:	Trauma (for example fractured skull), aneurysms (berry type), hypertension
Embolism:	Myocardial infarction, mitral stenosis, bacterial endocarditis, fat, air or tumour embolism

Source: Figures, Kurtze J.F. (1969) *Epidemiology of Cerebrovascular Disease*, Springer Verlag.

receives when trying to establish high standards of patient care (Kratz, 1978).

Stroke and the older person

It must not be assumed that the effects of a CVA on an older person's body image are unimportant. In earlier chapters it was argued that elderly people's body image is vitally important to them and something that they still seek to control and develop in daily life (see Chapter 3). Because of the impact of a stroke on the neurological control of the body, the effects upon body image are both widely disseminated and long lasting. While in some pathologies the patient may sustain problems predominantly in one area of body image (say body ideal), stroke affects all areas. As Piotrowski has said, the ageing body has imperfections and limitations, but the individual still seeks to maintain control over it. Self-esteem is based upon such control, at a time of life when control can seem to be slipping out of the elderly person's grasp in so many ways (Piotrowski, 1982).

Control and independence go together. Unfortunately, amongst the elderly, control post-stroke is not just a physical matter. In order to sustain an independent lifestyle, the patient needs a varied social support network. Death of peers may limit such options. Change in body image is difficult to accept at any age, but especially so when it has been rapid and when patients rely upon a limited number of caring individuals to help them build a new image. Therefore, it is impossible to address these body image problems of the elderly without considering the patient's circumstances. Society must revalue upwards its senior members if they are to rehabilitate successfully.

Rehabilitating the patient is a creative activity that starts immediately after the CVA (Stryker, 1972). It is essential to prevent further deterioration or complication to body reality, be this infection, contractures or increasing muscle wastage. Adams and Hurwitz outline steps in rehabilita-

Table 13.2 Common problems resulting from CVA

Unconsciousness
Hemiplegia/hemiparesis
Flaccid muscle tone giving way to spastic muscle tone and hyperactive reflexes
Dysphagia
Aphasia
Dysarthria
Hemianopia/diplopia
Incontinence
Constipation (linked to inactivity)
Emotional frustration

tion, such as sitting up, standing, and walking (Adams and Hurwitz, 1963). In order to achieve these physical goals body image barriers must be overcome, for instance altered perception of body space. The style of physical rehabilitation is open to some debate. Different authors support different therapies (Bobath, 1970; Stern *et al*, 1970), while yet others question whether physiotherapy actively improves patient recovery beyond limiting the complications that would hamper a degree of normal healing. What seems clear is that physical recovery is bound up with the need to create a new acceptable body image, itself an important motivator.

Body reality – problems and suggestions

While the effects of a CVA depend upon the area of the brain which is damaged, certain problems are commonly seen amongst most patients (see Table 13.2). These must be recognised promptly by the nurse. This chapter will look at a few suggestions on how to act. More detailed texts exist on many of the physical therapies and the reader is referred to the reference section of this chapter for complementary reading. As with all body image problems, attention must be paid to physical care if the foundations of a successful body presentation are to be laid. A body reality that is hopelessly out of synchronisation with the patient's body ideal is a recipe for depression and limited co-operation.

CVAs typically bring about a three stage effect. Cerebral ischaemia results in an initial period of unconsciousness, confusion or disorientation. At this stage muscle tone is flaccid, but paralysis or paresis will already be affecting one side of the body. In stage two, consciousness is typically regained, but during the post-stroke days the flaccid paralysis is replaced by spasticity of muscle tone, contorting the limbs into the classic stroke posture (see Figure 13.1). By stage three, the disorientated and anxious patient is attempting to deal with his new hospital surroundings and, the realisation that he is possibly incontinent, cannot speak or understand what is said to him, and has difficulties eating and swallowing.

The unconscious patient relies upon the nurse to protect his body from injury. While the principles of caring for the unconscious patient are directed at physical needs, they also meet body image needs too. Protection from joint contractures, pressure sores, skin trauma, deep vein thrombosis and opportunistic infections all serve to sustain the body, the vital material for the patient's new body image.

Elderly patients are prone to pressure sores, especially if they are malnourished and have poor circulation, for instance diabetic patients. By using pressure relief devices, such as air flow mattresses, and regular turning, bony prominences are protected and kept intact. Naso-gastric feeding may be important as nutrient intake is critical for a healthy skin.

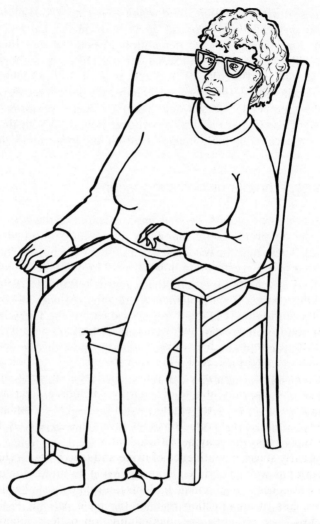

Fig. 13.1 Typical post-CVA posture. 1. Body leans toward the afflicted hemisphere (pressure sore and other risks). 2. Spasticity of affected hand – claw-like deformity may develop. 3. Inverted posture of affected leg – difficult to place foot flat on floor. (Risk of 'foot drop'.)

The nurse recognises that eating may be difficult for the patient, even weeks after the CVA. Because CVA victims are often aphasic, it is difficult to judge their experience of such protective measures. McNeil, another stroke victim, found that immobility was a source of great discomfort.

Beyond the two hour point, immobility resulted in considerable pain and anxiety for the patient (McNeil, 1975).

Passive physiotherapy to joints, especially while they are still comparatively free of spastic muscle tone problems, starts off the chain of rehabilitation that leads to dressing and walking later on. Putting joints through their full range of movements is very important if contractures are to be avoided (Kelly, 1966). When contractures have become established, subsequent physiotherapy and body reality rehabilitation becomes very much more difficult. Dressing and undressing, eating, writing and other avenues for body presentation are severely limited. The nurse should arrange for the patient's relatives and herself to receive instruction on any special exercises, so that support is sustained while the physiotherapist is absent.

Positioning the patient in a bed or chair three main goals should be borne in mind (see Figure 13.2). Firstly, to prevent additional trauma to limbs or pressure areas not felt by the patient (hemianaesthesia). Secondly, to place the affected limbs so that they are supported in a functional position – stroke victims tend to lean to the affected side, limiting later balance, gait and mobility. Thirdly, to place bedside locker, photographs and other possessions on the side of the patient's affected limbs. This encourages the patient to view his weakened or paralysed limb. It is important to recognise and to accept the affected limbs if physiotherapy is to develop and the patient is to create a new body ideal. Denial of the existence of the affected limbs (anosognosia) is a problem that the nurse must address from an early point. With this in mind, it is worth talking openly to the patient about his paralysed limbs. Embarrassment on the nurse's part is a block to rehabilitation. It should be emphasised that the limb is 'not dead' but robbed of some of its messages from the brain. Many of these messages may be restored later.

At this early stage, incontinence of urine and faeces pose a challenge to skin integrity as well as an infection risk. While an indwelling catheter is often seen as necessary for female patients, a uridom and collection system may prove less of an infection risk for the male patient. Following an assessment of the patient's previous elimination patterns many patients will benefit from bladder retraining (Nordmark and Rohweder, 1975). Toilet facilities, such as a urinal or commode, must be provided in private, at a time when the bladder is full and not just when it suits the ward routine. Palpating the bladder and assessing fluid intake should enable the patient and nurse gradually to establish a pattern of when to provide toilet facilities. In between times, protective measures, incontinence pants for instance, will be needed. These measures must keep the patient dry. Leaving him on a wet incontinence sheet destroys his morale and undermines his self-esteem (Bolwell, 1982).

If the patient's conception of his body contours and boundaries has been

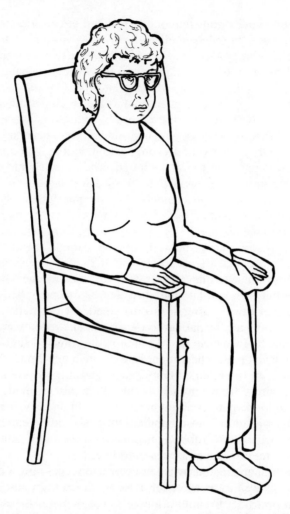

Fig. 13.2   Positioning the patient for good posture. 1. Patient sits upright (head in midline of body). 2. Affected (left) arm supported on pillows (slightly forward). 3. Knees and ankles properly flexed so that affected left foot is flat on the floor.

affected by the CVA, or he is confused, elimination retraining must take on a rather more formal format (see Table 13.3). This involves the nurse in praising success and tolerating toilet accidents. Angrily accusing the patient of letting you down presumes that the patient experiences his body and warning signs of abdominal fullness in the same way as you might. This is not the case. Accurate recording of the passage of urine or faeces enable the nurse to adjust an initial two hourly regime so as to avoid future embarrassment, with all that this implies for patient motivation.

Table 13.3 Elimination retraining

When patient confusion does not permit bladder palpation method:

Principles:
- Patients will need 2 litres fluid per day if dehydration is to be avoided
- The patient also needs rest and comfort, therefore plan fluids for earlier ⅔ day (so as to minimise problems for patient in the night)
- A wet and uncomfortable bed or chair is a negative stimulus and undermines patient motivation and co-operation
- Toileting should avoid other important highlights of the day (visiting, meal times)
- Fluid balance monitoring is important so that regime may be adjusted

Steps:
- Start with two-hourly regime, helping patient onto commode

- Facilities nearby and comfortable (for instance at room temperature)

- Explain what you are doing, ensure patient's comfort and dignity maintained

- Establish whether elimination has occurred. Measure quantity and chart. Praise success

- Review input and output of fluid at end of each shift. Note any accidents and adjust regime accordingly, for instance more frequent toileting as necessary

- Always anticipate the return of some control over micturition. Therefore ask patient if he senses the urge to visit the toilet (especially first thing each morning and post-meals)

Body ideal – rebuilding from the start

At the start of this book it was described how perceptions of the body are founded upon personal experiences of limb position and movement (body in space) and upon information gleaned by using the eyes. This picture of the body is then adjusted in order to approximate as closely as possible to an ideal, which often is culturally determined. The stroke victim may not have any of these components intact or in balance with one another. Firstly, the experience of body boundaries and personal space may be fundamentally disrupted. The patient may deny that there is anything wrong with the affected side. This denial is compounded by the lack of feeling in the affected limbs and a homonymous hemianopia, with perhaps a loss of 50 per cent of the visual information previously received. By talking to the patient from his affected side, the nurse's voice has the quality of an auditory hallucination because she is not seen. Watson groups these problems as neglect of the affected side, problems of recognition and spatial relationships, and problems of movement planning (Watson, 1987). Artwork produced by CVA victims illustrates the problem clearly (see Figure 13.3).

Spatial relationships of limbs – that is their perceived position, relative to one another, and other objects – are typically jumbled up. This has a

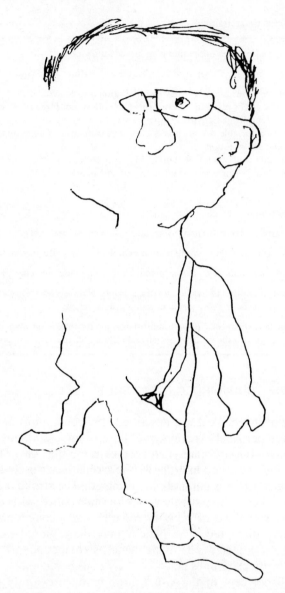

Fig. 13.3   Disruption to body schema (body boundaries) – patient's drawing.
Note the incomplete perceived body boundaries and asymmetrical
body proportions.

profound effect upon the efforts to form a new body ideal. Previous ideals
have been founded upon the certainty that we all have arms and legs in a
similar configuration, that we all know left from right and that our body
has a well demarcated boundary. This is not always true for the patient.

We normally feel different according to how we dress or groom ourselves. If body contours are not clearly identified it may be difficult to form a sense of our wholeness, let alone an identity that approaches the ideal (see Table 13.4). The incorporation of external objects into our body image, such as clothes and possessions, presumes that we make a distinction between ourselves and the rest of the world (Norris, 1978). The stroke victim may feel that all his 'edges' are blurred and that he has no such controllable boundary.

It is difficult to assess the damage done to body ideal because this usually calls for the patient to share his feelings. Aphasic patients may not be able to share ideas or attitudes, after all, body image is an abstract concept. In the early stages this picture may be complicated by the patient's disorientation and amnesia. He may have little idea of his identity and normal previous relationships. The previous body ideals may also have been lost as a result. While at first sight a further tragedy, this may in fact permit the nurse to work with the patient and relatives, to form a new ideal with a minimum of painful comparisons. The goals of patient dignity remain the same, but perhaps because the patient cannot easily make before and after comparisons, the progress may be more positive.

The nurse's body ideal interventions must therefore sometimes start at a very basic level. Before a new ideal can be built she must assist the patient

Table 13.4 Difficulties in forming body ideal

Steps	Attributes/qualities	Notes
Myself as a separate entity from the rest of the world	There are clear dividing lines where I end and the world 'out there' begins	The stroke victim may not recognise body boundaries, or even see these
Properties of my separate body (reality)	It moves to command, with co-ordination. It is animate and responsive. Unlike objects out there	Body movement and control disrupted in CVA victim (often at several different levels)
Possessions of my separate body (symbols of my nature)	I have clothes and personal possessions which are very much an expression of my personality, qualities, values	Personal possessions not recognised or not named. Therefore not easily admitted into body image (presentation)
Value of my body reality and its possessions and extensions (such as clothes) compared against the opinions of society, significant others	I find that I have much in common with others, we share much and value certain shapes, dress etc. more. Other values seem not to be like mine	The CVA victim does not have the raw material for such comparisons. Body boundaries and possessions are incomplete, so how can comparisons and ideals evolve?

to relearn the boundaries and properties of his own body and the objects he will regularly meet. It is as if the patient must once again take possession of his body. Using physiotherapy and occupational therapy settings, the nurse encourages the patient to touch and manipulate affected body parts. She reacquaints him with the textures of clothes, the contours of a comb or spectacles. These are named, their function and attractions reiterated repeatedly. Possessions are identified as such, 'this is your comb Mrs Duke, the red one with the long handle'. Accidents in manipulation of body or items are to be expected. The goal remains however to re-equip the patient with body attributes, properties and possessions, by which the patient may determine what is desirable and what is not. By which he may arrive at a new body ideal.

Relatives are extremely important in the search for a new body ideal. First reactions tend to involve a lament for the lost person and, later, tend to measure the new body image of their loved one in terms of the old one. Recall that the relatives' body images are often dependent upon projecting their ideals onto loved ones – supporting their own ideals through association with those who share such an ideal. It's not surprising, therefore, that the loss of the patient's distinctive image upsets their own equilibrium. The nurse must educate the relatives that in profound stroke, much of the patient's new self may be built from sources today, not memories of the life before. Some reference points may not be regained. Encouraging the patient to express likes and dislikes in current dress, grooming, posture, possessions, is a positive step. The patient may be surprised at how different the new body ideal may be. It is nonetheless valuable to the patient as he rehabilitates. Later, contact at home will offer new material for the formation of body ideal. It is then, at a pace the patient dictates, that many of the previous standards are once again relearned and revalued.

As with other patients, there must be an accomodation of body ideal with body reality. While recovery may continue for many months post-CVA, it is clear that not all physical function will be recaptured in every case. Speech may remain slurred, the gait uneven and balance uncertain. Accordingly, if the patient is to have success in body presentation and social interchange, body limitations must be recognised by patient and relatives. This may involve everyone learning to applaud achievements which would seem minor to the able bodied. We run a human race that should be judged by the challenge of the track rather than our time to the tape.

Body ideal incorporating the social graces, of movement, articulate speech and elimination control, may no longer be tenable. If the patient sets himself an unrealistic ideal, his frustrations may result in angry outbursts and self-destructive behaviour. Nurses are familiar with these emotions when the patient is thwarted, and must try to convey to relatives why they occur. It may take many months to accommodate body ideal and reality together. Understanding the frustrations of this process is important if the patient's family is to be helped to continue supporting the patient.

Aiding body presentation

The body presentation problems faced by the CVA victim can be grouped under the headings of mobility, dressing and hygiene, communication and control over possessions. There is a widely held public stereotype of the CVA patient's gait and speech. Difficulties in these respects can lead the public to the incorrect assumption that intellect is impaired. This is the beginning of a stigma that patient and family would prefer to avoid.

Improving hemiplegic gait starts from establishing good posture in bed. The patient is sat up with his affected arm resting on pillows. The patient is not allowed to lean towards the affected side as this affects balance when the patient comes to walk (Watson and Corlett, 1987). Mobilisation is planned to take place on a non-slip surface (Williams and Lissner, 1969). The nurse has already been re-acquainting the patient with his affected limbs. Acceptance of these limbs will be necessary for the first efforts now.

Before walking, the patient is acclimatised to sitting balanced on the bed or chair (Rantz and Courtial, 1978). Pace of mobilisation may be modified by any existing hypertension. Care is taken to 'rock' the patient forward onto his feet, once the floor beneath him is clear and the nurse's own stance balanced. It is important to allow the patient to stand supported until the feeling of giddiness has passed. Further transfer training under the guidance of the physiotherapist can then follow.

Once upright, patients are first encouraged to find the most stable posture possible. Myco recommends 'bed ending' to achieve this (Myco, 1983). Seated at the end of the bed the patient pulls himself to his feet, using the foot of the bed bar or board. A non-slip floor and appropriate footwear is important. Once on his feet, a stable position is then established by pushing or pulling against the bed end with the unaffected arm, until a more even keel is arrived at. If the patient keeps his head in the midline of his body, this should serve to reduce the tendency to tilt to the affected side.

Once balanced standing has been perfected, walking exercises may be attempted. The physiotherapist must advise on this as it is critical that the affected leg has been sufficiently strengthened to take a share of the patient's weight in motion. Ideally, the nurse guides the patient from behind, checking that the head is held up and the pelvis is kept as level as possible. The postural alignment is most important while the patient is shifting his weight forward. If a support is used it should be a rubber ended walking stick, held well forward in the midline for reassurance. It should be sufficiently long to avoid the patient stooping unnecessarily as this would bring the patient's centre of gravity to a point forward of the pelvis. The value of a standard pattern walking frame is doubtful because the pattern of mobility set up is unnatural and the control of such a frame with one active hand is precarious at best. In due course, the walking stick should also be abandoned as this also places restrictions on the use of the 'good' hand. The importance of mobility for body image cannot be over-estimated, since a number of the symbols of handicap are found in this area. The wheelchair and the walking frame have always figured high on the list. Even a poor gait permits some independent action and with it the chance for the patient to argue that further improvement may be on the way.

Dressing and hygiene are also important symbols of independence. It was a milestone in childhood when the patient took control of these and they remain important for body presentation after a CVA. This is parti-cularly so if the patient is dealing with incontinence aids. Adaptations to washing items and clothes facilitate self-care, reduce fatigue and enable the patient to prepare for more optimistic social engagements. Catches and attachments on clothes can be replaced by 'velcro' fastening which is available in a range of colours and is inexpensive enough to be replaced as it wears out. Brassieres with front fastenings should be chosen and the patient encouraged to choose clothes that require a minimum of disruption at toilet, for example avoid dungarees, or trousers and bracers which necessitate the removal of a jumper. Zips may be used, especially if a discreet toggle is attached to the zipper. Buttons should usually be avoided or replaced. The occupational therapist should be asked to instruct the patient, family and attending nurse on suggested dressing and undressing strategies. These include the use of a methodical step technique and some prior planning with reference to the patient's position and having clothes to hand. The institutional taint is removed from the patient when dressed in his own, suitably adapted clothes. It promises the return of something approaching a previous normality and gives the patient a reminder of his individuality, other patients probably having chosen very different garments and colours. The clothes are vital possessions, extensions of body image which can quite readily be adjusted or replaced. The opportunity of wearing bright clothes to reflect mood or personality tends to give back some control to the patient. It is also likely to encourage a more positive outlook on the part of visitors when they arrive. Colour co-ordination may prove a valuable aid until co-ordination of gait can once more be perfected. Where patient funds are limited, which is a common problem facing the elderly, relatives provide a great service by supplying the patient with attractive, well chosen items. These may be seen as rewards for rehabili-tation efforts.

Similar imagination needs to be shown with items for washing. A long loofah or sponge on a handle may usefully replace a flannel which can be difficult to manipulate. Small bath towels are easier to control than big ones. Non-slip mats and floors, additional hand holds or a call buzzer arrangement are useful too. Incontinence pants are chosen primarily for their ability to soak up urine, without excoriation to the skin. They can be relatively bulky, so the patient should be advised to choose fuller skirts or a looser fit of trousers to accommodate the extra padding. Combs on a longer, built up, handle and a small mobile mirror that can be stood on a surface, are better for the patient who might lose his balance while trying to groom using a conventional comb and wall mirror. A bend, or curve in the comb handle assists the patient to comb the hair properly.

Speech difficulties require the intervention of a trained speech therapist (Leche, 1974). The problems are varied and require expert diagnosis (see Table 13.5). Nevertheless, nursing staff should seek to reinforce the speech therapy lessons because communication facilitates learning about how the patient feels, including about his body image, and because communication is also an expression of the patient's self. Mannerisms of speech may have been lost, the accent distorted. However, characteristic ways of putting points, such as 'around the houses' or abruptly, may be a presentiment of the patient's neurological condition or his 'old self'. Relatives may recognise communication style as being characteristic and this helps them to encourage the patient further. If the order of ideas is distorted then such recognition may take longer.

Liaison in speech training is vital. If different health workers intervene to different purpose, the patient becomes frustrated and demotivated. He

Table 13.5 Speech problems post-stroke

Simple classification of speech problems:

Aphasia: either receptive or expressive
Dysarthria: difficulty in muscular production of speech
Dyspraxia: lost control over *purposeful* movements of speech musculature in the absence of a
    true paralysis

Initial assessment	*Interim assessment*
● Medical history	● Use of standardised screening tests
● Auditory/visual acuity	● For example, Boston test for aphasia
● Intellect/interests (motivation factors)	● Patient energy/concentration (during testing)
● Residual speech	● Any intellectual impairment?
● Degree of muscular weakness	● Highlight special problems, such as reading or writing
● Dysphagia?	● Memory
● Level of confusion?	● Jargon or repetitive utterances (seemingly meaningless phrases)
● Dentures?	● Respiratory control (essential for clear speech)

cannot develop the speech necessary for explaining his body image worries and gaining the help and empathy of the district nurse or relatives. Other helpers will start to anticipate the patient's wishes, and self-concept will be irreparably damaged. The need for basic speech training appreciation in nurse education remains largely unmet. In the interim nurses must seek out close guidance from the limited number of speech therapists, so that they might develop a channel through which to help the patient deal with body image and other problems.

Conclusion

From what has been stated it would seem that the stroke victim must be helped to build a new body image almost from scratch. It is often difficult to judge because of confusion and amnesia just what sort of body image does exist in the post-CVA days. The means of communication, both receptive and expressive, may have been damaged, so the nurse's first body image assessment might involve some presumptions and must rely heavily upon the history provided by any relatives to hand. When the patient becomes upset and emotional, it is hard to decipher to what extent such grief is body image related (Roaf and Hodkinson, 1977).

This chapter has suggested that a foundation for a new body image must be built upon a body reality that has been protected from further damage. It must be based upon efforts to regain continence, a degree of mobility and independence in grooming and dressing. There should be no delay in starting on these measures, so speech therapy (including early simple communication techniques) must be commenced alongside them, before a complete body image assessment can be made. There will have to be a note of realism in the efforts to establish body ideal, and the nurse must be prepared to encourage the relatives in this too. An elderly spouse may not regain their old partner, but one who has a new and still developing body ideal.

Restoration of body image will involve a team effort, the team comprising the patient, the nurse, the relatives and occupational, speech and physiotherapists. Because CVA victims may continue to improve their body image over a number of years and hospital stays tend to be limited, support must continue in the community. Family carers require support too. Community nurses and general practitioners should champion the benefits of day hospitals, clubs and peripatetic physio- and speech therapists. Contacts with peers, new and old friends, are opportunities for the patient to share his experiences and account for current problems or goals. Elderly colleagues may prove more intuitive and supportive than younger acquaintances. Over several years the grieving for lost function may be worked through, in an environment where nurses must learn from the patient as well as provide their own care contribution.

Review questions

1 List the factors that may make it difficult for the stroke victim to gain a clear idea of his body contours and boundaries.
2 This chapter argues that the complications of immobility must be avoided as part of the process of restoring the patient's damaged body image. Why is this important?
3 Why do you think that an elderly next of kin (seeking to help restore their loved one's body image) might require careful counselling and guidance by the nurse?
4 To what extent does rehabilitating in a strange hospital affect the patient's body image?
5 How does early passive physiotherapy contribute to a successful body presentation later on?
6 Why is it important to place the patient's locker and personal photographs on the affected side of his body?
7 Why might the patient find it difficult to incorporate clothing and possessions as part of a developing new body image?
8 If a relative offers to buy the patient some new clothes to cheer them up, what would you recommend?
9 What are the practical and body image disadvantages of the patient using a walking frame?
10 Why is receptive and expressive aphasia such a barrier to the nurse's assessment of the patient's body image needs?

Suggested exercises

Individual

1. Imagine that you have suffered a CVA and only have the full use of one of your hands. During your daily activities explore how easy it is to complete the following tasks one handed:
    (a) dressing and undressing
    (b) making a telephone call (number unknown)
    (c) writing a short note to a colleague
    Share with a friend how this made you feel about yourself. How did your body feel or look to you after these challenges?
2. Look through nursing textbooks and journals trying to find colour pictures of patients with a stroke or other handicap. Note what the

patients are wearing and what effect the style or colour of clothes might have upon their visitors. Share the pictures with other nurses. Find out to what extent they thought dress affected people's perception of the patient.

Group

3. In pairs visit a number of high street stores looking for suitable clothes that you would recommend be purchased for an imaginary 65 year old female CVA victim. Assume that she has a left hemiplegia and that you must work to a limited budget of money, previously agreed by all participants.

For each item of clothing recommended, note down the following:
(a) its advantages with reference design and function such as warmth, ease of putting on or taking off
(b) its durability or value for money
(c) its anticipated body image benefits.

Also note down its cost, the name of the store and whether purchase would be problematic for an elderly person, for instance awkward access, or cramped changing room facilities.

Return to the group to discuss your findings. The winning syndicate is the one that offers the most innovative and functional suggestions using the above criteria.

Suggested time scales are as follows:
(a) for field work, 2 to 3 hours
(b) for discussion and feedback, 20 minutes per syndicate.

Glossary of terms

Ageusia   impairment of taste.
Agnosia   failure to recognise previously familiar objects, such as a comb.
Agraphia   inability to communicate effectively through the written word.
Anomia   inability to put a name to familiar possessions or family names.
Anosognosia   patient neglects, denies or fails to recognise paralysed limbs.
Aphasia   inability to communicate using speech, either due to comprehension difficulties or expressive difficulties. Examples are:
   global: loss of all communication function
   Wernicke's or receptive: inability to comprehend written or spoken word
   Broca's or expressive: loss of powers of verbal expression
   syntactical: lost ability to put words in appropriate sequence
Apraxia   lost ability to perform co-ordinated purposeful movements, such as shaving.
Astereognosis   loss of ability to recognise, through touch, objects, when eyes are closed.

Asymbolia   lost ability to recognise and use symbols appropriately, for example gestures of pleasure or unhappiness
Ataxia   lost co-ordination during walking or other movement.
Diplopia   double vision.
Dysarthria   inability to control the mechanical/muscular production of speech, for example resulting in slurred difficult to understand speech.
Dysphagia   difficulty in swallowing.
Hemianaesthesia   disturbed sensation down one side of the body.
Hemianopia   defective vision of half the visual field in each eye (homonymous hemianopia).
Hemiparesis   weakness down one side of the body.
Hemiplegia   paralysis down one side of the body.
Paresis   a slight or incomplete paralysis.
Prosopagnosia   inability to recognise differences in facial features.
Somatognosia   inability to recognise body contours and boundaries. Where limbs are relative to one another.

References

Adams G. and Hurwitz L., 'Mental Barriers to Recovery from Strokes', *Lancet*, i, pp 533–7, 1963.
Bobath B., *Adult Hemiplegia – Evaluation and treatment*, William Heinemann Medical, 1970.
Bolwell J., 'Dignity at All Times', *Nursing Mirror*, 154(14), pp 51–4, 1982.
Kelly M.M., 'Exercises for the Bedfast Patient', *American Journal of Nursing*, 66, pp 2209–13, 1966.
Kratz C., *Care of the Long Term Sick in the Community*, Churchill Livingstone, Edinburgh, 1978.
Leche P.M., 'The Speech Therapist and Hemiplegia', *Physiotherapy*, 60(11), pp 346–9, 1974.
McNeil F., 'Stroke – Nursing insights from a stroke nurse victim', *Registered Nurse*, 387(Sept), pp 75–81, 1975.
Medawar P., Foreword to *Stroke, The Facts*, Rose F.C. and Capildeo R., Oxford University Press, Oxford, 1981.
Myco F., '*Nursing Care of the Hemiplegic Stroke Patient*', Harper & Row, London, 1983.
Nichols P.J., *Rehabilitation Medicine – The management of physical disabilities*, Butterworths, London, 1976.
Nordmark M.T. and Rohweder A.W., *Scientific Foundations of Nursing*, 3rd edn, Lippincott, Philadelphia, 1975.
Norris C.M., 'Body Image – It's relevance to professional nursing' in Carlson C.E. and Blackwell J.B. (eds) *Behavioural Concepts and Nursing Interventions*, 2nd edn, Lippincott, Philadelphia, 1978.
Piotrowski M., 'Body Image After a Stroke', *Rehabilitation Nursing*, Jan/Feb, pp 11–13, 1982
Politicoff L.D., 'The Philosophy of Stroke Rehabilitation', *Geriatrics*, 25,

pp 99–107, 1970

Rantz M.J. and Courtial D., *Lifting, Moving and Transferring Patients*, C.V. Mosby, St Louis, 1978.

Roaf R. and Hodkinson L.J., *The Paralysed Patient*, Blackwell Scientific Publications, 1977.

Stern P., McDowell F., Miller J. and Robinson M., 'Efficacy of Facilitation Exercise Techniques in Stroke Rehabilitation', *Archives of Physical Medicine and Rehabilitation*, 51, pp 526–31, 1970.

Stryker R.P., *Rehabilitative Aspects of Chronic Nursing Care*, WB Saunders, Philadelphia, 1972.

Wade D.T., 'Stroke' in Goodwill C.J. and Chamberlain M.A. (eds), *Rehabilitation of the Physically Disabled Adult*, pp 323–41, Croom Helm, London, 1988.

Watson P., 'Perceptual Problems' in Kamal A. (ed.) *A Colour Atlas of Stroke – Cerebro-vascular disease and its management*, Wolfe Medical, London, 1987.

Watson P. and Corlett J., 'Rehabilitation' in Kamal A. (ed.) *A Colour Atlas of Stroke – Cerebro-vascular disease and its management*, pp 147–77, Wolfe Medical, London, 1987.

WHO, 'Stroke – Treatment, rehabilitation and prevention', *WHO Chronicle*, 25 Oct, pp 466–9, 1971.

Williams M. and Lissner H., *Biomechanics of Human Motion*, WB Saunders, Philadelphia, 1969.

Further reading

Dardier W., *The Early Stroke Patient: Positioning and movement*, Bailliere Tindall, London, 1980.

Frazer F.W. (ed.) *Rehabilitation Within the Community*, Faber & Faber, London, 1982.

Hawker M., *Return To Mobility: Exercises for the stroke patient*, Chest, Heart and Stroke Association, London, 1978.

Law D. and Paterson B., *Living after a Stroke*, Souvenir Press, London, 1981.

Lubbock G. (ed.) *Stroke Care – An interdisciplinary approach*, Faber & Faber, London, 1983.

Mulley G., *Stroke – A handbook for the patient's family*, Chest, Heart and Stroke Association, London, 1978.

Mulley G.P., *Practical Management of Stroke*, Croom Helm, Beckenham, 1984.

14 The patient receiving radiotherapy or chemotherapy

Study of this chapter will enable you to:

1 Describe the major body image problems arising from radiotherapy or chemotherapy.
2 Discuss the research relating to measures designed to:
   (a) limit alopecia
   (b) limit oral hygiene problems
   (c) limit the incidence of nausea and vomiting
   (d) protect the skin during radiotherapy
3 Argue why body image support measures are important for the patient receiving longer term therapy.
4 Make a distinction between 'radical' and 'conservative' measures designed to reduce the effects of alopecia upon body image.
5 Suggest why the mouth is so important for the patient's body image.
6 Define simply the following, terms:
   (a) radiotherapy (external and internal sources)
   (b) chemotherapy (cytotoxic)
   (c) alopecia/stomatitis/xerostomia/trismus

For many patients, discovering that they have cancer may not immediately pose a body image problem. Cancer may throw up so many fears of pain and death that the individual has little time left to consider the body image implications. Nevertheless, cancer does pose immense altered body image challenges to the patient and the family. At some point during the illness they will become concerned with one or other aspect of body presentation. If the tumour itself does not occasion body image change, then therapy, surgery, chemotherapy or radiotherapy most certainly will. This chapter will concentrate upon the last two treatments, and highlight the nursing interventions that might limit the resulting body image problems.

It is important to realise that the patient's body image may already be damaged by the time treatment commences. A tumour may cause the patient weight loss (the classic cachexic appearance), lost neuro or endocrine control, or malfunction of one or more organs, for example the liver, kidneys or brain. The diagnosis of cancer may have been a blow to self-image (Welch, 1981) and to the family members (Dow, 1965), who may have limited faith in cancer therapy. Because the course of cancer illness and the efficacy of therapy is seen by many to be largely unpredictable, nursing interventions will have to address the family as a whole (Maxwell, 1982; Welch-McCaffrey, 1985). Most patients face an extended, if intermittent contact with the hospital. Both during such contacts and in between times, family support (see Chapter 7) can be vital to patient motivation.

The use of radiotherapy and cytotoxic drugs in the treatment of cancer has grown rapidly this century (Trester, 1982). Many tumours that were untreatable using surgery have proven susceptible to internal or external radiotherapy or combination cytotoxic therapy (Hassey, 1985; Hassey *et al*, 1983). While there have been some spectacular successes, for instance in testicular cancer or childhood leukaemia, there have been costs. Many of the treatments prove extremely toxic, resulting in side effects that both limit further therapy and undermine the maintenance of an acceptable body image (Dodd, 1987).

Radiotherapy

Radiation treatment or radiotherapy relies upon the disruptive effects upon tumour cell growth and replication caused by radioactive sources. These sources may be housed in a purpose built external treatment machine, or they may be implanted into or close to tumorous tissue as radioactive implants in pellets or needles. External radiotherapy involves patients visiting specialist and often frightening departments where they may have to wait for treatment time on one or other of the different machines (Eardley, 1986a; Holland *et al*, 1979). Internal radiotherapy involves a discrete surgical access operation and following this, the afterloading of radioactive implants when the patient has returned to his own room. Using a localised source of radiation, it is anticipated that long term side effects are minimised (Horiuchi *et al*, 1982; Unal *et al*, 1981). The more common, body image significant side effects of radiotherapy and chemotherapy are laid out in Table 14.1. The choice of which therapy will be offered depends upon the tumour, its size, location, spread and the patient's health. While it is a simplification, it would be fair to say that internal radiotherapy is usually employed for the more discrete and accessible tumours. Both therapies may be employed as potentially curative treatment, or as the means to palliate unpleasant symptoms or problems.

Table 14.1 Side effects of radiotherapy and chemotherapy

Side effect	Radiotherapy	Chemotherapy
Alopecia	Head and neck treatments	Yes
Nausea/vomiting	Yes	Yes
Anorexia	Yes	Yes
Altered bowel habits (such as constipation/diarrhoea)	Yes	Yes
Dysgusia	Yes	Yes
Stomatitis	Head and neck treatments	Yes
Skin reactions	Yes	Sometimes
Anaemia	Yes	Yes
Leucopenia	Yes	Yes (often profound)
Impaired fertility	Yes	Yes
Malaise/tiredness	Yes	Yes (especially secondary to malnutrition/vomiting)

Note: The extent of all side effects may be affected by the specific location of treatment, length of course and dosage.

Chemotherapy

Cytotoxic chemotherapy involves introducing into the patient's body, for example by means of a Hickman's line, one, or more often several, agents which interfere with cell growth and replication. There is now a substantial catalogue of cytotoxic drugs and combination therapy regimes. Unfortunately, such agents are not yet able to be completely specific about the cells that will be affected. Many healthy, rapidly dividing body cells, such as hair follicle or gastro-intestinal tract, will be affected. It is this non-specific cell toxicity that causes the majority of the body image complications of cytotoxic therapy. Efforts to limit the trauma to healthy cells through combination therapy or spreading the dosage pattern, has also enabled patients to sustain active life and in many cases to raise a realistic hope of cure. The overriding need to beat the tumour has, however, often meant that body image and comfort worries have been seen as of secondary concern. More modern research now addresses these comfort matters which is an important development as it is conceiveable that patients will continue to receive such therapy over a protracted time span (Raven, 1986).

Alopecia

It is not only Samson and women in shampoo advertisements who are deeply interested in retaining a good head of hair. The research indicates that head and body hair is important to a wide range of patients and especially those at risk of loosing part or all of it due to cancer therapy. Wilbur emphasizes the point vividly when he says, 'try to remember, when you were a teenager; hair loss was something you'd almost rather die than endure' (Wilbur, 1980).

The degree of hair loss depends upon the nature, dose and route of the treatment and the patient's health beforehand. Crounse and Van Scott noted that at any given time 90 per cent of human hair follicles are in the dividing phase and therefore susceptible to the effects of local radiotherapy or systemic cytotoxics (Crounse and Van Scott, 1960). Amongst the cyto-toxic drugs, doxorubicin (Blum and Carter, 1974; David and Speechley, 1987), and cyclophosphamide (Colvin, 1981), are both seen as likely to cause in excess of 75 per cent loss of hair. Other drugs causing alopecia to varying degrees are vincristine, actinomycin D, bleomycin, methotrexate and 5-fluorouracil (Cline, 1984). Radiotherapy to the head or neck may also produce a degree of alopecia. Uneven partial loss of hair may be more upsetting than a total loss of hair. Where hair loss is not complete, sur-viving hair may prove both brittle and fine.

The effects of hair loss upon body image appear to vary, both by patient's previous body image, age and social support, and the manner in which the hair loss occurred, for instance if forewarned by the nurse. Holmes revealed that cancer victims found alopecia very traumatic (Holmes W., 1979). Wagner and Bye reported that it usually caused anxiety in patients and that they frequently started to re-evaluate body image and self-image in terms of spiritual values rather than physical appearance (Wagner and Bye, 1979). Baxley *et al* found, rather surprisingly, that men with cancer had just as much difficulty adjusting to alopecia as women. Societal acceptance of naturally occurring bald men did not seem to help (Baxley *et al*, 1984).

Nursing interventions to limit the effects of treatment on the hair, and alopecia upon body image, may be divided into the radical and the con-servative. Radical measures address means of limiting the drug's effect upon the hair follicle (body reality) while the conservative approach em-phasises patient education (body ideal) or the use of camouflage, such as wigs or head scarves (body presentation). Two methods of protecting the scalp hair follicles are reported and in each case they are considered inappropriate in the case of leukaemia or other haematopoeic cancers as the measures might shield tumour cells in the scalp.

Scalp cooling consists of lowering temperature around the head to the point where vasoconstriction occurs and the metabolic demands of the hair follicle falls. If these conditions can be sustained before and during the active life span of a cytotoxic drug in the body (its plasma half-life), then alopecia may be limited. For success the cooling should be rapid, the drug half-life short (say, about one to two hours) and the cooling equipment such as gel packs efficient at maintaining cool temperatures (Dean et al, 1979). Most of the research has been directed at doxorubicin, and has usually admitted to limitations, such as controlling for the patient's liver function. Poor liver function means inefficient clearance of the drug from the blood and prolonged exposure of the scalp to cytotoxics after removal of the cooling device. In David and Speechley's study (op cit) only 12 per cent of patients with normal liver function suffered moderate or complete hair loss after using scalp cooling gel packs – the expected rate with doxorubicin was 95 per cent hair loss. When patients received doxorubicin and cyclophosphamide, 58 per cent lost moderate or complete amounts of hair. Providing cytotoxic drug dosages remained moderate, namely less than 50 mg doxorubicin, and the half-life of the combination drugs was short, considerable conservation of hair was possible. Other studies concerning doxorubicin have also been encouraging, although techniques and protocols of research have varied (Anderson et al, 1981; Cline, 1984). Subject to medical advice and type of tumour, it seems clear that the nurse might advocate the patient exploring such protective measures. This may be especially important for patients who have already suffered considerable alteration to body image through surgery or other treatments.

The second radical approach involves scalp tourniquets (Henessey, 1966; Holmes W., 1979; Lovejoy, 1979). As with scalp cooling, results are not totally conclusive, due to the range of research protocols followed. There was a reduction in hair loss for many patients, and amongst those patients who did lose significant amounts of hair, there was a useful delay until baldness resulted. At this juncture it seems unclear to what pressure the tourniquet must be inflated in order to achieve acceptable results. It may also be the case that only patients with comparatively healthy hair condition pre-treatment will obtain good results from this measure. The nurse might therefore bear this method in mind, but must be realistic about the variable results that may occur if the patient agrees the technique with the physician. One significant advantage is that if hair loss is delayed, the patient may more gradually accommodate his altered body reality and carefully choose a wig which suits his age, complexion and previous hair colour.

Conservative measures are probably still employed with the majority of patients. Scalp cooling and use of tourniquets are not always successful, nor always advisable. It is therefore important that the patient is given an honest appraisal of expected hair loss, including amount, rate, onset and duration. In the majority of instances hair regeneration occurs one to two months after discontinuation of chemotherapy (Cline and Haskell, 1975). As an interim measure body presentation might best be enhanced through choosing a degree of baldness. Many patients prefer to shave off oddments of surviving hair and present a totally bald crown – total baldness does have its folk heroes in television characters and sports stars.

Many patients find the use of brightly coloured head scarves (worn Romany style) or a colourful bobble hat an equally acceptable alternative. Some teenage patients have made a practice of collecting different coloured bobble hats, a different one for each day of the week! Other young adult patients have adjusted their dress to match their head gear, one patient even light heartedly setting herself up as the ward gypsy Lee.

The acceptability of wigs to patients seems to depend upon the anticipated period of hair loss, the fashionability or otherwise of wigs and the expertise of the wig fitter who serves the ward. It must be said that a badly fitted or matched wig is a body presentation disaster. The patient's eyebrow colour (if present) and complexion, as well as previous hair colour, whether dyed or natural, should be born in mind. It is worth discussing with the patient whether the wig will be openly seen as dress or as a pretense of normal hair condition. If the former is the case the patient may feel cheered by choosing a rather more flambouyant, fun style or colour. If the latter applies then careful colour matching is very important.

Oral problems

The mouth has an important effect upon body image. It is intimately involved with romantic and sexual expression, speech, social activity such as eating, and our earliest memories of pleasurable body experiences. Problems in the mouth are magnified in the mind (recall your last dental extraction), so that dentures, halitosis and stained or unattractive oral cavities become a source of embarassment. If the patient does not maintain a comfortable oral cavity, he may become anorexic and dehydrated. Infections, such as candida, may set in, progressing to septicaemia and even death (Eardley, 1986b). Radiotherapy to the mouth, head and neck can result in xerostomia (diminished production of saliva), mucositis (increased 'stickiness' of saliva), and stomatitis (soreness or inflammation of the mouth). These problems in turn may lead to mouth ulceration, altered taste sensation, trismus (inability to open mouth fully) and malnutrition (Bersani and Carl, 1983; Holmes S., 1986). Similarly, stomatitis, infection and ulceration may be expected with a variety of cytotoxic drug regimes (Daeffler, 1980a).

The patient experiencing oral discomfort is inhibited from conversing and even from smiling (body presentation). Because problems may have started in the first days after treatment commenced, been complicated by a dehydrated state and continued on for months post-radiotherapy, the mouth will take on increasing significance as body image recovers. The hair may have regrown, weight regained, but the mouth may still remind the patient of cancer, particularly if there has been loss of teeth or tissue.

Oral hygiene measures used by the nurse, therefore, should facilitate eating and drinking, talking, limit or exclude infection and encourage the patient to smile once more. Allbright recommends an oral hygiene programme based upon regular assessment of the patient's mouth, the nature of current therapy, for instance is the patient immunosuppressed, and the existence or otherwise of infection (Allbright, 1984). Oral care should be provided two hourly in the case of stomatitis. Dentures should be removed for the procedure and thrombin mouthwashes provided if the gums are bleeding. Pain should be controlled with a viscous xylocaine mouth wash or by systemic analgesia. Lips are protected from cracking with a thin application of vaseline. Artificial saliva is recommended in the case of xerostomia, but it is widely agreed that patients must also be rehydrated with fluids if the mouth condition is to improve (Daeffler, 1980b). Nystatin anti-fungal oral suspension is indicated if the patient suffers from candidiasis.

The choice of oral cleaning technique and mouth wash solution is rather less clear. A soft toothbrush may be useful for removing debris but is contraindicated if the patient suffers from thrombocytopenia or severe neutropenia (Trowbridge and Carl, 1975). An alternative might be toothetes or the use of a mouth wash by itself, short term. The mouth wash solution employed must suit oral circumstances. If stomatitis is *not* present, a dilute solution of hydrogen peroxide, one part H_2O_2 to four parts isotonic saline, may be used to loosen crusting or debris (Bruya and Madeira, 1975). It should not be employed on newly granulating oral tissues. Where the gums are inflamed, for example with leukaemic gingivitis, warm normal saline mouth washes are recommended (Segelman and Doku, 1977). Dilute sodium bicarbonate, one teaspoonful to one pint of warm water, is also widely accepted as an agent to loosen oral crusts (Maurer, 1977). Lemon–glycerine mouth washes are to be avoided. Their salivary stimulant effect is inadequate in the dehydrated cancer patient and there may be resultant drying and pH shift of the mucosa. Increased acid may damage the teeth and cause the patient discomfort.

In the light of this research it is important that each patient has a thorough oral hygiene assessment. If the patient can be encouraged to consume 2 to 3 litres of fluid daily, or receive a similar supplement intravenously, he may be assisted to maintain oral hygiene independently. If the nurse must intervene, then each hygiene session must be preceded by oral inspection and the careful selection of materials and techniques. For body image as well as comfort purposes, oral hygiene prior to meals and visiting times is especially recommended. Patients who reward visitors with conversation and a smile are likely to gain further family support. This should be borne in mind given that later therapy can be on an outpatient basis.

Nausea and vomiting

As with many other major illnesses, cancer threatens the patient's ability to control body function. Loss of control is stigmatising, making it difficult for the patient to retain dignity and a positive self-image. Patients receiving a wide range of cytotoxics and those undergoing radiotherapy to the gastro-intestinal tract may all experience nausea and vomiting. Because gastro-intestinal mucosal cells rapidly divide, they are very susceptible to the effects of drugs such as cisplatin and cyclophosphamide. Anticipatory nausea and vomiting may commence even before treatment is started (Redd and Hendler, 1983) and continue for several weeks after chemotherapy is completed (Whitehead, 1975). While the patient battles against nausea and the debilitating effects of repeated vomiting, he has little opportunity to develop body presentation ploys to improve his own and relatives' morale. He may see the lost control as degrading, and may resolutely refuse to be comforted by the explanations that point out the drug's effect upon the vomit reflex centre of the brain. To be told that vomiting is an 'acceptable toxicity' is not good enough (Scogna and Smalley, 1979). The nurse, patient and doctor must explore avenues to limit the side effect and to provide an opportunity for the patient to feel in control once more.

Anticipatory vomiting can be seen as a learned response, conditioned by previous experiences of treatment. If the first course of treatment is accompanied by prophylactic anti-emetic drugs (Warren, 1988a), then it is perhaps less likely to develop (Cockel, 1971; Donovan and Pierce, 1976). In Berry-Opersteny and Heusinkveld's study prophylactic anti-emetics reduced the incidence of vomiting, but did not reduce the patient's sense of nausea (Berry-Opersteny and Heusinkveld, 1983). Accordingly, it has been suggested that more holistic, nursing interventions should accompany these pharmaceutical measures (Contanch, 1983; Warren, 1988b). Contanch encouraged patients to use a relaxation programme that emphasised progressive tightening and then relaxation of muscles. Most patients in the study noted an improvement in the ability to control vomiting and, to a limited extent, nausea. All patients had an improved calorie intake during the 48 hours following chemotherapy. Other useful strategies would seem to include distraction therapy, guided imagery (Yasko, 1985) and self-hypnosis (Contanch et al, 1985). Such additional options might be seen as complementary to anti-emetic drugs and give that 'control' back to the patient which furnishes a little dignity as well.

When preventive measures have failed, body image concerns are still important. Discreet provision of a vomit bowl, tissues, an air freshener and clean sheets or clothing are all important if the patient is to feel comfortable. Relatives should be warned that vomiting is possible but that it is limited in most instances to the immediate treatment period. If a key relative can be encouraged to stay with the patient at this time, to comfort and help with tissues, an important bond may be supported. It is encouraging to be loved despite the vicissitudes of the body and the nurse must affirm this to the relative by her own presence wherever possible.

Skin changes

In the first chapter of this book it has already been established that the skin is of critical importance to body image. Patients undergoing cancer therapy experience a variety of skin problems either attributable to the preparation for therapy, the therapy itself or complications thereafter. Most skin problems have been traditionally associated with external radiotherapy (Walker, 1982), but the nurse should not forget that some cytotoxics also cause problems such as acne and dermatitis.

The degree of skin damage caused by radiotherapy depends upon the fractional radiation dose, the energy of the radiation source and the area of the skin treated – axilla, groin and other skin folds may cause more problems. The more severe reactions of previous years have now been limited by more sophisticated fractional dosage of tumours. Table 14.2 does, however, lay out the major possibilities, and nurses should not become complacent about the risks to patient's skin.

Before treatment has started, the patient may already have been 'marked up' for the radiotherapy. This involves marking upon the skin one or more target fields, areas where the therapy will be directed. Some markings will be very visible even when clothed. 'Martin Brown' was a young man being treated for Hodgkin's lymphoma. His neck was marked with a blue square, and this was partially visible even when wearing a collar. Such markings can be a badge for radiotherapy patients – a stigmata as damning as any slave's in a Roman market.

Unfortunately, there is little that can be done to disguise such markings. Tight clothing over the surface of the treatment area causes discomfort and the marks cannot be washed away if accurate treatment is to be continued. Most body image skin measures therefore are directed toward limiting damage, avoiding reactions worse than mild erythema. These measures may be important at both the entrance and exit sites of the ionising beam.

Firstly, it is important to avoid friction to the irradiated area. Rubbing the skin, wearing constrictive clothing or scrubbing the area with a flannel are all to be avoided. An eroded skin enhances the effects of radiation.

Table 14.2 Skin reactions associated with radiotherapy

Reaction	*Notes*
Erythema (redness of the skin). May later become oedematous and tender	Onset often within days of start of treatment. Mild erythema may last only a few days, but extent affected by the size and number of fractional doses
Dry desquamation (scaling of the skin)	Onset typically occurs after seven to ten days of treatment – sometimes following initial erythema
Moist desquamation (denudation of the skin – oozing of serum may be a rare presentation)	If this occurs considerable skin damage has resulted. Onset is usually after fourth week of treatment
Hyperpigmentation (due to increased synthesis of melanin)	Likely to occur (if at all) circa four weeks following resolution of initial erythema
Necrosis – tissue beakdown (very rare)	About two to three months past start of therapy. Pathogens may be found in wound. More common if patient malnourished

Secondly, cosmetics, talcum powder, soaps or creams should not be used on the affected area. These may contain metallic elements which would scatter the ionising beam. The dose of radiation to the tumour would fall and the damage to proximal skin increase as a result.

Patients undergoing radiotherapy will be more sensitive to sunlight. Exposure to the sun's direct rays should be limited and loose cotton clothing worn to control body temperature. Should the skin become dry and flaky, the doctor may prescribe an hydrocortisone cream as a notable exception to the general rule. Moist desquamation is usually best treated by cleansing the area with normal saline 0.9 per cent and then leaving the area exposed to the air. The condition of the skin should be reported to the radiotherapist.

If the patient is taught these precautions, the skin changes associated with radiotherapy may well not exceed erythema. Patients are familiar with the appearance of mild sun burn, so they might avoid significant body image problems. Closer attention will have to be paid to skin fold areas, such as the axilla, for if dryness or soreness occurs there medical advice may be necessary in order to limit the spread of infection or further breakdown of skin.

Fertility

Fertility, sexuality and body image are all bound together. Part of the adult's and the teenager's body ideal is founded upon notions of fertility –

the ability to become a mother or father. Both these roles are characterised by maturity, responsibility and control over life events. Many cancer therapies will limit or terminate the ability to reproduce. This is especially true if that treatment is aimed at reproductive organs or other structures within the pelvic region. Wilbur reported that treatment may not only affect primary gonadal organs, but may affect secondary sexual development as well (Wilbur, 1980). Treatment of ovarian tumours may inhibit breast development in the female teenage patient. Such traumas are made worse when parents do not know how to respond to such major altered body image and tend to resort to uneasy silence about the matter instead.

Nurses cannot afford to ignore discussion about fertility and sexual characteristics affected by treatment. While fertility cannot always be restored there may still be opportunities to bank sperm or ova before treatment occurs. This is an important option as it may allow a normal parental self-image many years later. Honest discussion about the limited development of breasts or secondary masculine characteristics is usually appreciated by teenagers who have often already talked openly about sexuality with their peers. It is certainly true that the adult population, which they observe closely, do not always develop sexual characteristics to equal degrees. This variety of standards, by which they may come to view their own bodies, may be the first comfort.

Because parents struggle to provide a tactful support to the teenager undergoing this sort of treatment, it is important to assign nurses who can understand the tensions that may occur. A younger, less experienced nurse may be more approachable for the patient. With this nurse they may share their fantasies and fears – the worries and anger at being cheated of a normal sexual development. A companion, more experienced nurse, might then act as counsellor to the parents and mentor to the junior primary nurse. Observation of interpersonal skills and actions is the key here. Choosing a nurse with good social skills and an empathetic disposition is important with regard to both of these nursing roles.

Conclusion

Part of the patient's ability to fight cancer depends on his willingness to cope with the treatment and its side effects. The battle has to be sustained over many months, through multiple treatment sessions, and alongside relatives who themselves may feel ill equipped to offer support. It is arguable that just surviving is often enough. Some will feel that body image has often to be sacrificed if a cure is to be achieved. Patient's must anticipate damage to body image, but its sacrifice is inadvisable. Part of the patient's recovery relies upon a personal dignity, and that in turn may stem from maintaining an acceptable appearance. Patients may be able to face another treatment if they can wear a bright headscarf to replace fallen hair, or smile despite the trauma to the mouth.

Body image can become a part of the patient's arsenal, his determination to win. Looking presentable may at the lowest moments, be a supreme expression of courage and an encouragement to relatives. As the nurse provides care to limit stomatitis, protect the skin and adorn the head, she may be helping the patient to resist the effects of the disease and highlighting the thoughtful measures which make body image care truly holistic.

Review questions

1 The course and progression of cancer is unpredictable, as may be the success of treatment. How do you think the resultant uncertainty may undermine the patient's body image or self-image?
2 Visiting a radiotherapy department the patient is likely to meet other patients showing some side effects of treatment. With this in mind, what body image points might ideally be made to a patient before starting the therapy?
3 Cancer may affect the body image of younger adults in special ways. Looking back over the chapter, can you suggest how?
4 Try to outline the 'conservative' measures used to tackle the alopecia problem and suggest why scalp cooling may not always be chosen.
5 It could be argued that few people normally see inside our mouth and that therefore its condition is not important for body image. How would you counter this argument?
6 Try to list those pre-treatment measures, such as staging investigations or skin marking, that you think might adversely affect the patient's body image.

Suggested exercises

Exercise 1
Conduct an informal survey amongst a dozen of your colleagues. Ask them the following questions (plus any others that you think important):

1. What are the advantages and disadvantages of a wig for a patient anticipating alopecia?
2. Are these affected by any of the following:
   (a) patient's age
   (b) patient's gender
   (c) patient's marital status
   (d) patient's previous experience of wigs as a fashion item

3. What points do you think should be made about the successful fitting of a wig? (for instance the role of the patient's next of kin, skills of nurse and wig fitter, resources available).

Note your findings down and bring these back to an informal group session. Discuss the views of your study population and try to decide whether these points would enable the patient to adopt a wig in your hospital successfully.

Allow 10 to 15 minutes for discussion for each members' survey report and the raising of issues.

Exercise 2
Using a reputable drug compendium, choose one or other cytotoxic drug regime (combination therapy). Note down the major side effects associated with this treatment.

With one or more colleagues briefly outline the body image implications of these side effects (you may like to look back over Chapter 14). Use your thoughts and notes to design an A3 size handout which you think might be used to advise a patient. Ensure that your patient education sheet meets the following criteria:

1. It is attractive to the eye (layout)
2. It is written in clear terminology (consider medical jargon and its effects on the cancer patient)
3. It is acurate according to the drug compendium
4. It would allow the nurse to use it in more than one way

Swap your sheet with another group and consider the different ways in which the information has been prepared. Try to decide what makes for an effective and sensitive patient education sheet? Consider asking the views of local oncology ward nurses or doctors. Suggested time allowance are as follows:

(a) for briefing/use of compendium, allow 30 minutes
(b) for planning the patient education sheet, allow about 60 minutes (home assignment?)
(c) for feedback discussion, allow about 10 to 15 minutes for each group

References

Allbright A., 'Oral Care for the Cancer Chemotherapy Patient', *Nursing Times*, 23 May, pp 20–3, 1984.

Anderson J.E., Hunt J.M. and Smith I.E., 'Prevention of Doxorubicin Induced Alopecia by Scalp Cooling in Patients with Advanced Breast Cancer', *British Medical Journal*, 282, pp 423–4, 1981.

Baxley K.O., Erdman L.K., Henry E.B. and Roof B.J., 'Alopecia: Effect on cancer patient's body image', *Cancer Nursing*, Dec, pp 499–503, 1984.

Berry-Opersteny D. and Heusinkveld K., 'Prophylactic Antiemetics for Chemotherapy Associated Nausea and Vomiting', *Cancer Nursing*, April, pp 117–23, 1983.

Bersani G. and Carl W., 'Oral Care For Cancer Patients', *American Journal of Nursing*, April, pp 533–6, 1983.

Blum R. and Carter S., 'Adriamycin: A new anti-cancer drug with significant clinical activity', *Annals of Internal Medicine*, 80, pp 249–259, 1974.

Bruya M.A. and Madeira N.P., 'Stomatitis after chemotherapy', *American Journal of Nursing*, 75, pp 1349–52, 1975.

Cline B., 'Prevention of Chemotherapy Induced Alopecia: A review of the literature', *Cancer Nursing*, June, pp 221–7, 1984.

Cline M. and Haskell C., *Cancer Chemotherapy*, WB Saunders, Philadelphia, 1975.

Cockel R., 'Antiemetics', *Practitioner*, 206, pp 56–63, 1971.

Colvin M., 'Cyclophosphamide and Analogues' in Crooke S. and Prestayko R. (eds) *Cancer and Chemotherapy*, Vol 3, pp 25–36, Academic Press, New York, 1981.

Contanch P., 'Relaxation Training for Control of Nausea and Vomiting in Patients Receiving Chemotherapy', *Cancer Nursing*, 6, pp 277–82, 1983.

Contanch P., Hockenberry M. and Herman, 'Self Hypnosis as Anti-Emetic Therapy in Children Receiving Chemotherapy', *Oncology Nurses Forum*, 12(4), pp 41–6, 1985.

Crounse R. and, Van Scott E., 'Changes in Scalp Hair Roots as Measure of Toxicity from Cancer Chemotherapy Drugs', *Journal of Investigative Dermatology*, 35, pp 83–90, 1960.

Daeffler R., 'Oral Hygiene Measures for Patients with Cancer I', *Cancer Nursing*, Oct, pp 347–55, 1980a.

Daeffler R., 'Oral Hygiene Measures for Patients with Cancer II', *Cancer Nursing*, Dec, pp 427–32, 1980b.

David J. and Speechley V., 'Scalp Cooling to Prevent Alopecia', *Nursing Times*, 83(32), pp 36–7, 1987.

Dean J.C., Salmon S.E. and Griffith K.S., 'Prevention of Doxorubicin-Induced Hair Loss with Scalp Hypothermia', *New England Journal of Medicine*, 301, pp 1427–9, 1979.

Dodd M., *Managing Side Effects of Chemotherapy and Radiation Therapy – A guide for nurses and patients*, Appleton and Lange, Norwalk, Connecticut, 1987.

Donovan M. and Pierce S., *Cancer Care Nursing*, Appleton Century Crofts, New York, 1976.

Dow T., 'Family Reaction to Crisis', *Journal of Marriage and the Family*, pp 363–6, 1965.

Eardley A., 'Radiotherapy: What do patients need to know?', *Nursing Times*, 16 April, pp 24–6, 1986a.

Eardley A., 'Radiotherapy: After the treatment's over...', *Nursing Times*, 30 April, pp 40–1, 1986b.

Hassey K., Bloom L. and Burgess S., 'Radiation – Alternative to mastectomy', *American Journal of Nursing*, Nov, pp 1567–9, 1983.

Hassey K., 'Demystifying Care of Patients With Radioactive Implants', *American*

Journal of Nursing, July, pp 788–92, 1985.

Henessey J., 'Alopecia and Cytotoxic Drugs', *British Medical Journal*, 2, p 1138, 1966.

Holland J.C., Rowland J., Lebovitz A. and Rusalem R., Reactions to Cancer Treatment – Assessment of emotional response to adjuvent radiotherapy as a guide for planned intervention', *Psychiatric Clinics of North America*, 2, pp 347–58, 1979.

Holmes S., 'Radiotherapy – Planning nutritional support', *Nursing Times*, 16 April, pp 26–9, 1986.

Holmes W., 'Alopecia From Chemotherapy: Can nursing measures help?', in *Clinical and Scientific Sessions*, pp 223–33, American Nurses Association, Kansas City, 1979.

Horiuchi J., Okuyama T., Shibuya H. and Takeda M., 'Results of Brachytherapy for Cancer of the Tongue with Special Emphasis on Local Prognosis', *International Journal of Radiation, Oncology, Biology, Physics*, May (8), pp 829–35, 1982.

Lovejoy N.C., 'Preventing Hair Loss During Adriamycin Therapy', *Cancer Nursing*, 2(2), pp 117–21, 1979.

Maurer J., 'Providing Optimal Oral Health', *Nursing Clinics of North America*, 12, pp 671–85, 1977.

Maxwell M., 'The Use of Social Networks to Help Cancer Patients Maximise Support', *Cancer Nursing*, Aug, pp 275–80, 1982.

Raven R., *Rehabilitation and Continuing Care in Cancer*, Parthenon Publishing, Carnforth, Lancs, 1986.

Redd W. and Hendler C., 'Behavioural Medicine in Comprehensive Cancer Treatment', *Journal of Psychosocial Oncology*, 1(2), pp 3–17, 1983.

Scogna D. and Smalley R., 'Chemotherapy Induced Nausea and Vomiting', *American Journal of Nursing*, 79(9), pp 1562–4, 1979.

Segelman A. and Doku H., 'Treatment of the Oral Complications of Leukaemia', *Journal of Oral Surgery*, 35, pp 469–77, 1977.

Trester A., 'Nursing Management of Patients Receiving Cancer Chemotherapy', *Cancer Nursing*, June, pp 201–10, 1982.

Trowbridge J. and Carl W., 'Oral Care of the Patient Having Head and Neck Irradiation', *American Journal of Nursing*, 75, pp 2146–9, 1975.

Unal A., Hamberger A.D., Seski J.C. and Fletcher G.H., (1981) 'An Analysis of the Severe Complications of Irradiation of Carcinoma of the Uterine Cervix: Treatment with intracavity radium and parametrical irradiation', *International Journal of Radiation, Oncology, Biology, Physics*, Aug (7), pp 999–1004, 1981.

Wagner L. and Bye M., 'Body Image and Patients Experiencing Alopecia as a Result of Cancer Chemotherapy', *Cancer Nursing*, Oct, pp 365–9, 1979.

Walker V., 'Skin Care During Radiotherapy', *Nursing Times*, 8 Dec, pp 2068–70, 1982.

Warren K., 'Will I Be Sick Nurse? Part 1', *Nursing Times*, 84(11), pp 30–2, 1988a.

Warren K., 'Will I Be Sick Nurse? Part 2', *Nursing Times*, 84(12), pp 53–4, 1988b.

Welch D., 'Planning Nursing Interventions for Family Members of Adult Cancer Patients', *Cancer Nursing*, Oct, pp 365–9, 1981.

Welch-McCaffrey D., 'Cancer Anxiety and Quality of Life', *Cancer Nursing*, June, pp 151–8, 1985.

Whitehead V., 'Cancer Treatment Needs Better Antiemetics', *New England Journal of Medicine*, 293(4), pp 199–200, 1975.

Wilbur J., 'Sexual Development and Body Image in the Teenager with Cancer', *Frontiers of Radiation Therapy and Oncology*, 14, pp 108–14, 1980.

Yasko J., 'Holistic Management of Nausea and Vomiting Caused by Chemotherapy', *Topics in Clinical Nursing*, 7, 1, 27, 1985.

15 The burned patient

Study of this chapter will enable you to:

1 Outline the special nursing challenge presented by providing body image care to the burned patient.
2 Indicate why it is important for the nurse to recognise her own stress needs and limitations, before caring for the patient.
3 Describe what is meant by the concept of a 'burn career'.
4 Describe the body image care priorities during the early or shock stage of the burn career.
5 Discuss how body image care is adjusted as the patient progresses through the intermediate or rehabilitation stage of the burn career.
6 Describe the nursing role, in support of patient and family, during the late stage of the burn career.
7 Suggest ways in which the burns unit environment contributes to the patient's altered body image.
8 Discuss the role of controlled exposure exercises and body image accounting in body image rehabilitation post-burn.
9 Suggest ways in which the body image needs of the burned child may be met.

Few greater body image catastrophes could be imagined than those associated with burns. Not only are large numbers of children and adults damaged in this way, but their injuries are often widespread, highly visible and rarely completely repairable. Meeting the body image needs of such patients is particularly difficult, both because of the condition and distress of the patients and because of the environment in which they must be cared for.

A large number of victims admitted to burns units have not enjoyed a stable normal body image before the burn. Patients may come from disturbed family backgrounds, where unemployment, poor housing and marital disharmony complicate the problem (Kolman, 1983). Individuals suffering from depression or psychoses are very prone to burn injury, either as a result of accident or through a self-destructive act (Noyes *et al,*

1979; Questad *et al*, 1976). Bowden points to a high incidence of burns amongst alcoholics (Bowden *et al*, 1980). Mental illness, alcoholism, and the low self-esteem associated with deprived backgrounds are all likely to mean that the patient faces the burn with few positive feelings about self-image and his ability to cope.

When a child is the victim, such as with scalding, the nurse finds herself attending to the needs of parents too (Galdston, 1972). There is a tendency for parents to blame themselves for all accidents, just at a time in their lives when they have invested a great deal of hope and pride in their off-spring. While the patient lies unconscious or shocked the full impact of injury falls upon the onlooking couple. The trauma is multiplied ten fold if one or more other family members have perished in the fire.

Delivering body image care to such patients is complicated by the burns unit surroundings. Nurses experience a dual stress; internal and external (Ashworth, 1976; Huckabay and Jagla, 1979; Tomlin, 1977). The nurse is surrounded by high technology facilities, working in a hot environment with patients and relatives who observe her every move. She must complete dressings which she knows will cause the patient pain. It is acknowledged that a percentage of children will die, and that if they don't they will be left with a body image that requires months or years of cosmetic surgery and psychological support. The nurse's means of coping with such stress may compromise the care delivered and her sensitivity to the patient's needs. Seeing the patient's problems in intellectual terms, concentrating upon the monitoring, mechanical support functions can limit active measures designed to alleviate body image problems (Clarke 1984; Marshall, 1980). Because of these recognised stressors it is important that nurses receive a planned programme of support (Crickmore, 1987). By facilitating nurse support groups, rotation of placements to other environments, continuing education in body image and burn psychology, the hospital will equip the nurse with the skills and energy to provide the type of body image care which will form a foundation for the patient's long term rehabilitation.

Burns patient careers

In Chapter 12 the notion of a patient career was introduced. The burns victim may also be said to have a 'career', with recognisable stages which often predate and then encompass those associated with plastic surgery. Mieszala has found that this typically consists of three stages, although other writers, such as Bernstein, have proposed more complex models (Bernstein *et al*, 1976; Mieszala, 1983). Each stage is characterised by particular patient health and body image problems, typical coping strategies, family needs and therapy (see Table 15.1).

Table 15.1 Stages in a burn patient's 'career'

	Early (shock) stage (circa first 72 hours post-burn)	Intermediate stage (following two to six weeks)	Late stage (later months/years)
Typical patient physical state	Life threatened, possibly unconscious, in pain, disorientated, hypovolaemic shock, oedematous	Pain, continuing oedema, loss of much tissue, gain of some (grafts), possible returning bowel, renal functions	Mobilising, still some pain, possible infections, effects of repeated surgery and anaesthetics, scar tissue
Typical patient mental state	Anxiety, delirium, confusion, sleep deprivation, sensory deprivation and overload, frustration (for instance with communicating)	Real onset of emotional reactions, flood response, depression, anger, regression, hostility, disordered sense of body space	Long term emotional trauma. Low self-esteem, risk of suicide, risk of withdrawal
Family/friends	Acute grief reactions, guilt feelings, feelings of impotence, bewilderment	Problems how to respond to and support patient, possible exhaustion, start to become part of patient care team	Need to learn and develop skills to help patient socialise/master encounters
Typical therapy events	Shock room treatment, airway protection, replacement of body fluids, early wound dressing, protected environment	Ongoing/developing wound management, early skin grafting, intensive physiotherapy, wound debridement, analgesia, nutritional replacement	Continuing cosmetic surgery, pressure bandages to scarring, occupational and physiotherapy

The early, shock stage may be said to coincide with the first 72 hours post-burn. The patient is receiving shock room treatment designed to support body organ function, fluid and electrolyte balance. He is often disorientated or unconscious and has made no self-appraisal of his body image. The effects of the trauma, sensory and sleep deprivation associated with therapy have all served to prevent the patient from orientating himself (Avni, 1980; Marvin and Heimbach, 1984; Patterson, 1987; Steiner and Clark, 1977; Zubek, 1969). Relatives meanwhile may be making a rapid assessment of current injuries and future body image (presentation) problems (Abramson, 1975; Brodland and Andreason, 1974; Woodward and Jackson, 1961).

The intermediate stage coincides with intensive wound care and the nurse's major efforts to rehabilitate the patient. The immediate threat to life has passed and with that the patient's attention focuses upon pain and discomfort. Pain reminds him of his body, how it feels and looks, so that emotional outbursts may become evident. There may be a 'flood response' with the patient eagerly talking out his anxieties. Stokes, Altman and Platzer all point to the fact that the patient's body experience is distorted by being attached to machines, nursed semi-naked, in an environment that has no day or night and which sustains a steady temperature. The patient may find it hard to distinguish where his body ends and the machine begins, especially where nerve endings have been destroyed (Altman, 1975; Platzer, 1987; Stokes, 1984).

In the third stage of the burn career the patient's life is punctuated, if not dominated, by the need to undergo plastic surgery, submit to regular physiotherapy and search for a new and acceptable body ideal. This stage may extend for many years, at a time when acute medical support services are rapidly being withdrawn, and when the family are ill equipped to take over the bulk of the patient's psycho–social support (Knudson-Cooper, 1982; Woodward, 1959; Wright and Fulwiler, 1974). Patients are likely to remain bitter and angry for years or even decades (Andreason and Norris, 1972). Because these stages are fairly well defined body image needs can be considered along the way. This chapter will discuss key issues and it is important to remember that the burn problems may later be complicated by changes in body image associated with ageing (see Chapter 3).

Dealing with body reality

Early stage body reality concerns are directly related to life saving measures (see Table 15.2). The patient has a primary need to maintain a clear airway and inhale sufficient oxygen to support tissue function. This often entails the fashioning of a tracheostomy, the use of intubation or ventilators. Providing the patient with humidified oxygen reduces the risk of

Table 15.2 Typical body reality concerns of a burn patient, by stage

Early	Intermediate	Late
• Maintaining airway/ oxygenation	• Maintaining wound toilet and dressings (painful)	• Intermittent surgery/ hospitalisation for reconstruction of body areas
• Maintaining fluid/ electrolyte balance	• Early skin grafting and first surgery to limit effects of contractures	• Continued physiotherapy
• Supporting circulation to limbs (for instance, escharotomies)	• Patient moves from shock room to side room in burns unit	• Possible retraining for new job/career
• Limiting/controlling pain	• Pain management reviewed and adjusted	• Use of pressure bandages to limit the effects of scarring
• Wound care (occlusive/ exposed, use of plastic bags for hands or feet)	• Intensive physiotherapy regime (hourly)	• Build up of nutrition – protein, carbohydrates etc.
• Maintaining a safe environment (infection control)	• First nutrition beyond intravenous infusion (parenteral support)	• Removal of all monitoring devices/ apparatus
• Monitoring vital functions	• Continued monitoring vital functions and efficacy or otherwise of pain control	

cerebral hypoxia. This is important if brain damage and associated body image problems are not to ensue. Careful hygiene measures used to clean and maintain the tracheostomy tube reduce the incidence of infection and may later leave a neater scar when the tube is removed. Similar principles underpin fluid and electrolyte replacements via an intravenous infusion. Inadequate replacement may threaten renal function with all the body image problems associated with the onset of acute, and then chronic renal failure.

Escharotomies (surgically incising constricting burns on arms or legs) may improve the circulation beyond the burn and limit the need for later radical surgery. While the incision of deeply burned tissue should not be painful, pain will be a feature of some erythematous areas of the burn and of the first wound dressing and cleaning procedures. Analgesia protocols will in part be dictated by the patient's respiratory and cardio-vascular state. They must also be adjusted so that the patient does not become excessively disorientated and sleepy. Experiences with pre-operation medications may remind us that our body does not feel our own under their effects.

While the patient will have to be nursed in a controlled environment, to assist body homeostasis and prevent infection, this should not preclude the nurse from establishing her own role and identity with the patient. At this stage he will not be able to concentrate upon all of his care plan, but simple and honest briefing about individual procedures should enable him to start to think about his condition, albeit piecemeal. Behind the mask and gown the nurse may look fairly anonymous, so it is helpful to establish the nurse's name and role. Hard badges may be an infection or injury risk, but large stick on material ones may assist the patient to sort out who is who – 'Nurse Robinson does a lot of my catheter care – she is the nurse with spectacles'. Establishing such first ideas about body reality may be critical when the patient's main attachments are to monitors, cannulas and catheters.

Intermediate body reality care is addressed at recapturing basic function of limbs and assisting the healing of wounds. Now body contact with the nurse is associated with pain. Use this challenge as the setting to start establishing some shared body image goals. The pain the patient feels now could be complicated and prolonged if active physiotherapy in the bath is abandoned. The patient faces a battle during which the burn has initially won territory. Reclaiming a stake on body tissue and body function is important if in the later stage of the struggle the patient is to use these resources to rebuild body image. Body image is not an abstract idea to such patients. The mirror reveals the initial assault, so encouraging patients with nutrition intake, physiotherapy and co-operation in wound care, is important if recovery is to include an improvement in appearance.

The nurse must explain that the oedematous, swollen and charred appearance of skin will improve with care. Intravenous fluids will initially provide rehydration and later oral food intake will provide tissue repairing protein. Fortitude during dressing changes may be more possible for the patient if the physical goals of care are explained. At this stage it is important that nurses set short realistic goals. The patient may not be able to envisage progress months in the future, so many early goals will be humble and targeted towards the next day or week. The first walk around the bed, the removal of intravenous infusions and the move to oral meals are all events which can be highlighted using a diary or calendar. Progress must be tangible to be tempting!

If the patient has been brave in the short term, he will need to be stoical in the long term. Late stage grafting of skin and further corrective surgery all take their toll on motivation and morale. As with so many cosmetic operations, it is important to establish just what change the patient expects from such surgery. This should then be discussed with the surgeon and the patient given the clearest, most realistic prognosis for appearance post-operation. A catalogue of photographs and line diagrams may be useful. The patient may follow through the illustrated steps involved in a pedicle graft and may anticipate the delays involved with further post-surgery oedema.

Not all late stage care is associated with surgical 'events'. The patient will need education about the formation of keloid scar tissue and its effects on the skin over time. He will also need to understand the benefits of wearing his pressure bandages properly and persistently. It is not enough to assure him that these will help with his later appearance. If he is to cope with the discomfort and inconvenience of wearing such appliances it is important that he can picture just how they combat raised scar tissue. Explaining that facial exercises such as facial grimaces assist this process, helps the patient to feel that there is a co-ordinated plan to his care.

Supporting body ideal

The early stage body ideal care should emphasise support for the relatives, and measures designed to limit the assault upon the patient's body space (see Table 15.3). In the early hours post-burn the patient will not be able to review all the implications of the burn for his body ideal. He will nonetheless feel invaded by machines, constant light and by staff who operate around him, much as mechanics might around an engine.

Relatives need to be carefully briefed about the patient's injuries, his appearance and the bedside equipment, before they see him. By accommodating their need to anticipate what they will see, what they will say and do when they visit, the relatives are helped to remain 'in control' and to be positive in their contribution to care. While they will be upset and shocked by the injury, they will not have lost the faculty to learn about the burn and how they may help the patient to combat it. Providing the relatives with hospital literature on the stages of burn care will help everyone to prepare for the steps that are taken to improve appearance and body function. During first interviews with the surgeon or nurse the relatives may not have been able to bring themselves to ask about scarring, or to vent their fears. Providing literature which anticipates typical questions (for instance 'how long will it take for the swelling to go down?') can help the family to resolve worries, to plan specific further questions and to start to think of themselves as part of the patient's support team.

Later, it will be the close relatives that assist the patient in piecing together a new ideal. From the earliest stages relatives may benefit from learning about facets of the body image and how in particular a positive body ideal can be rebuilt through their honest and constructive interest. Relatives are vitally important in helping the patient to sustain motivation. Frequent operations mean that the patient has constantly to revalue

Table 15.3 Typical body ideal concerns of a burn patient, by stage

Early	Intermediate	Late
• Emphasis upon family and supporters needs. These face full realisation of injury early on	• Patient may withdraw from first insights into injury/body ideal implications	• Early discharge from hospital means little time for social support network to support a new body ideal
• Invasion of body space (catheters, monitors etc)	• Taking stock of new body reality – first anxieties/trauma concerning self-image (unattractive = bad syndrome)	• Risk of developing stigma, patient assigned a poor social identity
• Body feels depersonalised – attached to monitors	• Feelings of lost control, dependency, of being exposed and vulnerable	• Need to refer to family or friends for cues on developing new body ideal
• Sensory deprivation – skin does not provide normal information, outside the environment is controlled – patient feels he has no control	• Dealing with pain. Pain affects our perception of our body and our self	• Search for new values, new criteria for self-valuation (for instance work, productivity, rather than appearance)
• Concerns with survival. It may be enough to simply preserve the self – in what form, that worry can come later	• Heightened awareness of others reactions to appearance of burn/skin	
	• First thoughts about sexuality, the future means of acceptable communication (rationalisation)	

himself – the new body ideal may have to start from humble beginnings. Relatives will have to accept that the patient's appearance will never again be completely the same. Cosmetic improvements must be applauded, but perhaps not so rapturously that the patient comes to doubt whether his relative's expectations are realistic!

The nurse attending the patient must regularly reaffirm with him that the monitors and catheters are really extra channels indicating his progress. Their purpose is limited and they will not remain *in situ* forever. In the intermediate stage this will be especially important, as the removal of such items may be one of the few ways in which the patient feels he is regaining control over his body.

At this time too the patient will start to watch eagerly for visitors' and nurses' reactions to his appearance and behaviour (Wallace, 1988). It is important that the nurse is open in talking about the trauma and that she is seen to value the positive attitudes he expresses toward therapy. At this point, self-image ideals of bravery, humour and sense of pragmatism may be developed as a support for new body image ideals. While it may be too early to analyse specific new body ideals, goals such as a return to work may help the patient to value yet more personal attributes of stamina, perseverance and inventiveness (Chang and Herzog, 1976; Hill, 1985). Body ideals may be improved through a resilient self-ideal – a perspective on the body that sees it as a servant to the self, that basic body functions may be as important as appearance.

Such respite as is offered by concentrating upon self-ideal cannot forever delay discussion of body ideal, as viewed in terms of body grace, movement, sexuality and reliability of body function. The ideal of smooth, supple skin has been shattered, and the hurt reinforced when loved ones recoil from touching the healing skin. The nurse may help the patient and relatives by touching his skin freely, explaining as she does so that visual expression of love, touch, gentle stroking, may be the first step toward normal intimate contact later. When such skin is seen not to be painful and that touching it can provide visual if not direct tactile messages of tenderness, the patient may be encouraged to explore his new skin surfaces with his loved one.

Aiding body presentation

It seems unreasonable for patients to rebuild new body ideals until such time as they have begun to master some aspects of body presentation (see Table 15.4). By achieving even moderate success here they can start to consider ideals which emphasise a flexible and open personal approach to social encounters. Relatives provide a useful testing ground for such presentation and that is why they must be welcomed quickly as members of the caring team.

During the shock phase, the patient's dignity is protected by the use of light coverings, a gown or sterile sheet being used wherever possible. If the circumstances permit, the patient is given a choice of which arm will be used for intravenous cannulation. The patient cannot forego the need for rehydrating fluids, but the nurse may be able to ensure that his favoured arm is kept free as possible. It should not be forgotten that such a small measure may be a big bonus to body presentation, especially as that hand is the contact point with family and the outside world.

While the patient is unconscious, basic grooming, mouth, nose and nail care are important. The patient will not wish to wake to a more dishevelled image than is necessary. Relatives too will appreciate the time taken to wash and arrange hair, clip nails and cleanse unburned skin. It may be one of the first positive messages that they receive in the midst of a major injury.

Helping the patient to communicate, perhaps by using pen and paper, or a simple yes/no code system, forms an early means of helping with

Table 15.4 Typical body presentation concerns of a burn patient, by stage

Early	Intermediate	Late
• Maintaining dignity ref exposure, reliance on machines and monitors, appearance of burns	• Change of dressings (smells, appearance)	• Need for support groups – the need to feel comfortable in company
• Basic grooming and hygiene needs (the smell of the burn)	• Need to see improvement in appearance (use of photographs, diary, mirror)	• Need for insight into the use limitations of cosmetic surgery
• Need to communicate clearly (communication through voice, touch, facial expression important as an avenue for the presentation of self)	• Need to play (children). Play is the classic expression of childhood and the means by which body presentation may be improved	• Need to establish a trusting relationship with significant others (such as work colleagues, teacher)
• Sensory deprivation. We have to sense our body and the environment if we are to express ourselves meaningfully using body presentation	• Discovers the benefits of clothing (a key body expression tool)	• Need for family support – to test out body presentation upon
	• Pace of exposure, meeting new people post-burn (can we really put on an adequate presentation quickly enough?)	• Need to express oneself sexually. Change in mating game rules – the way we relate to possible partners
	• Accounting adequately for appearance	
	• First prostheses (the use of pressure bandages, wigs, first camouflage makeup)	

presentation. Not only will the patient be able to start expressing pain or sensations, but also to start to express feelings, even comfort, for relatives who are very upset. A tracheostomy tube may be life-saving, but it severely limits the patient's opportunities to show others that he is alive and fighting within his damaged body. The expression of attitudes and emotions is a very human part of self expression. It is often this unique 'self' that nurses look to as a starting point for rehabilitation. Motivating the patient presumes that nurse's know something about him. Something, that in the first instance, is likely to come through, despite limitations of body presentation.

Changes of dressing and wound toilet do more than simply limit infection. They aid body presentation too. Hands or feet dressed in plastic bags accumulate unpleasant quantities of fluid, which is the result of silver sulphadiazine interacting with the burn. This may not hurt the hand but it is unpleasant to view. Patients would like to rid themselves of it on a regular basis. Soaked through dressings are not only an infection risk, but also unpleasant from a body presentation perspective. A clean dressing looks better and may smell better as well.

Amongst children, play is one of the best means of improving body presentation. Not only is it the means to achieve early physiotherapy, but it allows the burned child to express himself in the normal way for children. There may be limitations on the grasping of toys, restrictions in limb movement. Nevertheless play is such a fundamental part of child self-expression that opportunities should not be missed to encourage it. Through play the nurse may help the child to devise new ways of doing things such as toileting. The alternative way of moving toys about the bed may later become the strategies that enable the child to show off his body to best effect on a public stage. To this end, games and toys that involve easy to clean props, and which necessitate manipulation, even if through a plastic bag, are to be highly prized. Such toys may also help the child to act out his worst fears about the future physiotherapy and surgery. It may be advantageous at this point to work with the unit psychologist, drawing upon assessment expertise in order to plan a body image strategy that recognises the child's unique needs and fears.

Children and adult patients will both appreciate the chance to wear loose fitting and perhaps colourful clothing. The practicalities of dressing and undressing will suggest the need to choose clothes, that are not pulled on over the head, or which are made of looser fibres, irritating sensitive skin. It is important to choose clothes with a view to the patient's body experiences, as well as preferred colours or styles. Remember too that changes in skin colour and complexion may mean that the previous preferred colours will now look wrong. It may well be worth considering the purchase of one clothing item which especially suits current skin condition. Choosing this garment is important. For instance, a bright yellow top may look grotesque against the reds and blacks of a burned face. A white top may emphasise the red facial complexion but it may also represent freshness when the patient feels so crusty and uncomfortable elsewhere.

Two other body presentation strategies should be considered. These are a programme of controlled exposure to social encounters and assistance in accounting for the new body image (Bernstein and Cope, 1976; Price, 1986a,b). These strategies have been used very successfully by nurses and others in burns units, long before they received any formal titles. Bernstein has noted that the former of these strategies is critical if the patient is to develop assertive behaviour in outside hospital encounters.

Each controlled exposure programme must work from a basis of patient–relative–nurse trust, and must progress in manageable stages. The process of the programme is as useful as the product, for relatives may continue to assist the patient by continuing on with the principles long after he has been discharged from hospital. The programme is put into action as soon as staff contemplate moving the patient from his side room to the communal burns/plastics ward. The programme progresses further with his first trips outside into the main hospital and the local community. The nurse should begin by making a verbal contract of a specific objective, with the patient. For instance, he will be able to join the other patients to view the evening news on television; he will sit at the rear of the television lounge and be accompanied by his primary nurse. Note that the objectives are quite specific and have clear parameters, stating just what sort of support the patient may expect.

Having specified what is planned the nurse encourages the patient to anticipate what he will feel like, how others will react and what he will do in response. He must be reassured that the nurse will be with him, and that many of the other patients will have participated in earlier programmes. When he returns to his room the experience can then be reviewed and perhaps his feelings recorded upon a cassette tape or in a diary.

Patients are usually surprised to find just how well they coped. If patients have attended to them at all it has been to congratulate them on 'escaping the dungeon'! Where problems do arise it is important to help the patient to express worries and to try to identify just why the problem arose and how it was mishandled. In some instances a favoured relative may fill this role very ably. Indeed, given the short length of hospital stay, this may become a critical support as the patient contemplates socialising at large for the first time.

Burned patients are usually faced with accounting for an open altered body image. The account of such change must involve a more direct reference to injury, function and personal feelings about the same. It may seem cruel to take regular photographs of the patient's injuries, together with his encounter tapes or diaries. Nevertheless, these will in later weeks form a useful aid to showing progress in treatment and appearance. The stark reality of a burned face now, may be softened when the patient reviews a photograph of his oedematous, painful looking face of previous weeks or months. Sharing photographs that prove change for the better, helps everyone to anticipate realistic cosmetic improvement. It assures the relative or friend that here is a brave and very tenacious individual who recognises the injury, but who is able to strive for a more satisfying final appearance. This is not to suggest that each patient should have immediate recourse to a pocket book of snapshots. Rather, that the key relatives and friends may be helped to accommodate the new body presentation in this way. Cosmetic surgery, camouflage makeup and skin grafting will help, but these take time and the patient cannot remain a hermit meanwhile.

Towards the longer term

In the longer term, it is the patient's relatives and friends who will once again fulfil the major support role. Patients with poor social support networks are at a major disadvantage. It is important for the patient to once again become a member of a group. Group identity may enhance personal identity – the need to 'belong' may be met and the patient find at least some settings in daily life where the burn does not immediately intrude. Support groups, such as the American Phoenix Club, are important resources to patients and relatives alike (Wallace, 1988). They may offer expertise in cosmetic makeup, handling awkward questions or sustaining support links with regional burns centres. The nurse who facilitates such groups, supports the patient's individual body presentation and self-presentation through group activity.

In the final stage of the career the nurse will have become primarily a facilitator. Having taught all that she can in the burns unit, now she assists the patient by helping him to access other help and to identify a wider range of coping strategies. Children and school teachers may both need practical suggestions on how to handle the child's first post-burn lessons. Pre-term visits, by child to school or teacher to hospital, will enable the nurse to help both recognise and master their anxieties (Garrett and Levine, 1967). Sometimes the controlled exposure programme technique or the use of photographs may be of assistance.

Because the nurse has become a trusted friend and confidant it may be that the patient now describes his worries over sexual expression (Burleson, 1973). Whilst the nurse cannot replace the clinical psychologist's work here, it may be germane to help the patient to express his concerns. Relatives may be worried about this too, particularly if the patient's parents are elderly and perceive marriage, a committed relationship to be the best future for the patient. The nurse cannot promise that the patient will enjoy a full sex life. Previous partners may not be able to adapt to the new body presentation. The nurse must therefore help the patient with dress, makeup and grooming to enhance appearance. She will have to explain to partners that scarred tissue does improve in appearance, it still serves as a means of showing and receiving affection. By discussing visits that have been successful, or unsuccessful encounters between hospital admissions, the nurse may learn whether the patient has become disillusioned or depressed. Spotting growing difficulties, patient anger and withdrawal is important if sex counsellors or others are to be alerted.

The burn victim measures his body image problems in months and years. Contact with the nurse at key times, such as at admission and during subsequent stays for treatment, will provide the opportunity to monitor body image changes and to plan new goals. Behaviour toward the patient, communication with relatives and a willingness to work long term with the patient should provide a framework for building a new body image. Without such a continuity of nursing interest and effort, the scars may extend for years, into the patient's self and amongst his family.

Review questions

1 Why is it so important that the nurse is properly prepared to provide body image care to the burned patient?
2 What are the advantages of using a burn 'career' perspective when considering the patient's body image needs?
3 In what ways do machines and monitors interfere with the patient's body image?
4 Changing dressings and harvesting skin grafts are all painful. Why is pain important as a consideration in body image care?
5 Burned patients may spend a relatively short time in hospital. What are the body image advantages and disadvantages of this?
6 Why is so much attention paid to relatives when considering the body image support of the burned patient?
7 Briefly describe what is meant by a 'controlled exposure programme'.
8 To what use may photographs be put in the rehabilitation of the patient?
9 How are burned children's needs different with regard to body image support?

Suggested exercise

Imagine that you are caring for Elaine Norman, a 15 year old schoolgirl who suffered burns to both her hands and the right side of her face. Elaine is currently in the second stage of recovery and is now contemplating a series of visits around the hospital before she moves to a bed in one of the main ward bays. Assume that Elaine has the close support of a school friend (Anne), and her father.

Plan some objectives that will go to form your own controlled exposure programme for Elaine. These should include a trip into the main ward, a visit to the hospital newsagent and a short period in occupational therapy. Ensure that your objectives clearly state what is to be achieved, over what span of time, and assisted by whom. Having decided on four or five such objectives, try to place these in the order that you would present them to Elaine. (In reality, Elaine would be invited to share in the formulation of such objectives but for the purpose of this exercise proceed independently, 'assuming' that Elaine has identified the three visits stated above).

Share your objectives with one or more colleagues. Try to form one or more objectives which seem to meet common goals. Try to establish what it is that makes these so attractive to more than one within the group? Try also to describe the process by which individual objectives were modified to form the group suggested objectives. (This same negotiation would in reality take place with the patient.)

There is probably no 'correct' solution, and there are no naturally superior objectives. The process of arriving at workable, thoughtful objectives is at least as important as the final objectives themselves.

Suggested time scales are as follows:

(a) for the individual effort, allow 20 minutes
(b) for the group suggested objectives, allow 40 minutes
(c) for the discussion on the process of objective planning, allow up to 60 minutes depending on group size and experience

References

Abramson M., 'Group Treatment of Families of Burn-Injured Patients', *Social Casework*, 56, pp 235–41, 1975.

Altman I., *The Environment and Social Behaviour*, Wadsworth Publishing, Belmont, California, 1975.

Andreason N. and Norris A., 'Long Term Adjustment and Adaptation Mechanisms in Severely Burned Adults', *Journal of Nervous and Mental Disease*, 154, pp 352–62, 1972.

Ashworth P., *Care To Communicate*, Royal College of Nursing, London, 1976.

Avni J., 'The Severe Burns', *Advances in Psychosomatic Medicine*, 10, pp 57–77, 1980.

Bernstein N. and Cope O., *Burned and Disfigured*, Ch. 7, pp 125–45, Little Brown & Co., Boston, 1976.

Bowden M.L., Feller I., Tholen D., Davidson T.N. and James M.H. 'Self Esteem of Severely Burned Patients', *Archives of Physical Medicine and Rehabilitation*, 61, pp 449–52, 1980.

Brodland G. and Andreason N., 'Adjustment Problems of the Family of the Burn Patient', *Social Casework*, 55, pp 13–18, 1974.

Burleson D.L., 'Handicapped Aim For Normal Lives' Sex Information Council of the United States, *New York Times*, 14 Oct, 1973.

Chang F. and Herzog B., 'Burn Morbidity: A follow up study of physical and psychological disability', *Annals of Surgery*, 183, pp 34–7, 1976.

Clarke M. 'The Constructs "Stress" and "Coping" as a Rationale for Nursing Activities', *Journal of Advanced Nursing*, 9(3), pp 267–70, 1984.

Crickmore R., 'A Review of Stress in the Intensive Care Unit', *Intensive Care Nursing*, 3, pp 19–27, 1987.

Galdston R., 'The Burning and Healing of Children', *Psychiatry*, 35, pp 57–66, 1972.

Garrett J. and Levine L. (eds), *Psychiatry Practices with the Physically Disabled*, Columbia University Press, New York, 1967.

Hill C., 'Psychological Adjustment of Adult Burn Patients: Is it more difficult for people with visible scars?', *Occupational Therapy*, Sept, pp 281–3, 1985.

Huckabay L. and Jagla B., 'Nurses Stress Factors in the ICU', *Journal of Nursing Administration*, 9(2), pp 21–6, 1979.

Knudson-Cooper M., 'Burn Rounds: Emotional care of the hospitalised burned child', *Journal of Burn Care and Rehabilitation*, 3, pp 109–16, 1982.

Kolman P., 'The Incidence of Psychopathology in Burned Adult Patients: A critical review', *Journal of Burn Care and Rehabilitation*, 416, pp 430–6, 1983.

Marshall J., 'Stress Amongst Nurses' in Cooper C. and Marshall J. (eds) *White Collar and Professional Stress*, pp 19–59, John Wiley & Sons, London, 1980.

Marvin J. and Heimbach D., 'Pain Management' in Fisher S. and Helm P. (eds) *Comprehensive Rehabilitation of Burns*, Williams & Wilkins, Baltimore, 1984.

Mieszala P., 'The Stages of Stress', *Emergency Medicine*, Sept, pp 28–42, 1983.

Noyes R., Frye S. and Slymen D., 'Stressful Life Events & Burn Injuries', *Journal of Trauma*, 19, pp 141–4, 1979.

Patterson R., 'Psychological Management of the Burn Patient', *Topics in Acute Care and Trauma Rehabilitation*, 1(4), pp 25–39, 1987.

Platzer H., 'Body Image – A problem for intensive care patients (1)', *Intensive Care Nursing*, 3, pp 61–6, 1987.

Price B., 'Mirror, Mirror, On The Wall...' *Nursing Times*, 24 Sept, pp 30–2, 1986a.

Price B., 'Body Image: Keeping up appearances', *Nursing Times*, 1 Oct, pp 58–61, 1986b.

Questad K., Patterson D. and Boltwood M., 'Income, Preinjury Mental Health and Injury Factors as Predictors of Self Reported Health in Patients With Major Burns', Presented paper – *American Congress of Physical Medicine and Rehabilitation*, Kansas City, 19–21 Oct, 1976.

Steiner H. and Clarke W., 'Psychiatric Complications of Burned Adults: A classification', *Journal of Trauma*, 17, pp 134–43, 1977.

Stokes L., 'Thymectomy: On the receiving end', *Nursing Mirror*, 4 Jan, pp 87–8, 1984.

Tomlin J., 'Psychological Problems in Intensive Care', *British Medical Journal*, 2, pp 441–3, 1977.

Wallace L., 'Abandoned to a Social Death?', *Nursing Times*, 84(10), pp 34–7, 1988.

Woodward J., 'Emotional Disturbances of Burned Children', *British Medical Journal*, 1, pp 1009–13, 1959.

Woodward J. and Jackson D., 'Emotional Reactions in Burned Children and their Mothers', *British Journal of Plastic Surgery*, 13, pp 316, 1961.

Wright L. and Fulwiler R., 'Long Range Emotional Sequelae of Burns: Effects on children and their mothers', *Pediatric Research*, 8, pp 931–4, 1974.

Zubek J., *Sensory deprivation: Fifteen years of research*, Appleton, 1969.

16 Notes on eating disorders

Study of this chapter will enable you to:

1 With reference to the terms, body reality, body ideal and body presentation, outline the problems faced by an anorexia nervosa or a bulimia nervosa sufferer.

2 Outline the American Psychiatric Association diagnostic criteria for anorexia nervosa.

3 Suggest what effects the disordered body image of these patients will have upon their self-image.

4 Share the key nursing points about feeding anorexic patients.

5 Describe why variations in medical therapy may confuse the plans for nursing care of the patient.

6 Describe why the role of the occupational therapist is important.

7 Discuss why trust between patient and nurse is so difficult to establish, and yet so important for rehabilitation.

8 List at least three ways in which the anorexic or bulimic patient may be assessed.

Anorexia nervosa and bulimia nervosa

Julie was a 15 year old student who had been admitted to the psychiatric unit for treatment of anorexia nervosa. During her stay in hospital all food intake and elimination was to be carefully monitored. Previous attempts to vomit food into the toilet had been gently, but firmly forestalled. Julie seemed to be making moderate progress. Within her ward bay there was, however, a pervasive smell of vomit. A subsequent search of the area revealed that Julie had been regularly vomiting into the empty suitcase that she kept beneath her bed. Fifteen months after this event Julie died as a result of an overdose of tranquillisers.

Part of the tragedy of this teenager's death and that of others like her is the fact that both anorexia nervosa (AN) and bulimia nervosa (BN) are still contested concepts amongst the health professionals who seek to help the patient (Scott, 1988). AN and BN diagnostic criteria have varied and with it the treatment protocols favoured by the different groups such as psychoanalysts, feminists, and behavioural therapists. All of this has served to frustrate nurses and families alike and to limit the unqualified advice that can be offered within a text such as this.

Anorexia nervosa is very much a problem of control and the perception of body image and other controls in an adolescent or young adult's life. The majority of the patients have been female, from middle or upper class, educated family backgrounds (Crisp et al, 1976; Palmer, 1980). There is a growing incidence of AN amongst the general public (Duddle, 1973), and amongst male youth specifically (Crisp and Burns, 1983; Herzog et al, 1984; Vanderseycken and Van den Broucke, 1984). Lawrence argues that the high incidence of AN amongst middle class female adolescents may be as much to do with educational demands made upon the individual as their class background per se (Lawrence, 1987).

The American Psychiatric Association (APA) propose a number of diagnostic criteria for AN (APA, 1987). Firstly, the teenager refuses to maintain body weight, being 15 per cent or more below that expected for their age and height. Secondly, the patient expresses an intense fear of becoming overweight, even when the body reality is significantly underweight (Russell, 1970). Body ideal is disturbed, the patient perceiving that his or her body shape is grossly obese, particularly their waist, hips and thighs (Garner and Garfinkel, 1979; Garner and Garfinkel, 1982). In female patients amenorrhoea which is defined as the loss of three consecutive menstrual periods, is also present.

The AN patient appears to feel out of control, faced with the demands to be an assertive adult (the educational and other expectations), as well as more passive as a female or non-wage earner. The teenager may seek to delay the confusions that result, by delaying the changes of puberty which symbolise his or her change in physiological status. If the sexual characteristics of womanhood can be delayed, so might the dilemmas be (Edwards, 1987). Consciously or otherwise the individual begins selectively to starve herself of carbohydrates, to abuse laxatives and diuretics, and to vomit back meals that others have insisted she eat. This has profound implications for body presentation as they damage dental enamel (through gastric acid in the vomit), seek to control meal time behaviour and rid themselves of the food upon which they are proud to 'depend' less and less (Bruch, 1973).

Bulimia nervosa has a more recent recorded history, originally being thought of as part of AN. In this instance the patients may be a little older, perhaps in their twenties. They will have a normal age and height related body weight, and may even be mildly obese (Fairburn, 1982). These patients' behaviour alternates between binge eating sometimes a massive consumption of up to 20,000 calories per day, and bouts of remorse and associated induced vomiting. Large sums of money may be spent on food and a considerable guilt invested into the post-binge period. The extent of binge eating, vomiting and purging distinguish the bulimic patient from larger numbers of individuals who occasionally employ such measures for body weight control (Cooper and Fairburn, 1983). As with AN patients there is an obsessional interest in food and the control of eating. Many bulimics fear that they will not be able to control the consumption of some favoured food. 'Pigging out' only serves to confirm such fears and swing them towards a severe purging of the gastro-intestinal system. Men may also be affected, especially those living or working in areas where weight control may be important, for instance athletes, jockeys, and dancers (Rodin *et al*, 1985; Striegel-Moore *et al*, 1986). Usually the bulimic individual will have been dieting before he or she developed this chaotic cycle of consumption and elimination.

At varying points in the eating problem career both groups of patients experience depression and anxiety (Herzog, 1984). Depression may be associated with weight gain, the development of secondary sexual characteristics or the failure to prevent a major binge (Pyle *et al*, 1981). During such periods self-esteem (self-image) is low, the individual contemptuous of his lack of self-discipline.

Nursing assessment

The nursing assessment of patients with eating disorders is complicated by a number of factors. Firstly, the patient may be totally convinced that her own perception of body contour, weight and body space is accurate. She may not appreciate why she is in hospital or why so many others appear concerned at her condition. If the family or friends of the patient have reacted in a confused, frightened or prescriptive way towards the dietary habits, then the nurse may also have to work hard to win her trust and make an initial body image assessment.

Patients with rather more insight into others' perceptions of their condition may prove manipulative, trying to dupe the nurse with stories and explanations, or inviting her to take up an anorexic perspective herself (Biley and Savage, 1984, 1988). The hospital is an institution and this affects the patient's behaviour too. She may recognise the 'rules of the game', eating to gain weight rapidly and temporarily so that discharge might be effected.

The nurse may be requested to administer various anorexia inventories and questionnaire to the patient as part of the assessment strategy. The more well known of these are Slade's 'Anorexia Behaviour Scale', Garner and Garfinkel's 'Eating Attitudes Test' and Goldberg *et al*'s 'Anoretic Attitudes Questionnaire'. (Garner and Garfinkel, 1979; Goldberg *et al*, 1980; Slade, 1973). While such tools may give a first impression of how the patient feels about body shape, eating, and adult sexuality, they are still self-reported devices and therefore open to manipulation by the educated and articulate patient. Rather more scientific have been the invitations for patients to estimate various body widths such as head, shoulder, waist, and hips, using a technique reported by Slade and Russell (Slade and Russell, 1973). This involves the projection of a thin horizontal line of light onto a white wall in a semi-darkened room (Crisp and Kalucy, 1974). The line is 2 cm deep and is varied in its length between 0 and 100 cm by the projector operator. The height of the line on the wall is arranged to correspond to the height of the patient's head, shoulders, waist etc. in turn. The patient is invited, by using standard requests to instruct the projectionist, to adjust the line width until it corresponds to his own perceived width of body contours. The line can then be measured and the assessment repeated later in therapy. Changes toward a more accurate appraisal of body contours is thought to be a better prognostic sign than simple increase in body weight.

Because future therapy will often enlist the help of the patient's family, the nurse must also begin to assess family attitudes, visiting and interactions with the patient (Hoffman, 1986; Minuchin et al, 1978). In earlier chapters we have already recognised that much of body ideal is influenced by significant others, friends and relations. If the patient is to establish more than a tenuous grip on a new ideal body image and weight, it may be necessary to discover what role the family may have had in causing or exacerbating the body image disturbance. Space precludes family dynamics being considered here, but it has been argued that compliant daughters of high achieving families may be especially prone to anorexia nervosa.

Above and beyond assessing the patient's body ideal, through self-perception and the interplay with other patients, it is also important to assess body reality and body presentation. An accurate appraisal soon after admission will enable nurses to measure the success of nursing care, especially when the patient may see them as adversaries rather than friends. Anorexic patients may be in hospital for several weeks or months at a time. Close contact with the patient may blind the nurse to the gradual changes that occur, possibly demoralising staff in the process.

Body reality assessment must include an accurate weighing of the patient removing any hidden books, or other heavy objects the patient may have hidden on the body. A minimum of clothing should be worn by the patient when being weighed, and the clothing recorded together with the weight. A menstrual record may be taken by either the doctor or the nurse. Other observations may include the state of the patient's dentition – is dental decay due to vomiting? – and the condition of the patient's skin (risk of pressure sores). If the patient is extremely malnourished the nurse must look for signs of dehydration and vitamin deficiencies too.

Many patients are voluntarily admitted to hospital and arrive in reasonably good nutritional condition. The nurse may notice a number of body presentation points, including the style of clothes chosen by the patient. Patients eager to deny the development of secondary sexual characteristics may wear loose track suits to hide the changing contours. Where weight loss has been very rapid the patient may still be dressed in much larger sizes of clothing, emphasising the picture of a person lost in apparel.

The way in which the patient orders his appearance during group sessions, at meals times and leisure activity may also give insights into body image problems. Patients may show few problems eating with others, although eating may be a misnomer as they attempt to leave the carbohydrate foods and concentrate on salad or fluids. A passive, even pliable position taken in group therapy may be typical, until the patient is gradually invited to confront the inaccuracy of the body perception.

Body reality interventions

Body reality interventions centre around protecting the patient from complications of malnutrition, such as hypokalaemia, or self-destructive acts, promoting the restoration of body weight to agreed target levels and assisting the patient with the activities of living that he is too weak to achieve independently. While the patient starts out with a fundamentally disordered body image, pressure sores, unpleasant smelling skin or mouth should not necessarily result. Weight loss and often hunger may feature in the patient's dreams, disturbing his sleep. Many anorexics wake early and require company at a time when all is quiet and the night has left them sore and uncomfortable.

Feeding regimes are central to care and always affected to some extent by the other therapies planned, for instance behavioural techniques learning to recognise maladaptive behaviour (Garner and Bemis, 1985). Typically, however, patients are first served their meals alone and all food served is carefully planned with the hospital dietician. The 'regime' element of feeding may be softened by the negotiation of a target weight to be gained. Such a contract is best formalised in writing and strictly adhered to by the nurse. Many patients will try to negotiate concessions. Target weights are calculated with reference to the patient's height, age, sex and length of illness. A typical daily calorie intake may approach 3000 to 3500 calories and may be modified as progress is made beyond the first target weight.

If the patient cannot consume the food orally, then feeding by nasogastric tube or parenterally may be necessary. Such an invasion of the patient's body space often threatens the nurse's bond of trust with the patient, but may be life-saving. Frequent observation of tubes and intravenous infusion lines is mandatory, as patients will often sabotage equipment to avoid the dreaded weight gain. In providing such food, it is worth remembering that the manner in which it is served may be of great import- ance. A patient may previously have deceived the nurse or thrown it in her face; but the problem must still be approached as one concerning eating not as an interpersonal contest. Patients who meet a firm but sensitive nurse often appreciate the clear expectations laid down. There are goals to be met, but as far as possible the patient's individuality is respected.

Having contracted into achieving a target weight it is important that the nurse evaluates progress. She should note not only food eaten and weight gained, but also the patient's expressed attitudes toward food and eating. Sudden conversion to a hearty appetite should be viewed with suspicion. A patient may race toward a target weight anticipating an early discharge from hospital. In these circumstances the weight gain is 'cosmetic', more a ploy of body presentation than a sustainable change in body reality. It is important to explain that weight gain is only part of the therapy, and that changes in body ideal are also required.

Because of a risk that patient's will try to falsify weight gain, smuggle laxatives or diuretics into hospital, or induce vomiting, other observations are made on the patient. It may be hard for a patient to surrender privacy, even if it is to a specially selected primary nurse who tries to establish a good working rapport. However, recalling Julie, the observation and re- cording of elimination may be as important as those of eating.

Body ideal interventions

The nurse's body ideal interventions are profoundly affected by the local psychiatrist's therapy and the nurse's commitment to, or distrust of the same. It seems crucial that, as a variety of health professionals will care for the patient, they should be able to agree a cogent protocol for the individual circumstances of each patient. If such is not clear, or apparently arbitrary changes are made to the protocol, then it is a professional responsibil- ity that the nurse seeks clarification so that care may be effective and unambiguous.

In order to establish just what perceptions of body reality the patient does have, the nurse should spend a considerable amount of time listening to the patient. Following group therapy the patient may start to reflect upon previous family arguments, personal beliefs or feelings about binge- ing food. It is not at all certain that the patient's body ideal has remained constant throughout the illness. Helping the patient to recall the chang- ing ideas of what he wanted to feel or look like may provide a degree of personal insight for the patient, and facilitate the psychiatrist's course of therapy.

As the patient regains weight, secondary sexual characteristics may re- appear, as will menstruation in female patients. This may precipitate a crisis so that the nurse has to once again encourage the patient to express the threat that this seems to pose. Reactions of other family members to such progress will also be noted by patient and nurse. Because family and patient may be emotionally entrenched in arguments over eating and body weight, it may be important for the nurse to interview parents and learn just what beliefs and anxieties they hold. It has already been argued that body ideal is not only learnt in part from others, but that our own body ideals are projected toward intimate others (see Chapter 1). Given this, the nature of family expectations may either hinder or help recovery. Involving family and patient together in a group discussion may enable taboo conflicts to be aired safely and completely (Russell et al, 1988).

In cognitive therapy, the patient is invited to consider perceptions of personal body shape as a maladaptive response to the changes of puberty and adolescence. The patient is asked to share openly thoughts about fatness, body shape and eating, and is then encouraged by the nurse to make connections between such disordered body ideal thoughts and his or her current dependent position (Garner and Bemis, 1985). The patient's beliefs about attractive body shapes are challenged. In some instances the care team may focus upon key words associated with such beliefs – 'must', 'should' or 'can't' relative to food or dieting are reconsidered. Each of these words are absolutes, often based upon a perfectionist standard which the patient manipulates to limit lifestyle. Substituting words like 'won't' for 'can't', remind patients that they own their own attitudes, constructive or otherwise. In time the word 'won't' may come to be applied to purgatives, vomiting and bingeing, rather than eating.

Body presentation interventions

Anorexic individuals (both AN and BN) have become trapped by their food rituals and obsessions, so it is important that body presentation activities remind them of other life domains. It should start to make them feel confident enough to enjoy experiencing their body changes, posture and movement. Later, practical steps concerning dress may help them to send the right interpersonal, gender signals, right for them as individuals, rather than right for a societal stereotype.

Occupational therapists play a fundamental and often undervalued role here (Allen et al, 1988). One group of activities will help to develop the skills necessary for independent living, such as cooking, cleaning, and shopping, and others are designed to encourage the patient to express feelings through art or dance. In settings far removed from the psychiatrist's couch, a patient will often reveal a great deal about current mood. Through practical activities others may demonstrate that they respect and value the patient.

In the early stages of therapy the patient may have come to depend heavily upon the nurse for approval, so the nurse's role in changing body presentation is very important. Choice of dress for discharge, discussion about body posture and what this means sexually to the adolescent may be areas where the nurse can support recovery. It would be naive to believe that all patients will emerge from hospital socially skilled. They may however feel more secure, for instance that it is fine for them to dress in ways that suit their taste and circumstances. Advocating this independence to parents may sometimes be necessary.

Conclusion

While the aetiology, development and treatment of eating disorders are still debated hotly by therapists, patients continue to suffer and in some instances, to die. It seems clear that a large number of young people will remain vulnerable, especially in a modern world that makes such great demands on body image. It also seems clear that both anorexia nervosa and bulimia nervosa involve a radical disruption of body image, centred upon the body ideal. This disordered ideal is no longer referenced against widely accepted social norms, but against perfectionist standards drawn from a confusing array of personal, family and societal sources. The struggle to meet the ascetic abnormal body ideal results in considerable damage to the patient's health (body reality) and a growing conviction that body presentation must neither be overtly sexual, nor conform to the demands of previously dominant others, perhaps a parent.

The alternative model of control, symbolised for the patient by control of eating and body weight, is a cruel deception. The triangular balance between body ideal, body reality and body presentation is soon disrupted as the patient becomes obsessed with weight control, or in the bulimic's case, bingeing and purging. It is the nurse's role to try and help the patient to re-establish more viable body ideals, to protect this body reality and to help in choosing a body presentation that offers control beyond that expressed through starving. To do this nurses must recognise the different therapies promoted, and share their perceptions of the problem honestly with others. To clarify the body image problem in our own minds may have already been an important aspect of that.

Review questions

1 What principle body image differences would you wish to highlight between anorexia nervosa and bulimia nervosa sufferers?
2 Why is it difficult to offer a definitive nursing body image intervention for anorexia patients under current circumstances?

3 What body reality problems result from eating disorders such as AN and BN?
4 What is the nurse's role with regard to helping to protect and support the patient's body reality? (Consider dietary contract.)
5 How and why might an anorexia nervosa patient try to deceive a nurse caring for him or her in hospital?
6 What pubertal events may be said to contribute to the onset of eating disorders?

Suggested exercises

Exercise 1
This first exercise is really a longer term one, necessitating a little preparation. Form a reading group and ask one or more members to read the following texts.

1. Dunbar M., *Catherine*, Penguin, Harmondsworth, 1987. (A story of an anorexic girl who began her illness to protect her mother from a depressed and at times violent father.)
2. Szmukler G.I., 'Anorexia Nervosa: A clinical view' In R.A. Boakes *et al* (eds) *Eating Habits*, Wiley, New York, 1985. (A family therapy perspective.)
3. Fairburn C.G., 'A Cognitive-Behavioural Approach to the Treatment of Bulimia', *Psychological Medicine*, 11, pp 707–11, 1981. (A rather clear account of diet and eating programmes from a cognitive – behavioural approach.)

As you read your relevant text, bear these two questions in mind.

1. What are the implications for the way in which the nurse should provide care?
2. Is the body image problem explicit, or subsumed under other considerations, such as family dynamics, complications of malnutrition or others?

Make notes on these points and then share your summaries with others in group discussion. You will probably notice how varied the approaches to care might have to be!
Suggested time scales are as follows:

(a) for reading the text and making notes, allow 1 to 2 weeks
(b) for presenting the summaries, allow 60 minutes
(c) for discussing care implications, allow 60 minutes

Exercise 2
Look through the nursing journals and select all the articles that have recently addressed care studies/histories of AN or BN patients, say, for the

last five years. Using some blank sheets, rule three columns and then label them with the following headings: 'body image problem' (reality, ideal or presentation), 'family or friends' reactions', and finally 'nurse reactions'. If your literature search draws a lot of promising material, share these articles with colleagues.

In a group seminar share the items you have found under the three headings described. Try to discover what the common denominators are. Consider in particular the role of the kin and the nurse – do they work together to assist the patient to recover? Finally, are the body image problems so varied that it is almost impossible to formulate useful guidelines on how the nurse might assess the patient?

Suggested time scales are as follows:

(a) for the literature search, this will depend upon the local library
(b) for writing notes, allow about one week
(c) for discussion, allow one to two hours depending upon group size

References

Allen M., Giles G. and Scott D., 'Occupational Therapy in the Rehabilitation of the Eating Disordered Patient' in Scott D. (ed.) *Anorexia and Bulimia Nervosa: Practical approaches*, Croom Helm, London, 1988.

American Psychiatric Association, *Diagnostic and Statistical Manual of Mental Disorders*' 3rd (revised) edn, American Psychiatric Association, Washington DC, 1987.

Biley F. and Savage S., 'Anorexia Nervosa', *Nursing Times*, 1 Aug, pp 227–330, 1984.

Biley F. and Savage S., 'The Role of the Nurse in Eating Disorders' in Scott D. (ed.) *Anorexia and Bulimia Nervosa: Practical approaches*, Croom Helm, London, 1988.

Bruch H., *Eating Disorders*, Basic Books, New York, 1973.

Cooper P. and Fairburn C., 'Binge Eating and Self Induced Vomiting in the Community: A preliminary study', *British Journal of Psychiatry*, 142, pp 139–44, 1983.

Crisp A. and Burns T. 'Primary Anorexia Nervosa in the Male and Female – A comparison of clinical features and prognosis, *International Journal of Eating Disorders*, 2, pp 5–10, 1983.

Crisp A. and Kalucy R., 'Aspects of the Perceptual Disorder in Anorexia Nervosa', *British Journal of Medical Psychology*, 47, pp 349–61, 1974.

Crisp A., Palmer R. and Kalucy R., 'How Common is Anorexia Nervosa? A Prevalance Study', *British Journal of Psychology*, 218, pp 549–54, 1976.

Duddle M., 'An Increase of Anorexia Nervosa in a University Population', *British Journal of Psychiatry*, 123, pp 711–12, 1973.

Edwards G., 'Anorexia and the Family' in Lawrence M. (ed.) *Fed Up and Hungry: Women, oppression and food*, Women's Press, London, 1987.

Fairburn C., *Binge Eating and Bulimia Nervosa*, Smith, Kline & French, London, 1982.

Garner D. and Bemis K., 'Cognitive Therapy For Anorexia Nervosa' in Garner D. and Garfinkel P. (eds), *Handbook of Psychotherapy for Anorexia and Bulimia*, Guildford Press, New York, 1985.

Garner D. and Garfinkel P., 'The Eating Attitudes Test: An index of symptoms of anorexia nervosa', *Psychological Medicine*, 9, pp 273–9, 1979.

Garner D. and Garfinkel P., *Anorexia Nervosa: A multidimensional perspective*, Brunner/Mazel, New York, 1982.

Goldberg, S.C., Halmi K.A., Eckert E.D., Caspar R.C., Davis J.M. and Roper M., 'Attitudinal Dimensions in Anorexia Nervosa', *Journal of Psychiatric Research*, 15, pp 239–51, 1980.

Herzog D., 'Are Anorexics and Bulimics Depressed?', *American Journal of Psychiatry*, 141, pp 21–4, 1984.

Herzog D.B., Norman D.K., Gordon C. and Pepose M., 'Sexual Conflict and Eating Disorders in 27 Males', *American Journal of Psychiatry*, 141, pp 989–90, 1984.

Hoffman L., 'Beyond Power and Control: Toward a "second order" family systems therapy', *Family Systems Medicine*, 3, pp 381–96, 1986.

Lawrence M., 'Education and Identity: The social origins of anorexia' in Lawrence M. (ed.) *Fed Up and Hungry: Women, oppression and food*, Women's Press, London, 1987.

Minuchin S., Rosman B. and Baker L., *Psychosomatic Families: Anorexia nervosa in context*, Harvard University Press, Cambridge, Mass, 1978.

Palmer R., *Anorexia Nervosa*, Penguin, Harmondsworth, 1980.

Pyle R.L., Mitchell J.E. and Eckert E.D., 'Bulimia: A report of 34 cases', *Journal of Clinical Psychiatry*, 42, pp 60–4, 1981.

Rodin J. *et al*, 'Women and Weight: A normative discontent' in Sonderegger T. (ed.) *Psychology & Gender: 1984 Nebraska Symposium on Motivation*, University of Nebraska Press, Lincoln, 1985.

Russell G., 'Anorexia Nervosa: Its identity as an illness and its treatment' in Price J. (ed.) *Modern Trends in Psychological Medicine*, Butterworth, London, 1970.

Scott D. (ed.), *Anorexia and Bulimia Nervosa: Practical approaches*, Croom Helm, London, 1988.

Slade P., 'A Short Anorexic Behaviour Scale', *British Journal of Psychiatry*, 122, pp 83–5, 1973.

Slade P. and Russell G., 'Awareness of Body Dimensions in Anorexia Nervosa: Cross-sectional and longitudinal studies', *Psychological Medicine*, 3, pp 188–99, 1973.

Striegel-Moore R., Silbesstein L. and Rodin J., 'Towards an Understanding of Risk Factors for Bulimia', *American Psychologist*, 41, pp 246–63, 1986.

Vanderseycken W. and Van den Broucke S., 'Anorexia Nervosa in Males', *Acta Psychiatrica Scandinavica*, 70, pp 447–54, 1984.

17 The terminally ill patient

Study of this chapter will enable you to:

1 Describe how body image remains an important concept beyond death.
2 Describe some typical body image rituals associated with last offices and death.
3 Outline the importance of each of the following in the body image of the dying patient and his family:
    (a) coping strategies (grief response)
    (b) social support networks
    (c) living–dying patterns (dying trajectories)
    (d) pain and associated symptoms
4 Suggest ways in which pain relief may also meet body image goals for the dying patient.
5 Appreciate points about the importance of the patient's religion or culture, when considering body image care.
6 Describe the important body presentation problems that arise during the terminal stages of an illness.

If could be said that there can be little body image interest when a patient dies. After all, the dead person can no longer possess a body image – body reality is ended and, with that, any sensible notion of body ideal or body presentation. The terminally ill patient may be thought to be in little better a position. The failure of body systems and the radical disruption of life functions may conspire to make body image concerns rather superfluous, an incidental concern beside more important matters. Such a first impression is understandable but nonetheless misguided. Matters of body image do affect both death and dying. They are important to the patient, relatives and nurses, and may later facilitate an understanding of what makes for a good, a dignified and a peaceful death.

If is important to make a clear distinction between death the dying, because the emphasis of body image care shifts once the patient has died. Death is the permanent cessation of all body functions. It is an event, which is sometimes difficult to affirm clinically, and a state – being dead (Martocchio, 1982). Dying, in contrast, is a process in life – a journey toward death. This apparently obvious distinction has several body image implications. It follows that in dying the patient still possesses a body image and may, to varying degrees invest time and energy into its maintenance. It has already been suggested that body image is a dynamic phenomenon (see Chapter 3), changing as individuals age, as circumstances demand. When we are dead however, the investment of time, love and care in personal body image is that of the relatives. Because we share a personal body image with intimate others, dressing to please a spouse, seeking approval, as patient or relative we later have a right to order an acceptable body image in death. This may be a fundamental need if grieving is to be successfully concluded.

When a relative dies, it is a widespread western custom to dress and prepare the body as though the person was merely sleeping. Female deceased may have hair arranged and makeup applied, dentures may be replaced in the mouth, nails clipped and perhaps coloured. The body may be dressed in fine clothes and a flower or favoured momento placed in the hands of the deceased. These are elaborate body presentation measures which have symbolic rather than practical meaning. The body (as presented) may then lie in state and be viewed by relatives – a last clear image before kin must rely upon photographs and memories.

The importance of such a last body presentation has been emphasised in the case of the stillborn or a perinatal death (Lovell et al, 1986; McMeeking, 1985). Where the parents have not been allowed to hold and see their stillborn child, grieving has subsequently been inhibited. This problem has been compounded if the child has not been allotted a personal, marked burial plot (an extension of body space?). It seems crucial that we are able to preserve in memory a last peaceful image of a loved one. If the child was deformed, for instance with anacephaly, then a body presentation adjustment, such as a dressing) may have assisted the mother to hold that memory – through a photograph if preferred.

It has been argued by Kubler Ross and others that western society is a death-denying society and that the elaborate ritual associated with death is a way of disowning our own inescapable mortality (Becker, 1973; Kubler Ross, 1969; Robbins, 1983). This would certainly seem to be true when recalling the body image emphasis upon youth, vigour, beauty and physical control. It should be pointed out though that some other cultures which are traditionally seen as more death affirming, also utilise body image rituals within the rite of passage (Neuberger, 1987).

Amongst orthodox Jews and devout Muslims the ordering of the dead body is closely dictated by scripture or custom (McGinn and Robbins, 1983). With the former patient, the nurse should only perform limited last offices. This consists of closing the eyes, bandaging the mouth shut and straightening the limbs to the side of the body. Similar constraints attend a Muslim's death. The relatives of the deceased will wash the body and dress it in specially prepared cloth. Burial takes place as promptly as possible after death and does not include a coffin which is only a part of western burial custom. A last postural consideration is that the body should be arranged facing the holy city of Mecca. This may place constraints on the use of room space, but it is of considerable religious importance to the deceased and the living relatives.

Other body presentation rituals attend the Indian and Asian religions. Both Hindus and Buddhists believe that the body is a temporary shell for a transmigrating soul. While this usually means that it is not the seat of the soul, it nevertheless follows that rebirth into another body may be affected by attitudes to the last home of the soul. Just as the Muslim's body is viewed as the personal temple or mosque of Islam, so the Buddhist deeply respects the body through which he or she has sought to understand suffering, the confusion of desires, pleasures and pains. Specific rituals may vary with sect and local advice should be sought. In Buddhism it may be traditional that the body is dressed in white, not black. With Hindus it is the husband who cuts the marriage thread that has been worn continually by his wife since their wedding day.

Body image and dying

Just as body image is profoundly affected by the process of ageing, so it is by dying. Body reality is affected by the failure of organs or body systems, so that control is lost altogether or only partially possible. The patient may become incontinent, lose control of mobility or speech and exhibit frightening signs associated with terminal illness, for instance haemorrhage or the 'death rattle' of laboured breathing. Owing to previous surgery or treatment body reality may not be complete – there may have been amputation, stoma formation and other wounds. These may be seen as symbols of failure and damage to body image which is now all in vain.

Body ideal will also have suffered. Cultural based ideals, western ideals at least, will be unrealistic. The patient may have spent a long time searching fruitlessly for adequate alternatives. That ideal of control over the body, which has so often been used to replace physical beauty or grace, will also have been threatened. Even so simple and human a phenomenon as crying may remind the patient that dignity is hard to preserve. Body space has usually been breached by a number of hospital measures. The patient may be catheterised, have a naso-gastric tube *in situ* or wound drains protruding. Dressings to pressure sores, two hourly turns and the noise of the ripple mattress or monitors all regularly invade the patient's space, either physical or emotional. Such measures are well intentioned –

an emphasis on physical comfort and freedom from pain is worth having. The measures do, however, still incur body image costs.

Body presentation is increasingly in the hands of the nurse and the patient's relatives. As the patient loses strength and consciousness, 'how they look' comes down to the dedication and values held by carers. Considerable body presentation challenges abound when the patient's tissues have been increasingly denied adequate oxygen and nutrients. One patient, a lady with well advanced fungating carcinoma of the breast illustrates the point. She was admitted to the hospice for terminal care with an unpleasant smelling wound and a chest infection. Expectorating purulent sputum was both difficult and painful. Limited fluid intake had left her with a dry and unpleasant tasting mouth. She had a pressure sore in her sacrum and her right heel. As she soon became incontinent of urine she was catheterised to improve her comfort and remove the smell that quickly permeated her clothing and bedding. Realistically, the nursing staff had to find a trade-off position, intervening to improve her comfort and appearance, the experience she had of her failing body. This intervention could not be so frequent and disruptive that it denied her rest, dignity and a degree of privacy with relatives and friends.

Just how body image is affected by the process of dying seems to depend upon the coping strategies and the social support network of the patient (Price, 1986) and what has often been called rather ineloquently 'the dying trajectory'. It is also affected by the age of the patient, though there is little research evidence of this in the area of child death (Lansdown, 1985). Kubler Ross has outlined six stages of response common in dying patients (see Table 17.1). It is important to remember that these are not static responses and that the patient may move backwards and forwards through them at different times. Recognising which of the coping strategies is currently being used may help us to understand the patient's response to altered body reality. In denying terminal illness the patient may have very optimistic body ideals and endeavour to present a well groomed and well dressed appearance. However, a depressed patient may show a lack of attention to body presentation, even though the patient is physically capable of doing so.

Table 17.1 The Kubler Ross stages of dying

Shock and disbelief
Denial
Anger
Bargaining
Depression
Acceptance

When patients can call upon an extended group of kin and friends (social support network), the efforts to maintain body presentation are both assisted and more frequently rewarded. Assisting the patient to groom himself or perform basic skin or oral care may be a useful contribution by the relative, and one that leaves the relative feeling less impotent in the face of impending death. We should not forget that it is emotionally taxing to hold vigil at the bedside, to try and affirm ideals of dignity and calm for the patient's sake. If the process of dying is an extended one, multiple close relatives may be able to offer a constant support. Once, in caring for a traveller (gypsy) woman, nurse colleagues were struck by the large number of relatives who took part in her care. It was important that she not only felt comfortable, but that she looked 'presentable' too. The confidence that this seemed to give her did appear to make her last hours dignified, even serene.

Just how well such patients and relatives can cope depends in part on how much time they are given to respond. Martocchio reports four patterns of 'living–dying'. The first, 'peaks and valleys' is typical of the relapses and rallies associated with cancer. At one moment the patient is building up his hopes, only to have these dashed by a new setback. The 'descending plateaus pattern' describes a general downward trend in independence, with periods where the patient 'holds his own'. This can be typical of some degenerative neurone conditions and often the patient is acutely aware of the deterioration.

What Martocchio describes as a 'downward slope' is more commonly encountered in the acute care setting. The body fails so rapidly that body ideals cannot be adjusted and the efforts to compensate through body presentation are overtaken by a pre-death coma. Patients who have been poisoned or suffered major trauma may experience this pattern.

The 'gradual slants' pattern of living–dying is characterised by a low ebb of life gradually fading toward death. Many of these patients suffer from organ failure, such as liver or kidney. Their final days may be spent on a life support machine with all the ethical dilemmas that this implies. While the patient may not consciously express or experience a body image, his relatives do. They become distressed at his dependence upon pumps and tubes and the unpredictability of the outcome (Martocchio, 1982).

Even after death, body image concerns may press in upon the relatives. Surgeons and nurses may wish to offer relatives the opportunity to consider organ donation. In this instance the relatives may feel consoled that others have benefited from their loved one's death, but they must still be prepared to sanction the invasion of his body so that organs can be removed. This may not be at all easy.

It would seem reasonable to expect that the more gradual the decay in the life force, the more easily the patient and relatives might come to terms with alterations in body image. By and large this is probably true, especially if the care team provide empathetic support. Still, there are a number of experiences associated with dying that may disrupt both patient comfort and body image. Reference has already been made in Chapter 14 to the importance of oral hygiene and hair care. These matters concern the dying patient too. The remainer of this chapter will concentrate on the problem of pain. While pain is not invariably present during terminal illness, it is feared and will disrupt body image considerably. The patient perceives his body negatively when it causes him chronic discomfort. The extinction of such pain should be a prime nursing goal in caring for the terminally ill.

Pain – a body image challenge

For the purposes of this chapter, pain will be defined as an unpleasant experience, associated with major or minor changes in body reality, or the environment around body reality. It is a uniquely personal experience, mediated by the individual's socialisation and culture, and by his personality (Zbrowski, 1952). It is therefore largely what the patient says it is (McCaffery, 1979). In addition to physical pain, patient and relatives may face emotional or spiritual pain, which may in turn undermine the patient's self-image. Pain may be caused by failing body organs, the growth of tumours, trauma or the complications that accompany immobility (Norton et al, 1975; Waterlow, 1985). It is likely to be exacerbated by patient anxiety and the removal of the patient to strange new settings. When the pain is episodic or chronic he begins not to trust his body, which now ambushes him unexpectedly or leaves him with constant, meaningless aches. The ideal of body under control can never be contemplated when the patient is in constant pain. The way he moves, communicates, dresses, or positions himself may be dictated by that pain.

The apparently simple things, such as dressing, sitting comfortably, and taking a short walk, become major goals for many terminally ill patients. Such humble body presentation goals are made possible when the nurse actively assesses the pain and plans care that is based upon a philosophy that says all patients have a right to comfort.

A first point concerning pain in terminal illness, is that it is often multifocal and does not necessarily arise because of the patient's primary tumour or injury. A dehydrated patient, with mouth ulcers and a pressure sore on the left buttock suffers pain as a result of all these causes.

The second point is, that if the pain origins are multi-factorial, then so should be the nurse's responses. While an opiate drug may reduce the general experience of pain, it may not resolve the constipation that has contributed toward it! It is not always necessary to rush to the most sophisticated pharmacological answer, but one may provide simpler care measures in conjunction with medication. This means that the nurse must invest time

and energy in this care, and should not presume that it is a poor investment of limited value because the patient is soon to die. The giving of
care in the form of oral hygiene and pressure area relief, is a therapeutic
act beyond the physical activity. The nurse is saying to the patient, 'you are
important and loved, I must ensure that you can be comfortable'.

A third point is, that few patients' body ideals include a 'drugged up to
the eyeballs' stupor. The patient and his relatives want to achieve pain
relief but still to be able to communicate. Body presentation is not enhanced when the patient is so sedated that the response to visitors is
negligible. An excessively sedated patient may sense his unpleasant appearance, but be powerless to do anything about it. Relatives are upset
by a heavily sedated patient, unless this is the only alternative to prolonged
and agonising pain.

Having assessed the patient's pain and its likely origins, the nurse can
begin to relieve the more accessible problems. Norton and Waterlow have
both pointed out how we can anticipate pressure sore risks (Norton et al,
1975; Waterlow, 1985). Relieving that pressure through the use of air flow
or ripple mattresses is the next step. While conventional turning of the
patient has a lot to commend it, this does disrupt the patient's sleep and
any comfortable position found. Therefore, pressure relief devices should
be used to supplement such turns, reserving major disruption for times
when the skin is to be inspected, washed and a new comfortable position
established. Pressure sores, once formed, are easily infected and enlarged,
limiting the posture that the patient can comfortably adopt. Their prevention or limitation is a major nursing goal.

If the patient is catheterised, or has an intravenous infusion in situ, both
catheter and cannula should be checked for sources of discomfort. While
silastic catheters are expensive, they do limit the number of repeat cathe-
terisations necessary during the patient's final months (McGilly and Egan,
1983). For male patients a uridom may be more suitable as it is an easily
removed intrusion into body space. The nurse must assess the patient's
state of fluid balance. Is urine output sufficient to inhibit infection, the
formation of catheter tip calculi? It is important to check that the catheter
is properly secured and the drainage bag adequately supported. Look too
for any signs of a catheter bypass leak – incontinence multiplies ten fold
any perineal discomfort.

While the patient may prove to be anorexic, the successful ingestion of
fluids, trace elements such as zinc, and protein will have a good effect upon
patient well-being. Malnutrition delays wound healing, enhances the risk
of pressure sores and increases the incidence of complications such as
constipation. All of these are associated with pain and a negative body
image.

Other control measures are less concerned with removing the origins of
pain. Relaxation exercises come in various forms but all tend to contrast

the poor body experiences with more pleasurable ones (Sweeney, 1978). The patient is taught progressively how to tense and then release different muscle groups. He is encouraged to note the feelings of warmth and heaviness after muscle tension. Distraction therapy redirects the patient's attention to other external or body matters. Distraction may take the form of rhythmic breathing, or a concentration upon something else, perhaps fundamental to body presentation such as clothing. Naish used a clothes analogy to illustrate the principles of distraction. It was pointed out that if a strap or belt caused us intense discomfort, we would tend to focus our attention upon it (Naish, 1975). The more we concentrate upon the irritant, the more annoying it seems. By implication, if that irritant is a body one, concentration upon another aspect, like clothing, should enable the patient to limit the irritant's impact upon him.

With reference to the use of analgesics, the nurse should employ this principle – control pain, do not chase it. If a patient commences on a four to six hourly prn (i.e. if required) regime he experiences periods when the analgesia no longer supports a comfortable state. He watches and waits for the next dose. The body is once more an unpredictable and unpleasant home to be in. It is better instead to establish a regular analgesia regime, with a reserve, complementary drug for painful procedures or specific problems. Oral analgesia is preferred while drug absorption through this route remains high.

In many instances, non-narcotic agents, including anti-inflammatory drugs, provide adequate pain relief (Goodinson, 1986). Whichever agent is prescribed, its primary and side effects must be carefully monitored. The London Hospital Pain Observation Chart offers a useful format for such evaluation (Nursing, 1986). Inviting the patient to record his experience of pain relief measures enables an accurate assessment to be made. The patient's involvement in this offers some hope of personal influence over a failing body.

Conclusion

Even in dying and death, body image is important. Investments in body presentation extend beyond the grave, in family memories. Following a period when pain may have been a daunting enemy, relatives like to remember their loved one with an expression of peace on his face. In dying the patient surrenders the last vestiges of the body ideals he cherished in youth and early adulthood. The opportunities to express body presentation in an attractive way may have been limited, and reliant upon the help of others. There are many ways to die and we should all like to feel that it was with dignity, serenity and support. The self-image is reliant upon body image – that which the patient has learnt about body function and appearance.

The nurse who respects the body image concerns of the patient and his kin, contributes to a peaceful end. Contrary to some opinion, the body image rituals of death are a constructive way of dealing with loss. Relieving pain, helping the patient with hygiene and simple body care beforehand is a part of that respect. Nurses should invest in the images of dignified death – the traveller lady who died in hospital had been right.

Review questions

1 How are body presentation issues important to relatives during last offices and after the death of their loved one?
2 Why do you think coping strategies, such as those described in Kubler Ross's grief reaction, are important in assessing body image needs?
3 Why is pain such an important challenge to the dying patient's body image?
4 Patient die under different circumstances and in different settings. How is body image affected when the patient dies:
   (a) in the intensive care department?
   (b) with a small social support network?
   (c) after a sudden trauma (downward slope)?
5 How does a patient's religious or cultural background affect body image while he is dying?
6 List the living–dying patterns (Martocchio) which Chapter 17 argues are important to the body image.
7 Which non-analgesia care measures might be utilised to provide comfort and limit alterations to body image?

Suggested exercise

Complete a literature search on one of the following themes:

1. Parental grieving/response to death of a child for instance stillborn or cot death.
2. Grief responses associated with the elderly widow.
3. Attitudes of next of kin after donation of body organs.

Obtain a cross-section of available literature and prepare cards with the following questions, on which you will note ideas from your reading.

1. What evidence did you find of the importance of body image matters (for example, body presentation–preserved memories)?

2. Did there seem to be any relationship between active body image rituals while the patient was dying, or last offices, and the relative's ability to grieve adequately?
3. Did the manner of dying, or organ donation, affect the image which the relative held in his or her memory?

Record the full details of resources used. File this information and apply it to a care study or project as offered within your course.

References

Becker E., *The Denial of Death*, The Free Press, Riverside, NJ, 1973.

Goodinson S., 'Pain Relief: Pharmacological interventions', *Nursing: Add on Journal of Clinical Nursing*, 3(11), pp 415–19, 421–3, 1986.

Kubler Ross E., *On Death and Dying*, Macmillan Publishing Co, New York, 1969.

Lansdown R., 'Coping With Child Death: A child's view', *Nursing: Add on Journal of Clinical Nursing*, 2(43), pp 1264–6, 1985.

Lovell H. *et al*, 'Mothers' Reactions to a Perinatal Death', *Nursing Times*, 82(46), pp 40–2, 1986.

Martocchio B., *Living While Dying*, Robert J. Brady Co., Bowie, Md, 1982.

McCaffery M., *Nursing the Patient in Pain*, Harper & Row, London, 1979.

McGilly H. and Egan C., 'Nursing Aims and Giving Care 1' in Robbins J. (ed.) *Caring for the Dying Patient and the Family*. Harper & Row, London, 1983.

McGinn P. and Robbins J., 'Religious Beliefs and Practices' in Robbins J. (ed.) *Caring for the Dying Patient and the Family*, pp 174–80, Harper & Row, London, 1983.

McMeeking A., 'Is Death Before Birth a Non-Event?', *Nursing: Add on Journal of Clinical Nursing*, 2(43), pp 1267–9, 1985.

Naish J., 'Discomfort After Food', *Nursing Times*, 71, pp 2060–2, 1975.

Neuberger J., *Caring for Dying People of Different Faiths*, The Lisa Sainsbury Foundation Series, 1987.

Norton D. *et al*, *An Investigation of Geriatric Nursing Problems in Hospital*, Churchill Livingstone, Edinburgh, 1975.

Nursing, 'Use of the London Hospital Pain Observation Chart', *Nursing: Add on Journal of Clinical Nursing*, 3(11), pp 415–19, 421–3, 1986.

Price B., 'Peacefully At Home', *Nursing Times*, 82(1), pp 22–4, 1986.

Robbins J., 'Attitudes to Death and Dying' in Robbins J. (ed.) *Caring for the Dying Patient and the Family*, pp 1–8, Harper & Row, London, 1983.

Sweeney S., 'Relaxation' in Carlson C. and Blackwell B. (eds), *Behavioural Concepts and Nursing Intervention*, pp 240–52, Lippincott, Philadelphia, 1978.

Waterlow J., 'A Risk Assessment Card', *Nursing Times*, 81(48), pp 49, 51, 55, 1985.

Zbrowski M., 'Cultural Components in Responses to Pain', *Journal of Social Issues*, 8, pp 16–30, 1952.

Unit 5
Sexuality and body image

Human beings are sexual beings. That is, they have sexual characteristics which define them as either masculine or feminine (sexual gender), and an internal sense of a 'sexual identity'. This sexual identity evolves throughout life and will enable each person to formulate opinions, orientations and attitudes towards his or her own gender and that of others. Part of sexual identity relies upon personal body experiences and upon body image. When we formulate body ideal, this will include notions of how we should look sexually. It will include norms of dress, grooming, movement and function which serve the need to act as sexual beings. Body ideal must take account of body reality. Does the individual live in a body which includes clear and unambiguous gender organs? Is body reality able to support a body presentation which makes the individual feel masculine, feminine, sexy or sensual?

Unit 5 looks at altered body image circumstances which threaten sexual identity. These may have been brought about as a result of treatment for cancer, or through a variety of other measures designed to sustain health. In some cases, surgery will be used to adjust body reality so that gender and sexual identity match more closely (see Chapter 21). What is common to all such patients, is the need to re-establish a satisfactory body image, so that their sexuality is not impaired. In helping the patient to do this, the nurse faces one of her greatest body image care challenges.

18 Body image – the hysterectomy challenge

Study of this chapter will enable you to:

1 Discuss briefly the importance of body image as a part of human sexuality.
2 Discuss why the uterus and associated reproductive organs are invested with so many emotions, fears and aspirations.
3 Outline the physiological changes that may occur following hysterectomy.
4 Describe the three groups of variables (Wassner) that will determine what effect hysterectomy has upon a woman's body image.
5 List simple body reality interventions which will serve to improve the patient's health and her ability to sustain a satisfactory body image.
6 Describe how the nurse may help the patient to develop a new body ideal, and one that still includes sexual activity should she so wish.
7 Argue why the body image care of hysterectomy patients should take into account their loved ones, and should start prior to hospital admission.
8 Discuss why addressing personal fears about intimate matters may prove an important aspect of supporting the patient's body presentation.

Despite the heartfelt pleas of modern and informed feminist writers, female sexuality has largely been defined by fertility, the coital act and the physical attributes that are associated with 'having sex' (Webb, 1987). Much less has been said about the wider aspects of female sexuality – the characteristics, expressions and priorities that are specifically associated with being a woman (Lion, 1982). If we talk about expressing sexuality most people will think directly of the sexual act or acts, and this may be

223

seen to be an entirely inappropriate concern for a woman who is ill or who has undergone surgery (Webb, 1983a,b; Webb, 1985a,b). These rather limited perspectives have involved, and had a profound effect upon, women's body image. Indeed, the expression of human sexuality and body image are virtually inseparable, both in health and illness (McKenzie, 1988).

Psychoanalytic theory apart, it seems clear that the changes of the menarche and puberty in general accelerate a woman's concern with her reproductive organs and associated fertility. The function of the female reproductive system causes a mixture of pride and misplaced shame. The adolescent finds herself becoming an adult woman, with potential for all the female reproductive miracles that science can explain. Equally however this same system provides the monthly menstrual period, the 'curse' that will plague many women, more or less regularly, until the menopause. Menstruation has been seen as dirty and unpleasant. In some cultures it has even led to women's social freedoms being limited. A menstruating woman may be precluded from preparing food, social engagements and religious rituals.

In many ways the female reproductive organs make it difficult to maintain a stable, healthy body image. Both menarche and menopause have a profound effect upon reality. Changes in body shape, stature and function cause women to reconsider their body ideal, often to adjust body presentation. Many fears and fantasies accompany the notion of female fertility and menstruation (Glover, 1985). 'Old wives tales' and folklore offer a rich source of mystique about associated powers (witchcraft or otherwise), and this too may affect the woman's sense of body ideal. Pregnancy brings about radical alterations in body image, forcing the purchase of maternity clothes and the acceptance of a body shape which will probably extend into her previous normal body space. The pregnant woman is bombarded with social interest in 'her condition', and is reminded of changed contours (body presentation) every time she takes a seat on bus or train (Berry, 1983; Hughes, 1984; Strang and Sullivan, 1985).

Pregnancy is just one stage of a woman's emotional investment in reproductive function. Even before conception girls are taught to view their reproductive organs as special, something that must be preserved and protected in an insensitive world. These are the organs that permit pregnancy and by implication, make the woman of reproductive value to society. Changing gender expectations, the use of contraceptive devices and sterilisation operations have modified this stance, but it remains important in many quarters. The reproductive organs may be valued because of motherhood potential, even if she is not inclined to take up this option. In addition they are organs associated with erogenous zones and therefore a source of possible pleasure (Masserman, 1966).

Hysterectomy as altered body image

There are many surgical and other traumas to the female reproductive system which may bring about an altered body image. Still, because of the symbolic value of the uterus and the ovaries, their complete or partial removal offers the best example of body image trauma. Wassner has pointed out several key variables that determine the impact of surgery upon the patient's body image (Wassner, 1982). Firstly, variables concerning the patient herself such as age, personality, beliefs, expectations, the symbolic or other significance of her uterus. As hysterectomy operations involve differing degrees of tissue loss, for different reasons this will be important (see Table 18.1). The impact of operation upon a woman who has passed through her menopause, has proudly raised three children and who is supported by a caring family may be less than for a woman with a less developed or satisfying reproductive history. Alternatively, the loss of the uterus just when it has ceased to produce the monthly period, may seem a sad irony. It is important that we learn as tactfully and as thoroughly as we can, what meaning the reproductive organs have for the individual patient. While the skills of sexual history taking are not well developed in nurses, some insight into her feelings is essential if care is to be effective (Webb, 1985b). We cannot always assume that the loss of the uterus is a grievous one. Years of pain and poorly controlled menstrual periods may have forced the patient to hold a very different perspective. The hysterectomy may represent the starting point for a new freedom and a more positive body image.

Wassner's second variable concerns the preparation of patient and relatives for the changes that will result from the operation. The importance of supportive, significant others is reiterated, as is the patient education promoted elsewhere in this book. Part of this preparation must include education about sexual life beyond surgery. It must include direct reference to any hormonal changes anticipated (post-oophorectomy) and how these may be modified by hormone replacement therapy. Preparation of the patient for changes in body image implies that the nurse is familiar with the different types of operation. It also means that she must be prepared to establish a close and trusting relationship which facilitates a full body image assessment (see Chapter 7).

The third Wassner variable is the health team's understanding of body image matters. Despite the appearance of 'altered body image' as a nursing diagnosis in records, the nurse's knowledge about this topic is often very limited. The amount of insight shown by physicians and other paramedical staff is likely to be less still. This text argues for the use of a body image model in planning care and will be discussed next.

Table 18.1 Hysterectomy operations – indications and possible implications

Operation	Indications	Extent of surgery	Possible implications
Total hysterectomy	Fibroids, uterine trauma, tumours	Complete removal of uterus, and cervix. May involve the loss of upper third vagina	Fallopian tubes/ovaries left intact, hormonal disruption slight or non-existent. Potential dyspareunia
Hysterectomy/salpingo-oophorectomy	Malignant tumours, ovarian/tubal disease (including malignant ovarian cysts)	Removal of uterus, fallopian tubes and ovaries	If both ovaries removed, female hormone production disrupted and onset of menopause iminent. Consideration of hormonal replacement therapy
Wertheim's hysterectomy	Carcinoma (advanced) of the cervix	Total excision of uterus, bilateral salpingo-oophorectomy, upper third vagina and pelvic lymph glands	Major surgery involving hormone disruption and shortening of the vagina (potential dyspareunia). Temporary atonia of bladder and abdominal distension. Risk of thrombophlebitis in pelvic or leg blood vessels
Total pelvic exenteration	Malignant tumours (advanced) of the cervix or other reproductive structures	Excision of all pelvic reproductive organs, removal of pelvic lymph nodes, internal iliac vessels, pelvic peritoneum, levator muscles and perineum. Excision of rectum and distal sigmoid colon, urinary bladder and lower third ureters	Major surgical shock. Hormonal disruption, early onset of menopause in younger woman (unless replacement therapy started). Sigmoid colostomy. Ileal conduit (urostomy)

Body reality interventions

Depending upon the patient's pre-operational health, for instance is she fighting cancer, and her social circumstances, she should be admitted to the ward at least 48 hours prior to surgery. This will allow her to acclimatise to the ward, its staff and her fellow patients. It will also enable the nurses to assess her physical condition, particularly her nutritional state, fluid balance, pain experiences and menstrual history. Because of menorrhagia, the nature of surgery (extensive excision of tissue) and possible malnutrition, it may be discovered that anaemia is a problem. The anaemic patient feels tired and lethargic, the skin looks pale, and in extreme cases will be immobile. Looking in the mirror the patient appears ill as well as feeling it. Efforts to arrange makeup or hair may simply be too much and this can be distressing as she contemplates surgery. A blood transfusion is often commenced pre-operatively to relieve this problem. The sense of improved well being that follows may benefit the patient both because she now has the energy to self-care and because she can anticipate a more active post-operative recovery.

Because the patient may well be immobilised short term post-operatively, and have a urinary catheter and drains *in situ*, it is important to provide her with a high protein, high fibre diet. A fluid balance record should be kept and the patient encouraged to consume 2 to 3 litres of favoured non-alcoholic fluids each day. The complications of immobility, such as pressure sores, constipation, and urine retention, are all very real risks post-operatively, and likely to limit the return of a healthy body image just as much as physical well being.

Explaining the practical procedures and equipment associated with surgery also starts pre-operatively. Where possible, the patient is introduced to a patient who has already undergone surgery and who is successfully adapting to changes in body image. Hygiene of the perineal region and appropriate aseptic techniques are explained with regard to avoiding infection. If the surgery is accompanied by other adjuvent treatment, such as cytotoxic chemotherapy, then the effects of these must also be discussed.

While it can be said that most women show a considerable interest in their uterus, the nurse should not assume that they necessarily understand the physiology of the female reproductive system. This may be an important point to remember, for it is only through an understanding of normal reproductive function that the patient understands what results from surgery. The fear of hormonal changes and premature menopause is a case in point. Many patients will not have anticipated that preservation of the ovaries permits normal hormonal production, even if no periods follow. They will often have 'known someone' who went 'through the change' as the result of a more extensive operation. The distinction between operative effects becomes clear when she understands which organs are responsible for what function. A range of irrational mythical beliefs may have to be dispelled, if physical recovery is to be unhindered (Clarke, 1975).

Supporting body ideal

No patient cherishes a body that is painful, losing blood or serous fluid, and which has two or more drains protruding from it. While the appeal of fertility (evidenced by child-bearing) will depend upon the patient's circumstances, few women savour the loss of body tissues which may or may not affect their femininity and their appeal to partners. Many patients have reported a sense of hollowness, a feeling that major working parts of their body have been wrenched from their pelvis. One woman likened it to the bottom of a car. You could not 'underseal' the body – the space left behind would always leave a worry that other organs might displace or come into contact with the last vestiges of tumorous tissue. When these patients have been invited to draw full scale the size of their uterus or uterus and associated ovaries, they have tended to grossly overestimate their size. More realistic drawings, and an explanation of the elastic capacity of the uterus in pregnancy, have often helped these patients to put the challenge to body ideal in perspective.

Establishing a new and confident body ideal depends upon the nurse helping the patient to establish new criteria of self-worth. Patently, if the patient has previously been sterilised, or if a couple are currently practising determined contraception, the child-bearing role of the uterus is less apparent. In this instance the patient's body ideal may especially emphasise the coital role of the reproductive tract. It should be firmly pointed out that hysterectomy need not be an end to pleasurable coital experiences. While some patients may need vaginal dilatation to reduce dyspareunia (painful intercourse), the facility for orgasm is not necessarily physically impaired. Even amongst patients undergoing total pelvic exenteration, pleasurable coitus may be achieved within weeks or months of surgery (Lamont et al, 1978).

What seems to be critical in establishing such a satisfactory post-operative body ideal is the support of a partner and appropriate pre-operative sexual counselling. Such counselling should be undertaken with both partners present and should preferably begin before the patient's admission to hospital. Sharing intimate fears about the body and its sexual function is probably easiest while on home territory. Being assertive, asking sensible questions, may be more difficult in a clinic with a doctor or nurse dressed in their respective uniforms.

A good starting point is often the 'debunking' of the terms sexuality, sex and gender. The partners should be helped to understand that sexuality and sexual expression are not purely coital/genital in nature. Sexuality extends beyond reproductive role and a partner's ability to achieve orgasm. If it is explained that the loss of the uterus does not mean the loss of even coital function, and that this in any case is only a part of sexuality, then the operation may seem more manageable. This counselling need not involve medical staff trampling over previously held body ideals and beliefs. Many patients will have grown up in cultures that emphasised the coital definition of sexuality. It is good counselling technique to start by listening attentively to the patient's views and beliefs. The wider definition of sexuality may then be introduced as an alternative point of view.

Early counselling sessions will also permit the patient to anticipate her own feelings and the reactions of relatives post-operatively. The nurse may point out that post-operative mood changes are associated as much with the physiological effects of surgery, for example steroid and adrenaline production, and the move into a strange environment, as the loss of the uterus *per se*. When patients anticipate a trauma, learn as much as possible about the best ways to cope with it physically, they often make a more effective post-operative recovery (Hayward, 1975). Knowing that 'post-operative blues' are not solely to do with grieving for lost reproductive function, often helps.

Reviewing just what the new body ideal can be like will usually encourage everyone. It can still be an ideal that includes active coital function, a feminine appearance, perhaps with the aid of hormone replacements, and all the other new found freedoms that the operation may represent. Weight gain post-operatively can be controlled – it is in any case precipitated by anxiety and 'comfort eating'. If the patient's partner is able to grasp these essentials and to anticipate a fruitful ongoing caring relationship, anxiety is reduced and the need to eat so much is removed (Fisher and Levin, 1983).

Body presentation – revealing the hidden?

In some respects, hysterectomy is the classic hidden altered body image problem. Provided that wound care has been properly delivered and hormone or other therapy provided, many patients will show no outward body change. Only in the case of premature menopause or total pelvic exenteration does an open altered body image challenge really arise. Despite this, most women will experience some body presentation worries. This chapter deals with just two, one very intimate, the second much more public.

The intimate problem concerns the patient's and her partner's fears about resuming coitus. Many women wonder how penetration will feel and how they will control expressions of discomfort. Both partners may be seeking to make coitus a success once more, eager not to dampen, enthusiasm with expressions of pain or comments about being disappointed. Some patients wonder where the ejaculate can now go; will it cause internal damage? Many men are fearful that they may injure their partner. It is important to resolve this presentation problem by a combination of strategies. The first, pre-operatively, is to talk frankly about future coitus, to anticipate the risk that at first it may be a little uncomfortable. An agreement to proceed with coitus firmly, but sensitively, and that it will not immediately be wonderful, is a useful first step. Advice on when to recommence coitus must depend upon the nature of surgery and the patient's response to previous counselling and support. Different operations will have varying impacts upon the vagina. A second strategy is the use of vaginal dilatation. Couples who have experienced painful coitus in the past may gain confidence from knowing that the nurse has helped the patient to regularly dilate the vagina. Dilatation is achieved using a suitable guage dilator and may also involve the use of a lubricating gel (subject to medical advice).

The third recommended strategy refers back to the importance of patient education. It should be explained just what does happen to sperm, lubricating fluids and the vagina during intercourse. Reference to a clear line diagram is often a great help. This will enable the patient to see that the vagina is now sutured in a pouch like fashion, and despite this, there are adequate elastic tissues within the vaginal wall to permit penile penetration. Most of the ejaculate is contained within the pouch and then eventually lost back to the external environment. Given adequate postoperative healing time, the vaginal suture line should withstand normal coital activity. These are admittedly very practical and intimate ideas to share. Experience with worried post-vasectomy patients has demonstrated that the practical and the intimate often must be addressed.

The more public worry concerns the way the patient may adopt what may be described as 'symbols of mourning' post-operation. As has been seen in earlier chapters, a patient's clothing, makeup, and grooming, may indicate a lot about feelings about the body. Amongst some patients posthysterectomy, the choice of clothing can become a marked display of grief. A previously outgoing confident young woman, who had a total hysterectomy illustrates the point. Pre-operatively this woman dressed fashionably and was obviously conscious of a need to 'look her best' at visiting times. Post-operatively she confined herself to a dressing gown until her last two days on the ward. It was noticed that she had a number of arguments with her husband when he visited. She did not share the nature of these disagreements with the nurses, even when they enquired if she was unhappy. On her penultimate last morning on the ward she dressed in a heavy jumper and long tweed skirt that her husband had brought in the evening before. The cloth of the skirt looked rather worn and there were buttons missing. The clothes were a drab brown or green and quite unlike the style of dress which the nurses had seen her adopt previously. She did however continue to pay close attention to her grooming, and applied a sparing amount of makeup to her face. For this patient, the switch to drab, rather uncharacteristic clothes was an expression of mourning. She did not want to highlight her sexuality, or to offer a confident outward appearance to society. Her husband confided his regret to the ward sister, explaining that he had tried to persuade his wife to stick to her usual confident image. The nurses had not spotted the change quickly enough and now her imminent discharge from hospital limited what they could realistically do to help patient or husband.

It is not suggested that the patient should have been more actively encouraged to have dressed brightly. Neither is it proposed that nurses can in a limited span of time, move a patient through all stages of grieving. However nursing action (or in this case inaction) must always be referenced against assessment of the patient's and relative's responses. The nurse must be aware of the patient's coping strategies, the pre-operative counselling and its success or otherwise. The new body presentation that this patient chose may have been a useful coping strategy until new body ideals were in place. Unfortunately, her husband had not been helped to understand this and perhaps she was not fully aware of it either! More awareness all round might have helped the nurses to anticipate the problems the couple might face post-discharge. Further counselling or support may then have been suggested.

Conclusion

There are considerable limitations upon the nurse's opportunity to help the hysterectomy patient with body image problems. Hospital stay may be short, the patient and her partner (if she has one) may feel inhibited about talking over body image concerns. Despite these limitations it seems clear that there is a need for body image care and this must involve the nurse much more in patient education, counselling and practical demonstration. Not all nurses are as yet happy with these roles. This is a deficit that should be addressed now, for if it is not, it is hard to imagine other health professionals dealing with problems which could in the patient's future lead to misery, feelings of guilt, shame and even to an eventual divorce.

Review questions

1 To what extent do you think feminism has helped us to reappraise the term sexuality? (Is this important for nurses?).

2 Pregnancy and hysterectomy both occasion drastic change for the woman's body image. How would you compare and contrast these changes?

3 What are Wassner's three sets of variables affecting a patient's response to body image trauma?

4 Hysterectomy may be described as a hidden altered body image. Does this make matters any easier for a patient?

5 What are the arguments for starting counselling and patient education well in advance of the patient's operation?

6 How does anaemia contribute to a more negative body image?

7 In most instances the patient's closest relative will be her husband. How does the relative being a man facilitate or inhibit the nurse from giving effective body image care?

8 Chapter 18 describes how one woman's post-operative coping strategies were shown through her change in dress. Why do you think nurses might not pick up such useful messages post-operatively?

Suggested exercises

In this exercise you are invited to consider the body image implications of a different violation of the female reproductive system – rape. Rape, rather like hysterectomy, leaves the victim with considerable psychological scars which may take years to heal (if they ever heal at all). Unlike hysterectomy there are no clear benefits involved in the trauma, it is totally untherapeutic.

Complete a literature search on the psychological and body image effects of rape using two distinctly different sources:

1. The nursing press (journals)
2. The newspaper or magazine press

Collect your points on cards, or as cuttings, remembering to record the full details of your sources. Then in group discussion try to answer the following questions:

1. With reference to body reality, body ideal and body presentation what are the effects of rape upon the victim and upon other women?
2. How would you contrast the effects of hysterectomy and rape?
3. How are the psychological/body image effects of rape described in the two different types of press? Do any differences matter?

Suggested time allocation

There is a considerable literature on rape and its effects, so group members may need to confine themselves strictly to subject matter and try to avoid lengthy discussion on the circumstances of the rape and sentencing policy.

For the group literature search, allow 2 to 4 weeks. Nursing journal material is easier to trace, the newspaper material may take a little longer. Try a visit to the local newspaper offices.

For the group discussion, allow 2 hours. This subject usually engenders considerable comment and debate. You will need time to explore this, and to resolve members' major differences of opinion.

References

Berry K., 'The Body Image of a Primagravida Following Cesarian Delivery', *Issues in Health Care of Women*, 6, pp 367–76, 1983.

Clarke M., 'Psycho-social Problems of Patients Following Radical Cancer Surgery' in Proceedings Nursing Mirror/Royal Marsden Hospital International Conference, *Cancer Nursing*, London, 1975.

Fisher S. and Levin D., 'The Sexual Knowledge and Attitudes of Professional Nurses Caring for Oncology Patients', *Cancer Nursing*, 6, pp 55–61, 1983.

Glover J., *Human Sexuality in Nursing Care*, Croom Helm, London, 1985.

Hayward J., *Information: A prescription against pain*, Royal College of Nursing, London, 1975.

Hughes R., 'Satisfaction with One's Body and Success in Breastfeeding', *Issues in Comprehensive Pediatric Nursing*, 7, pp 141–53, 1984.

Lamont J.A., De Petrillo A.D., Sargeant E.J., 'Psychosexual Rehabilitation and Exenteration Surgery', *Gynaecologic Oncology*, 6, pp 236–42, 1978.

Lion E.M., *Human Sexuality in Nursing Process*, John Wiley, New York, 1982.

Masserman J.H., *Sexuality of Women*, Grune & Stratton, New York, 1966.

McKenzie F., 'Sexuality after Total Pelvic Exenteration', *Nursing Times*, 84(20), pp 27–30, 1988.

Strang V. and Sullivan P., 'Body Image Attitudes During Pregnancy and the Postpartum Period', *Journal of Obstetric, Gynecologic and Neonatal Nursing*, July/Aug, pp 332–7, 1985.

Wassner A., 'The Impact of Mutilating Surgery or Trauma on Body Image', *International Nursing Review*, 29(3), pp 86–90, 1982.

Webb C., 'Hysterectomy: Dispelling the myths, part 1', *Nursing Times Occasional Papers*, 79(30), pp 52–4, 1983a.

Webb C., 'Hysterectomy: Dispelling the myths, part 2', *Nursing Times Occasional Papers*, 79(31), pp 44–6, 1983b.

Webb C., *Sexuality, Nursing and Health*, John Wiley & Sons, Chichester, 1985a.

Webb C., 'Gynaecological Nursing: A compromising situation', *Journal of Advanced Nursing*, pp 47–54, 1985b.

Webb C., 'Sexuality. Sexual healing', *Nursing Times* 83(32), pp 28–30, 1987.

19 Body image – the mastectomy challenge

Study of this chapter will enable you to:

1 Outline the historic importance of the breast as an symbol of womanhood.
2 Discuss the factors which will determine how a woman may react to the prospect of a mastectomy.
3 Describe physical care measures designed to help the patient regain an acceptable body image.
4 Describe the importance of assessment as a prerequisite to providing care supportive to body ideal.
5 Offer practical points concerning breast prostheses, their fitting and associated advice to women.
6 Identify a range of advantages and possible disadvantages in the use of reconstructive surgery.
7 Offer a full range of practical measures designed to help the patient use dress to enhance her body presentation.
8 Identify other agencies (professional or lay, in the hospital or community) which may play a part in the patient's body image rehabilitation.

For centuries the female breast has been seen as important, for both women and men. Pagan statuettes have emphasised it as a symbol of fertility. In oil paintings, sculpture and the cinema, the breast has been viewed as the most obvious expression of female sexuality, of femininity. Equally, breast feeding is frequently seen as the archetypal nurturing activity. Even the feminist movement of the 1960s and 1970s, intent upon rejecting male sexist attitudes, concentrated upon the breast as a symbol of the growing confidence of women. The discarding of brassieres rejected attitudes toward the breast, it did not dislodge the breast from its central place in women's self-image.

The complete or partial loss of one or both breasts (mastectomy) may be anticipated to be a disaster for the patient and her most intimate others (Bard and Sutherland, 1955; Fortune, 1979; Maguire *et al*, 1978). The surgery alters in a stark way the contours of the woman's body, removing a part that has been invested with cultural and sexual value (Carroll, 1981). The nurse might expect that the patient will fear that she is no longer sexually attractive. It is possible to imagine that the woman will feel that the lost 'female shape' will make her sexual role ambiguous, or that she will withdraw from sexual activities. In reality, the body implications of mastectomy are rarely obvious or straightforward (Krouse and Krouse, 1981). To understand why, it is necessary to appreciate something about the woman's attitude towards her own breasts, the circumstances of her surgery and the degree of social support that she can rely upon.

Contrary to popular belief, women hold widely differing feelings about their breasts. For some, their breasts have never been what they think others would, or they should, believe they should be. Large breasts may prove uncomfortable, particularly if the woman is exercising. Other women with smaller breasts may feel that the loss of the breast tissue is a marginal issue. As the breast has not been considered one of their 'best features', its loss may seem less significant. Body ideal may be based upon clothes, fashions or styles that emphasise a 'flat chest'. This was a popular image in the 1920s and 1960s. Other women's body ideal may be influenced by the more ample figures of some cinema stars and the relatively popular pastime of topless bathing.

Goin has described the often pragmatic attitude that many women have toward their breasts and surgical changes thereto (Goin, 1982). Plastic surgeons have for a long time been able to reduce or enlarge breasts (breast augmentation), and such adjustments have sometimes been achieved for essentially fashionable rather than mental health reasons. Many women take a surprisingly confident approach to breast surgery, reacting to change on the basis of how results match up to some clearly formed ideas on 'the ideal'.

Even when breast surgery is offered as treatment for cancer, it does not automatically follow that the body image will suffer irreparably (Anderson, 1988; Jenkins, 1980; Worden and Weisman, 1977). Anderson discovered that many mastectomy patients recovered from surgery remarkably well, despite a lack of patient education, counselling and prosthetic support. While immediately post-operation, the wound might be described as a 'grotesque disfigurement', four weeks later most of the patients were 'learning to live with it'. A significant number of patients reported feeling quite positive about the surgery, it having removed the worst immediate threats of a tumour. Seventy per cent of the patients who were sexually active, reported little or no change in their intimate relationships.

It can be argued that such a good response to breast surgery depends in part upon the woman's circumstances and her experiences of hospital.

Table 19.1 Mastectomy operations

'Lumpectomy' (tylectomy): simple excision of discrete tumour tissue

Partial mastectomy: removal of tumour and margin section of surrounding tissue (typically 5 cm)

Subcutaneous mastectomy: removal of underlying breast tissue, but leaving skin, areola and nipple intact

Simple mastectomy: removal of main breast tissue, but not overlying skin, underlying intercostal muscles or axilla lymph nodes

Modified radical mastectomy: complete removal of breast, including nipple, some skin and adjacent soft tissue

Halstead (radical) mastectomy: complete removal of breast, nipple, some skin, pectoral muscles, adjacent fat and axilla lymph nodes

---

Several authors record that it is not just the operation itself which may affect body image (Moetzinger and Dauber, 1982; Tait, 1988). Many of the patients will have undergone a mammogram, doctor's examination and a breast biopsy (Forrest Report, 1987). These are worrying procedures in themselves, each invading the patient's body space, forcing her to review her control over an intimate part of her anatomy. Statistically many of the doctors will have been male. Most of the patients will have carried the fear that they may suffer, and later die from breast cancer.

If the patient has previously practised regular breast self-examination, she may have developed a greater confidence in dealing with such intrusions into her body space. She may even have developed a rationalistic approach to surgery itself. Self-examination will not however have prepared her for the range of possible operations (see Table 19.1) or the wound drains, physiotherapy and prostheses that may follow.

Patients undergo mastectomy at different ages and in different family or social circumstances. Many woman will discover a lump in their breast during, or soon after the menopause. Then the diagnosis of cancer and prospect of mastectomy or radiotherapy may come as a double blow. Their ideals of femininity have already been threatened by all that the menopause is supposed to imply. Now surgery will alter body reality too. Younger women who face mastectomy may have other concerns. For some, the loss of a breast will rule out their plans for breast feeding – a cherished dream. They may even envy the older woman whom they perceive to have problems after having had the joy of motherhood and active marital relationships. Each woman brings to surgery very personal fears, prejudices, worries and support. Not all patients will have a caring husband, friend, mother or lover. This can be a profound disadvantage for it seems likely that to fight breast cancer, mutilating surgery, the patient must adopt a positive, even combat ready, body image and self-image. That is easier to achieve when the social circumstances are in the patient's favour. Several months after she has left the direct care of the hospital nurse, she may face her greatest crisis of self-confidence (Polivy, 1977). It is then that family or friends, and a counselling community nurse may play an important role.

Practical points for body reality care

The loss of a breast and associated axilla lymph glands (radical mastectomy) is a major piece of surgery. It poses immediate body reality problems which, if left unresolved, will undermine the recovery of the patient's total body image. Body reality measures should be directed at four major concerns.

Wound care

The patient will usually return from theatre with a suction wound drain and, if tissue loss has been considerable, a skin graft and pressure dressing too. There may be a tendency for the patient's proximal arm to become engorged and swollen which is the result of poor lymphatic drainage after surgery. Firstly, it is important that the patient is educated about these difficulties pre-operatively. If she is able to anticipate the problems, and the means of response, she will experience less anxiety as a result. Talking with a well adjusted, positive, fellow post-operative patient may be beneficial. Knowing that a kindred spirit has overcome similar challenges helps to engender a more optimistic attitude. Secondly, the nurse must ensure that the drainage tube remains patent and that the dressings are not dislodged until wound inspection becomes due. Should a haematoma form under the suture line, or infection attack the wound or graft, healing may be prolonged and painful. A longer stay in hospital is unlikely to enhance the patient's self-image.

Comfort

Helping the patient to remain comfortable is equally important. She will have been positioned sitting upright and helped to move so as to avoid the complications of immobility. This will not be easy – the nurse must ensure that drainage tubes are not blocked or allowed to drag, and that shearing forces against the dressing are avoided when she is moved. Because breathing will be uncomfortable and perhaps limited in depth by the wound site, sutures and drains, it is necessary to support the patient in an upright position.

Because pain is likely to inhibit physiotherapy, appetite, sleep and a recovering body image, prescribed analgesia is given regularly at first. Later, specific doses of analgesia may be planned for dressing changes, blanket baths or major sessions of chest physiotherapy. In the light of analgesics used, respiratory rate, depth and character are carefully monitored. If the patient's arm does start to become swollen it may be supported on pillows or in a bedside sling. In doing so the nurse makes regular checks on the circulation to the patient's hand, reporting any signs of cyanosis or symptoms such as paraesthesia. Blood pressure recordings are taken on the unaffected arm. Hygiene care, for skin, mouth and hair also becomes a priority. The immobile patient, dehydrated after surgery, perhaps receiving oxygen therapy, will appreciate a body that feels fresher, even if movement is limited by drains and intravenous infusions.

Nutrition

At least three factors conspire to make nutrition a body reality concern. The patient may well be elderly and may, pre-admission, have already become malnourished. The malnourished patient is more at risk of pressure sores and other complications. Secondly, the patient is often battling against cancer and may already be cachexic. The effects of the tumour upon the body can inhibit appetite and certainly sap the energy necessary to prepare or eat food. Thirdly, the metabolic adjustments necessary after surgery, usually mean that the patient is anorexic immediately post-operation. Soon however, the body will need protein, vitamins and trace minerals to heal the wound, and carbohydrates for energy. It is important that the nurse provides these nutrients to the patient in the most attractive and efficient forms possible. This may take the form of supplements, sip feeds or frequent small portions of a favourite food. Weight loss undermines body image and body recovery.

Activity and rest

In the early post-operative period the patient will have little energy for extensive exercise or activities. Sleep will be important. Even then however, chest physiotherapy, in the form of deep breathing exercises and assistance with expectorating will be a priority (Markowski et al, 1981). The patient may be provided with anti-embolism stockings and invited to complete arm and shoulder range of movement (ROM) exercises. The latter are designed to reduce arm oedema and prevent shoulder stiffness.

Later, exercise can be promoted through encouraging the patient to play a part in her own washes and toileting. The patient's energy reserve should not be overestimated, she may need to rest frequently and to accept (albeit grudgingly), that she must permit her body time to heal. Regaining even a limited mobility is a positive body image step. The patient will have been surprised to find just how her operation drained her. Now, going for even a short walk to the ward lounge symbolises the return of independence.

Practical points about body ideal support

Throughout, this book has considered the relationship between body ideal and patient coping strategies. The two come together again in the care of mastectomy patients. From the outset it is sensible to assess as carefully as possible, just what part the breast plays in the patient's body ideal (Woods, 1975). This means that pre-operatively the nurse must help the patient to explore her hopes and fears about the surgery. It involves the nurse in enquiring the circumstances of how 'the lump' was discovered and what this has meant for her and any partner she may have. Often an anxious patient is eager to recount the events leading to her admission, rationalising her actions or inactions en route. This forms an excellent opportunity to judge the importance of the breast to her. The story of Mrs Lewis makes the point.

Mrs Lewis   I took a month to tell my husband about the lump. I was so scared, so upset that he might notice that I undressed with the light off each night.

Nurse   So you were worried about your husband's feelings, his reactions as well as the lump itself?

Mrs Lewis   Yes. I know it's daft, but he was always so proud of my figure. I know he'd be disappointed if something happened to me.

Nurse   When your husband did find out, at the clinic, did he seem upset?

Mrs Lewis   Yes, but in a nice way. He was cross with me for not seeing the doctor earlier. He said that he'd started to worry I didn't find him attractive anymore – I was always turning out the light!

Nurse   So the delay had caused confusion in several ways?

Mrs Lewis   Yes, it was stupid. We're better about it now though. We haven't stopped talking since I got the biopsy result.

Nurse   Good – I'm glad.

In this sort of assessment, Mrs Lewis has already given early hints on the importance of her breast to her husband. By implication it seems important to her for similar reasons, as a part of their marital bonding. The nurse has also started to learn about the Lewis's coping style which is a positive one.

In talking openly about her worries, Mrs Lewis gives permission to her husband to help. She may not have realised just how important that will be to them both in the future.

Where the assault on body ideal has had a more traumatic effect, patients and relatives may not be so ready to receive the nurse's advice and support. Instead, she may have to concentrate upon empathetic listening, giving tacit permission for the patient to work through the grief reaction at a pace she can handle. All nurses may be able to quote examples where a patient did not display obvious 'third day post-operative blues', seeming to deny the problems or challenges to be faced. It would be easy for the nurse to feel that she had failed if she did not coax the patient toward a more open acceptance of her wound, the prosthesis and any necessary change in dress or lifestyle. That, bluntly done, would in any case be unwise. For some patients, denial is a crutch that must be kept close by until they are once again home, on known territory, hopefully with a supportive friend nearby. Forcing care and rehabilitation to suit a short hospital stay may be fruitless, even dangerous. It may be better to acquaint a community colleague or caring relative with continuing needs and to help the patient access other support agencies at a time of her choice.

Where patients seem more eager to explore their feelings; the nurse might encourage the formation of a ward support group. This is a psychological equivalent of the patient's physical support as she explores her wound. In this setting fellow patients share their emotions and newer patients learn how grief may be worked through. It is often useful to review just how body ideal has been influenced by other people's opinions, by the media and by fashion. Clearly, examples may be found of alternative perspectives on body shape and contours. Body image is only one aspect of self-image and collectively other qualities such as bravery, determination and dignity, exhibited while being a patient, may be valued by the group. Asking the mastectomy nurse or visitor, a psychologist or experienced counsellor to join the group may enhance the patient's confidence. The nurse should be prepared to facilitate group development, and this may demand the addition of new helpers and new skills.

Presenting a new image

Practical measures designed to help the patient present a new body image to the world must address prostheses, prosthetic fitting and dress. The provision of prostheses in Britain is not yet developed to a state where all mastectomy patients receive individualised, professional attention (Pendleton and Smith, 1986). Sampling London and Scottish populations of patients Anderson, found that large numbers of women (25 per cent of the Scottish group) had no prosthesis four months after surgery. London women were found to be better served and to be more knowledgeable about the prosthesis as a result of patient education before hospital admission. A smaller percentage of the sample had read literature about prostheses and adaptation to the loss of a breast, such as the Health Education Authority booklet *Living with the loss of a breast*. These are significant findings when Anderson adds that, of those women fitted with a prosthesis, 80 per cent found them satisfactory, and 60 per cent of them found the prosthesis comfortable (Anderson, 1988).

The first prosthesis offered is usually a soft fibrous pad which may be worn inside the brassiere as soon as the patient is comfortable with this post-operatively. Pope has suggested that such a temporary prosthesis can be attached inside night wear even before a brassiere is tolerated (Pope, 1981). Whichever method is employed, it is useful to advise the patient pre-admission to bring her most comfortable brassiere with her. Experimenting with new brassieres post-operatively is both uncomfortable and possibly embarrassing. The hospital surgical fitter can normally arrange adaptations of the patient's own brassiere so that the prosthesis can be inserted snugly and unnecessary cost avoided.

More permanent, silicone based prostheses are offered a little later, when the wound is healing well and when the patient has started to take charge of her own personal hygiene. Radiotherapy treatment, or complications with skin grafts may necessarily delay the fitting of a long term prosthesis. When fitting is completed and the patient starts to wear her new silicone prosthesis beneath day clothes, it is important to remind her of the Breast Care and Mastectomy Association (BCMA). This organisation may already have proved supportive pre-operatively, but now it can offer further advice on all aspects of prostheses and associated problems. As with other patient support organisations, the BCMA offers a range of free, practical advice literature. Because it is a non-medical organisation, the patient may feel that its advice is both more useful and empathetic.

As the patient chooses a prosthesis it is worth bearing in mind that it will not only be experienced visually, but through touch as well. When checking contour appearance in the mirror it should be suggested that the prosthesis is gently pressed, flattened and moved, to see how it behaves. A prosthesis that leaves the patient fearful of giving or receiving a cuddle, or entering a crowded room is a prosthesis that has limited value.

In addition to these prostheses, a number of patients may be offered one of the implanted varieties, a breast reconstruction operation. When surgery is suggested it is ethical that the nurse acquaints the patient with the possibility that the cosmetic result may not be perfect. The consistency, appearance and weight of the reconstructed breast may not match the unaffected breast. In particular, the creation of a new nipple and dark areolar tissue is difficult. Apart from the cosmetic effects, perceived benefits of surgery, in terms of the patient's sex life, may not be straightforward either. Shain found that there was no difference in the degree of self-esteem, satisfaction with sex life and 'zest for living' between women who had undergone reconstructive surgery and those who had not (Shain, 1979).

Practical help with choosing or adapting clothing complements the efforts made with prosthesis choice and fitting. At this juncture it is helpful sometimes to invite the patient's partner to become involved. It may be possible that jointly choosing new clothes and styles may enable a husband to feel that he is affirming his love for his wife. The partner's constructive and sensitive interest in clothing and his wife's appearance might prove to be one avenue whereby a couple develop new coping strategies post-discharge from hospital.

Both Anderson, and Feather and Lanigan highlight patients' concern with choosing appropriate clothes post mastectomy. Most patients feel that the operation poses significant limitations on what they can safely or comfortably wear. With a well fitted prosthesis, a supportive family and an imaginative mind the restrictions may not be as severe as they first seem (Anderson, 1988; Feather and Lanigan, 1987). Several principles are outlined here, a starting point for the patient education programme that you might devise locally (see Table 19.2).

Firstly, in anticipation of post-operative lymphoedema, it is wise to advise the patient to bring at least one wide sleeve garment to hospital with her. Dolman or kimono style sleeves permit early dressing in attractive clothes, facilitate undressing and provide a welcome boost to self-esteem. Later, a tighter sleeve may once again be possible.

Table 19.2 Practical dress advice post-mastectomy

---

1. In the early days do consider comfort in dressing and undressing. Wide sleeves, simple popper fastenings or even velcro fastening might be preferable.
2. Do not choose clothes that cling closely to the body outline – look for fuller lines, perhaps using a belt on a large size blouse to create a cossack top effect.
3. Do choose bright colours and varied patterns – they break up contour outlines.
4. Use vertical lines to divert the eye up and down the figure – rather than across, from breast to breast.
5. Consider asymmetrical patterns, fastenings and styles. A button line down the centre of the blouse or dress invites comparison of the sides of the body.
6. Always consider the purpose of the clothes, where they will be worn. Will particular fabrics prove irritating or unmanageable against the wound or prosthesis.
7. Look for interesting accessories and necklines – the principle of distraction. Avoid V neck lines where possible.
8. Consider shopping by post. You may want longer trying out the dress, checking its appearance, gaining the opinion of a loved one. Home shopping may be more convenient, especially until you have regained confidence.
9. Enlist a seamstress as a friend. Many clothes can be adapted, new ones need not always or immediately be bought.

Secondly, it should be remembered that camouflage can be just as effective with clothing as makeup. Try to break up the contour lines of the body, to emphasise new attractive body attributes, colours or textures. Such camouflage departs from that used by the hunter or soldier. The nurse should seek to draw a planned attention to the patient's femininity, to control the perception, not to elude it! This is best achieved by choosing randomly patterned fabrics. Plain ones allow the eye to concentrate rather more exclusively upon contour. Bright colours emphasise a positive disposition and the pattern may also make it difficult to compare one side of the body with the other. Vertical lines 'break' the contours of the bust line, the eye being directed along the line, rather than horizontally from breast to breast.

Developing the principle of asymmetry, it is also worth considering blouses and other tops that do not feature buttons or zips down the centre. If the fastenings are offset to one side and if they are also set at a slight angle, it is much less likely that a comparison of breast contours will be made. In addition to the use of asymmetrical features, the patient may use additions to neckline, hem line or sleeves that attract the eye. Necklines might feature high collars, a necklace or an extravagant bow. 'V' neck and round neck collars are much less satisfactory. Distracting attention to stylish hair arrangements, fashion accessories such as handbags or footwear is another aspect of this general strategy.

The rather greater challenge of swimwear demands that the patient consider whether their clothes are for swimming or sunbathing in. Choosing a snug fitting, stretch nylon swimsuit may enable the patient to support a waterproof prosthesis firmly beneath it. Before buying the garment, the patient should be encouraged to note what happens to it when it becomes wet. To what extent does it show details through? Does it look tighter or looser fitting when wet? Some of the problems may be compensated for by choosing a one piece patterned suit. If the suit is solely for sun lounging, matters are a little easier. Many one piece suits are available with matching jackets or towelling tops. A combination of the two may be suitable for even the more crowded beach.

Conclusion

It is by no means certain that women will tend toward a major grief response at the loss of a breast, or that this will necessarily bring an end to sexual relations. This said however, it is the nurse's responsibility to anticipate that mastectomy may produce a profound altered body image problem and that this might be delayed post-operatively. Therefore, pay close attention to the assessment of the patient, her attitudes, explanations, questions and body language. Only once a clear assessment has been made can the nurse start to adjust care to include recognition of the meaning of the breast and its loss, in this particular patient's world. Mastectomy (even partial) remains a significant physical trauma to a woman's body. Given time, changing relationships and perhaps a continuing threat of recurrent cancer, the nurse should expect to deliver some form of body image care. Such care may have to extend beyond the period of hospitalisation and take account of the patient's kin and prognosis.

Review questions

1 In what ways does our society emphasise and value the female breast as an aspect of a woman's femininity?
2 The chapter suggests that the patient's age may affect her attitude toward mastectomy. In what ways?
3 To what extent do you think that:
(a) modern cosmetic breast surgery
(b) the threat of cancer
may affect a woman's attitude towards mastectomy?
4 To what degree do you think feminism has affected the breast as an aspect of women's and men's body ideals?
5 How does a breast biopsy, physical examination and mammogram affect a woman's body image?
6 Why are the following so important in restoring the patient's body image:
(a) wound care?
(b) physiotherapy?
(c) pain relief?
7 How does taking a patient history contribute to the assessment of a woman's body ideal?
8 List ten pieces of advice that you would offer a patient concerning body presentation.

Suggested exercise

For this exercise you will need a discarded 'clothes by post' catalogue or similar women's fashion publication. Scissors, imagination, some white card and a careful review of the body presentation points in Chapter 19 complete your requirements. Imagine that you are creating a catalogue of garments that will be marketed for patients who have undergone mastectomy. Remember that the catalogue must cater for different age groups of women, and for those that are large and small. The catalogue must include items that could be termed, day wear, evening wear and sports/leisure wear. Make up your catalogue selection by sticking the images to plain white card background. Add any notes on garment adjustments that you would recommend before the item was finally included in the selection.

Now discuss your portfolio with colleagues, perhaps making up a fuller group catalogue. Try to identify the strengths and weaknesses of your catalogue range. Allow one to two hours for discussion.

Possible developments/applications

1. The creation of a clothes booklet or handout for use on the ward.
2. Surveying clothes styles in a major high street chain store. Show your 'catalogue' to store representatives and monitor their reaction to patient's needs.
3. Invite post-mastectomy patients to suggest clothing hints which you will use to form a patient advice sheet.

References

Anderson J., 'Coming to Terms with Mastectomy', *Nursing Times*, 84(4), pp 41–4, 1988.

Bard M. and Sutherland A., 'Psychological Impact of Cancer and its Treatment: Adaptation to radical mastectomy', *Cancer*, 8(4), p 656–72, 1955.

Carroll R.M., 'The Impact of Mastectomy on Body Image', *Oncology Nursing Forum*, 8(4), pp 29–32, 1981.

Feather B. and Lanigan C., 'Looking Good After Your Mastectomy', *American Journal of Nursing*, pp 1048–9, 1987.

Forrest P. (Chair) *et al*, *Breast Cancer Screening*, DHSS, HMSO, London, 1987.

Fortune E., 'A Nursing Approach to Body Image and Sexuality Adaptation in the Mastectomy Patient', *Sexuality and Disability*, 2(1), pp 47–53, 1979.

Goin M.K., 'Psychological Reactions to Surgery of the Breast', *Clinics in Plastic Surgery*, 9(3), pp 347–54, 1982.

Health Education Authority, *Living With The Loss Of A Breast*, London, 1986.

Jenkins H., 'Self Concept and Mastectomy', *Journal of Obstetric, Gynecologic and Neonatal Nursing*, Jan/Feb, pp 38–42, 1980.

Krouse H. and Krouse J., 'Psychological Factors in Postmastectomy Adjustment', *Psychological Reports*, 48, pp 275–8, 1981.

Maguire G.P., Lee E.G., Bevinghon D.J., Kuchemann C.S., Crabtree R.J. and Cornell C.E., 'Psychiatric Problems in the First Year after Mastectomy', *British Medical Journal*, 1, pp 963–5, 1978.

Markowski J., Wilcox J. and Helm P., 'Lymphoedema Incidence after Special Post Mastectomy Therapy', *Archives of Physical Rehabilitation*, 62, pp 449–52, 1981.

Moetzinger C. and Dauber L., 'The Management of the Patient with Breast Cancer', *Cancer Nursing*, Aug, pp 287–91, 1982.

Pendleton L. and Smith G., 'Provisions of Breast Prostheses', *Nursing Times*, 82(22), pp 37–9, 1986.

Polivy J., 'Psychological Effects of Mastectomy on a Woman's Feminine Self Concept', *Journal of Nervous and Mental Disease*, 164(2), pp 77–87, 1977.

Pope B., 'After the Mastectomy, Prostheses and Clothing', *Nursing Times*, 82(22), pp 37–9, 1981.

Shain W., *Facts Every Woman Should Know About Breast Reconstruction*, American Cancer Society, New York, 1979.

Tait A., 'Whole or Partial Breast Loss: The threat to womanhood' in Salter M. (ed.) *Altered Body Image – The nurse's role*, pp 167–77. John Wiley & Sons, Chichester, 1988.

Woods N.F., 'Influences on Sexual Adaptation to Mastectomy', *Journal of Obstetric, Gynaecologic and Neonatal Nursing*, 4, pp 33–7, 1975.

Worden J.W. and Weisman A., 'The Fallacy in Postmastectomy Depression', *American Journal of the Medical Sciences*, 273, pp 169–75, 1977.

Further reading

Hassey K., Bloom L. and Burgess S., 'Radiation Alternative to Mastectomy', *American Journal of Nursing*, Nov, pp 1567–9, 1983.

Maxwell M., 'The Use of Social Networks to Help Cancer Patients Maximise Support', *Cancer Nursing*, Aug, pp 275–80, 1982.

Norbeck J.S., 'Social Support: A model for clinical research and application', *Advances in Nursing Science*, pp 43–59, 1981.

Northouse L., 'Mastectomy Patients and the Fear of Cancer Recurrence', *Cancer Nursing*, 4, pp 213–22, 1981.

Stanway A. and Stanway P., *The Breast: What every woman needs to know from youth to old age*, Granada, London, 1982.

Stillman M.J., 'Women's Health Beliefs About Breast Cancer and Breast Self Examination', *Nursing Research*, 26, pp 121–7, 1977.

Tait A., Maguire P., Faulkner A., Brooke M., Wilkinson S., Thomson L. and Sellwood R., 'Improving Communication Skills: The use of a standardised assessment for mastectomy patients', *Nursing Times*, 78(51), pp 2181–4, 1982.

Welch D., 'Planning Nursing Interventions for Family Members of Advanced Cancer Patients', *Cancer Nursing*, Oct, pp 365–9, 1981.

Winkler W.A., 'Choosing the Prosthesis and Clothing', *American Journal of Nursing*, 77, pp 1433–6, 1977.

20 Male sexuality and body image

Study of this chapter will enable you to:

1 Discuss briefly why men have become more body image conscious during recent decades.
2 Describe the importance of body function as an aspect of male body image.
3 Offer examples of modern health education campaigns which may sensitise men to body image issues.
4 Offer typical examples of diseases, treatments or operations that may affect male body image at different stages of life.
5 Discuss the importance of patient education to men's body image.
6 Describe briefly the part that toileting and grooming play in male body presentation.
7 Suggest the advantages and disadvantages of female nurses providing care to male patients with body image problems.

It is often argued that men experience their bodies in a totally different way to women. Male children are socialised in a different way to female children. Boys are encouraged to value body function, athletic achievement, strength and endurance. In school, youth club and the community at large, a relatively plain boy may still gain acclaim if he is a high achiever. For many parents this is essential for life training, the boy will grow up to be an important, if not the sole, breadwinner for a family. In more modern times it is increasingly clear that other aspects of body image are also important to men. A major fashion industry has grown up surrounding men's grooming, clothing, toiletries and jewellery. While this industry has not grown to the size of that supplying women, it is nonetheless substantial. Advertising, manufacturers and the media provide messages about how the modern man should look no matter what his age. The demand for designer clothes focuses attention on body proportions, shape and size, as well as function. We cannot any longer make a significant distinction between the different sex's interests in body image. Both men and women are intensely concerned with appearance, only the emphasis of interest may differ.

Male interest in body form and function extends beyond work and fashion. There has been a concerted effort to educate men about self-examination, as one means to avoid illness (Heidenstam, 1976). Testicular self-examination may not be as widely employed as breast self-examination, but it is gradually coming to be seen as a worthwhile way of detecting tumours. Early detection may provide a much improved chance of cure, especially as the whole of the scrotal contents are identifiable with a little instruction. Equally, men and women are starting to monitor skin moles for possible malignant melanoma and stools for blood loss (bowel cancer). The process of self-examination relies upon men being confident and comfortable enough to explore their own bodies. This seems increasingly possible given modern sex education and knowledge about human anatomy and physiology.

Increased body awareness can come from a sense of vulnerability to disease or trauma. Amongst gay men the threat of Acquired Immune Deficiency Syndrome (AIDS) has heightened the need to care for and protect the body. AIDS threatens life itself, but before that body image may be undermined by opportunistic infections, malignancy and disordered body control. Relationships with partners of necessity, are affected. Fears about infection, about hurting a loved one can lead to increasing physical or emotional isolation (Kassler, 1983; Miller, 1987). It is no coincidence that groups gathered to support gay men highlight body concerns through such titles as 'Body Positive'.

Contraception is also a field where body image concerns arise (Draper, 1972). Historically the onus of contraceptive precautions has fallen unevenly upon women (Guillebaud, 1985). The encumbrance of planning a sexual encounter, encasing the penis in a rubber sheath, has limited the sense of freedom which seems bound up in traditional concepts of male sexuality. It is only more recently that they have taken an increasing control over contraception. This has been because there is a growing sense of male responsibility, partly through the greater availability of vasectomy operations and recently because of the prominence of the condom as a defence against incurable sexually transmitted disease. Vasectomy may profoundly affect the way in which a man feels about his body. Some patients report mild post-operative depression – feeling 'less of a man' once sterile. Others record a feeling of surprising abandonment, of being freed at last from contraception worries. Perceptions of body reality and body ideal are both altered because the operation might not be reversible. Body presentation may be adjusted too. One patient known to the author sported a T-shirt with the caption 'I fire blanks'.

Altered body image

A variety of diseases and operations may seriously disrupt a man's body image (see Figure 20.1). This chapter will concentrate on genito-urinary problems. The reader is referred to other chapters in this book for orthopaedic, neurological and traumatology examples. Irrespective of age, men are worried about the body image effects of genito-urinary pathology or surgery. An elderly man receiving female hormone treatment for carcinoma of the prostate may well fear body presentation changes, especially gynaecomastia. A middle aged executive is embarrassed by the continuous drainage system *in situ* following a trans-urethral resection of the prostate (TURP). A young man facing surgery and chemotherapy for teratoma testes is in an unenviable body image dilemma. What complicates each

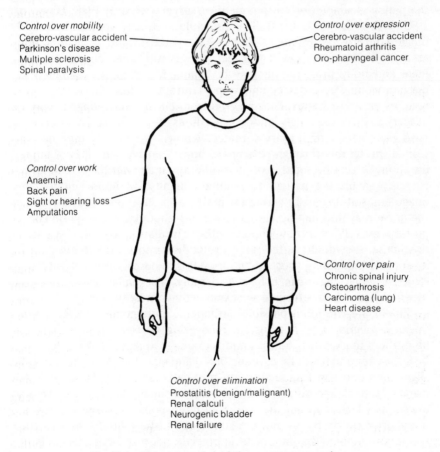

Control over mobility
Cerebro-vascular accident
Parkinson's disease
Multiple sclerosis
Spinal paralysis

Control over expression
Cerebro-vascular accident
Rheumatoid arthritis
Oro-pharyngeal cancer

Control over work
Anaemia
Back pain
Sight or hearing loss
Amputations

Control over pain
Chronic spinal injury
Osteoarthrosis
Carcinoma (lung)
Heart disease

Control over elimination
Prostatitis (benign/malignant)
Renal calculi
Neurogenic bladder
Renal failure

Fig. 20.1   Threats to male body image – some examples.

man's problems is that personal control over his body is severely limited. Such control has always been an important part of his sexuality.

The ward environment, where the patient receives body image care is staffed predominantly with female nurses. For many of these nurses ritual care has been used to limit their own personal embarrassment over 'men's problems' (Menzies, 1961). The patient lying in the communal ward may not have developed such defences. Convention dictates that a man should not show too much embarrassment or fear. It does not follow that these emotions are unknown to him as he awaits surgery.

Nursing interventions

It has previously been established that early patient education facilitates the patient's adaptation to treatment or surgery (Boore, 1978; Hayward, 1975; Wilson-Barnett, 1979). This principle is equally applicable to body image concerns. The patient should be assisted to anticipate how body reality will alter and how it will feel. In this way some changes in body ideal and body presentation may be planned. Telling the patient what discomfort may be expected and, importantly, how this will be combatted is an essential first step. Pain may be transient but terrifying. It may be exacerbated by seemingly minor procedures, for instance by inserting a naso-gastric tube or urinary catheter. Knowing that pain may be controlled, preferably through patient's actions, that typically it is of limited duration, or that pre-operative physiotherapy may limit the risk of its occurrence, helps the patient to maintain dignity, so important to body image and self-image. In caring for patients about to undergo vasectomy, the nurse may find that he knows something about checking sperm counts post-operatively. Very few know whether ejaculation will later be painful or whether they might suffer more scrotal discomfort through not wearing a support. Explaining procedures, physiology and previous patients' constructive experiences can help considerably. The embarrassing question of will it hurt when returning to sexual activity must be answered.

Similar preparation is possible for patients undergoing a TURP. In this instance meeting a well adjusted, recovering post-operative patient enables them to examine the continuous drainage apparatus. Yes, there will be a catheter and it will be draining blood and clots too. Yes, there may be slight discomfort at first micturition post-catheter removal. No, it is not usual to suffer a recurrence of the prostate problem. These are answers to questions which map out the body and its response to surgery. Knowing the short term problems and the staff's optimistic attitude towards their resolution enables the patient to appreciate his own body, its resilience and promise of a new body image ahead.

As with female patients dealing with mutilating surgery, male patients require assistance to adjust to a disrupted body image. This may take the form of body camouflage or help with body ideal. Camouflaging a catheter and urinary drainage bag may involve the use of a suitable holster or holder that may be strapped to the leg or suspended beneath the dressing gown. Many men are not comfortable carrying a bag in hand. The fact that it contains urine adds to the unease. For good or ill, the British male has not been socialised to carry a 'hand bag'. The bag and catheter may be associated in his mind with senescence and terminal incontinence. Therefore, do not assume that visiting time and mobilising around the ward are easy for the patient. Arrange his clothes, his camouflage, before you help him to the day room.

Enhancing body presentation should extend to grooming and hygiene matters as well. There has been a previous assumption that men are not as 'fussy' about their hair, nails and body odours. This is not an assumption that a professional nurse can make. Convention may suggest that men do not make a flamboyant display of grooming and toilet, nonetheless they are concerned about it. Washing, combing hair, applying hair lacquer or spray, aftershave and even male makeup can make him feel more attractive, even though beneath the cover there is a catheter *in situ*. The daily or twice daily shave, trimming of beard and moustache are also important. At a time when movement is limited and pyjamas worn, the grooming of his hair, cleaning of teeth and cleansing of his skin may be one of the best statements about dignity and respect that the nurse might make toward the patient. It is important to anticipate his concerns and to stand in for his senses when he does not note body odour or halitosis. Anaesthesia may limit his sense of smell or taste but his relatives may however register 'bad breath' and wonder how well he really is.

Body ideal support includes points of concern about fertility and genital appearance. Patients preparing for orchidectomy or amputation of the penis, anticipate a terrible mutilation. It is critical that before giving consent to operation, such patients form a clear picture of genital appearance and function after surgery. Nursing staff should be prepared to advocate the patient's concern to the surgeon, who may have afforded the patient only a limited time in which to explore his body image worries. It is often helpful to encourage patients and relatives to write down their questions, so that these might be cogently raised at the next interview with the surgeon. Sometimes putting pencil and sketch pad in the hands of the doctor is the next step. A line diagram clarifies how the operation will work and can be left with the patient should he wish to share this with his spouse. Observation at visiting time will help the nurse to spot whether such drawn explanations raise problems for the patient's partner. It is worth remembering that the partner also invests a body ideal of the patient into their relationship. It may be necessary to spend as much time briefing and counselling the partner regarding surgery as the patient himself. Will for instance, the operation or treatment render him infertile? Will it end his sex drive or function? If the treatment will leave him infertile, might sperm be banked for later use? As with other patient problems discussed within this book, such body ideal dilemmas may not always be resolved in hospital. Rather, what the nurse should attempt to do is facilitate communication, so that patients can avail themselves of their support network.

Conclusion

Ever since Samson was weakened by the loss of his hair, men have been either overtly or covertly concerned with their body image. How the body looks, functions and feels is important for their sense of sexuality, whether they are homosexual or heterosexual. Expression of male fashion has changed with time. Traditionally, male body presentation is understated in western civilisation, although this differs elsewhere. When a man faces treatment for genito-urinary problems, either in a clinic or the hospital, he is forced to review the body image he has built up over time. This process may be brief as treatment of sexually transmitted disease is often quickly accomplished. It may however, involve a radical rethink of his image and his sexuality. Carcinoma of the genito-urinary tract threatens permanent change in body reality with all that might entail for body ideal and body presentation.

At this point, the male patient realises that any new body image will be explored in the company of female, as well as male nurses. It is in this professional, but perhaps worrying setting, that foundations may be laid or the opportunity lost, depending on whether male body image is taken seriously. It should be accepted that for men an emphasis on body function rather than body feature may be more usual. However, body function is an aspect of body presentation, and leaves the patient reflecting on how he feels about his body home. It is important then, to establish the right atmosphere, that the patient is given explicit encouragement and permission to express body image concerns. He should be helped to prepare for body image change and then to enhance personal and social support coping strategies which seem to promote rehabilitation. Empathising with the patient's concerns is possible, whether the nurse is male or female. This can be achieved by believing that male body image concerns may show different emphases, but that they are just as real and just as important.

Review questions

1 Consider your own education and upbringing. Recall whether you were exposed to health education or screening. Did either of these cause you

to start reviewing how you felt about your body, whether you really knew and understood it?

2 It is implicitly argued that men experience their bodies as healthy, functional 'machines'. Men are not reminded of body change in quite the same way as women might be, say through the menstrual cycle. How does this affect their body image, their experience of illness in general?

3 What factors have played a part in promoting male contraception? How has body image been involved in this?

4 How does personal grooming and hygiene contribute to men's body image when they are sick?

5 Why is it so important to provide thorough and understandable patient education for men about to undergo mutilating genito-urinary surgery?

Suggested exercises

Exercise 1

Think back to when you have been nursing patients who have either been catheterised or have undergone genito-urinary surgery. Draw up a list of terminology, approaches that you habitually use when referring to or dealing with genital issues, for instance blanket bath, catheter care, and passing urine. Now add an 'F' to those terms or approaches that you would use for female patients, and an 'M' for those usually employed with male patients. Try to discern if there is a difference in your approach or attitude. If so, decide to what extent your care is affected by:

1. Your sex in relation to that of the patient's
2. Ritualistic nursing care, namely care that is done in a standard, unswerving pattern
3. Confusion or beliefs that you hold concerning men's body image or attitudes

Share your ideas with a trusted colleague or counsellor/tutor. There are no right answers, save that it is constructive to consider your own attitudes carefully and thoughtfully.

Suggested time scales are as follows:

(a) for drawing up your list/first thoughts, allow 20 minutes
(b) for a chat with counsellor/tutor (straight after), allow 30 minutes

Exercise 2

Men from different cultures and different times have not always followed the same standards of dress, grooming and other body presentation matters. Visit the local public library and research a non-western and/or non-contemporary group of men, for instance tribesmen, men from asiatic cultures, or Elizabethan men. Try to collect pictures of the men and their typical modes of dress and grooming. Read what you can about their personal body care, health habits and attitudes.

Present to the wider group your report on the body image of men from a different time or place. Consider through discussion how such men might respond to altered body image, assuming of course that they benefited from modern nursing care!

For the research period allow two to three weeks (directed in terms of depth by group leader/tutor). For the discussion, allow 30 to 40 minutes per presentation, depending upon group size.

References

Boore, J.R., 'Pre-operative Care of Patients', *Nursing Times*, 73(12), pp 409–11, 1978.

Draper E., *Birth Control in the Modern World*, 2nd edn, Penguin Books, Harmondsworth, 1972.

Guillebaud J., *Contraception – Your questions answered*, Churchill Livingstone, Edinburgh, 1985.

Hayward J., *Information – A prescription against pain*, Royal College of Nursing, London, 1975.

Heidenstam D. (ed), *Man's Body – An owner's manual*, Diagram Group, Paddington Press Ltd, London, 1976.

Kassler J., *Gay Men's Health*, Harper & Row, London, 1983.

Menzies I., *A Case Study in the Functioning of Social Systems as a Defence Against Anxiety*, Tavistock Institute, London, 1961.

Miller D., *Living With AIDS and HIV*, Macmillan Education, Basingstoke, 1987.

Wilson-Barnett J., *Stress in Hospital*, Churchill Livingstone, Edinburgh, 1979.

21 Changing gender

Study of this chapter will enable you to:

1 Identify what is meant by the term *transsexual*.
2 Outline briefly the common components that are associated with most transexual surgery.
3 Understand some of the loneliness, if not confusion, which may be experienced by a transexual before coming to understand his or her sexuality, and hence realising that his or her feelings and experiences are shared by others.
4 Discuss some of the arguments on why preparation for transsexual surgery takes so long.
5 Review how sexual stereotyping may play a part in everybody's upbringing.
6 Consider critically some of the prejudices that may relate to transsexuals and their surgery.
7 By using a degree of imagination, empathetically consider the challenges that the transsexual faces both before and after surgery.

When a patient gives consent to an operation which removes or augments their sexual organs, a profound change in body image has to be faced. The surgery itself will have been planned in response to a body image that includes a body ideal of the opposite sex. Caring for such patients requires that the nurse must understand the transsexual's perspective and feelings toward his or her current body reality. In recognition of this profoundly different care need, this chapter will concentrate upon one patient's personal recollections and experiences. It is a very different approach to meet a very unusual and important body image care challenge.

In the early 1970s Jan Morris published her by now famous account of transsexual life and surgery (Morris, 1974). In 1971 Helen Lovell underwent surgery, leaving behind a life as a husband, father and male army officer to become a woman. A cool January morning found me seated in the living room of her ground floor flat, sipping tea as we planned the interview which would become the basis of this chapter. It is hoped that the review of just a few of Helen Lovell's life experiences will help nurses to understand a transsexual perspective, and through that to anticipate the needs of others, before or after transsexual surgery. As you read through this rather different chapter, try to review in your mind what sort of response you are feeling. The questions and exercises at the end of the chapter are arranged to help you develop insight and empathy.

Transsexual surgery

A number of centres throughout the world now perform transsexual surgery. Such operations fundamentally alter body reality by creating or removing sexual organs, adjusting secondary sexual characteristics, providing the means to operate a substantially masculine or feminine (as sought) body presentation. The surgery is but one facet of a total package.

A transsexual is someone who is firmly convinced that his or her current body reality does not match actual sexual orientation (body ideal). Over a protracted period of time the transsexual comes to realise that he or she 'should have been born as a member of the opposite sex'. Because this is, by any standards a momentous conclusion, the care and surgery must be planned gradually, even cautiously. Neither patient, surgeon nor nurse would wish to contemplate surgery lightly. Four components are in any case involved in the patient's total management (see Table 21.1).

The first of these is that the patient is assisted to clarify his or her ideal, and to be sure of the wish to proceed with mutilating and possibly painful surgery. The assistance usually takes the form of multiple sessions of professional counselling from psychologists and consultant psychiatrist or surgeon. The patient is referred to such counselling perhaps several weeks earlier, by a doctor who will have established the sincerity of the patient's requests. In conjunction with counselling, the patient is also required to 'cross-dress' in the clothes of the intended gender for a period of (typically) one to two years. This is a prescription to live and work, as far as possible, the life of the opposite sex – experiencing the attitudes, problems and joys in degree! It is an extended opportunity for the patient to confirm or abandon the goal of gender change.

The third component includes both hormonal therapy and a range of discreet measures designed to aid a new body presentation, such as the removal of facial hair by using electrolysis. Hormone therapy is taken over a protracted period of time, both before and coinciding with the wearing of the preferred gender clothing. Hormone therapy brings with it considerable physiological change, although this often results in a patient's relief rather than distress. The fourth and final component, surgery itself, is often not a single operative procedure. Instead it proceeds in steps,

Table 21.1 Major components in support of transsexual patient contemplating sex change

Component	Notes
Professional counselling	Transsexual surgery is major surgery, and not as such reversible. The psychological health of the patient is seen as key to successful adaptation.
Period of cross-dressing	This may seen as the field work of the preparation. The prospective patient needs a continuous period experiencing life in the opposite gender clothing, to gain the clearest impression of what life will be like later.
Adjuvent therapy (for example hormone therapy, electrolysis)	Body presentation is strongly affected by those hormones controlling secondary sexual characteristics. These are adjusted in order to support change brought about by surgery.
Serial surgery	The surgery itself is often a multiple number of operations. The majority of these will be addressed to body sex organs, but other cosmetic surgery may also be envisaged. Like all surgery, there is the risk that the operation will not be completely successful, that complications may intervene.

sometimes over months. A patient seeking male assignment will undergo mastectomy, hysterectomy as well as surgery to fashion a penis. The operations carry the usual discomforts, worries and challenges associated with surgery.

Caring for the patient undergoing transsexual surgery must of necessity take into account more than these essentially practical patient concerns. The nurse should anticipate multiple contacts with the patient, at different stages of surgery and in different settings (ward, clinic, out patient department). The nurse must recognise that the patient may be prone to all the fears and anxieties about hospitals, and perhaps about the staff who will care for him or her. The nurse will also have to come to terms with her own feelings and beliefs about transsexual surgery and its place in a total health care service.

Several principles are helpful to the nurse in such circumstances. The first is that of ethically based care. Each patient is entitled to care that will enrich his or her life, and this must be interpreted with the patient's experiences and sexual orientation in mind. The principle of beneficence underpins ethical nursing care, and the patient's lengthy preparation for surgery has been designed to assist in making a considered consent to surgery. As elsewhere the nurse has advocated the patient's hopes and needs to others, this approach should be supported again.

The second guiding principle is that nurses should adopt an honest and enquiring attitude towards the patient. By the time the patient has been admitted to hospital, he or she will have accumulated a great deal of knowledge about, and insight into, the ramifications of transsexual surgery (Hodgkinson, 1987). It seems clear then that while the nurse contributes a great deal in terms of practical surgical care, she would be wise to learn from the patient about the emotional elements that are felt to be important. In the professional nursing relationship, there should be room for humility, and a willingness to listen and learn.

Thirdly, we should be prepared to consider the interest and support offered by the patient's friends, relatives and self-help agencies. Each will bring, with the patient's consent, some insights that will be helpful when providing care. Because the patient's preparation for gender change has been detailed, and body image carefully considered, assessment and care planning may be complex. Much of the early work will have been completed by others, including psychologists and counsellors, and the opposite sex body ideal explicitly stated. Nevertheless, care may have to be adjusted, fine tuned in the light of surgical or other complications, so adequate liaison with the patient and other privileged parties remains very important.

A patient's story

Nearly twenty years ago, Helen Lovell began to finalise her plans to undergo surgery to become a woman. Prior to then she had received a public school education, travelled widely, fought in the second world war, married and parented three children, all as a man. A talented artist, she now leads a busy life directing a sculpture workshop and before that, the activities of SHAFT, the Self Help Association For Transsexuals, in which she was a prominent figure. While Helen Lovell was not at the outset of interview familiar with all the modern body image terminology, she had patently thought with care and humility about her personal body image concerns. Seated before me was an obviously articulate, humorous and worldly wise woman who had much to offer nursing.

BP   (Bob Price)   It must seem a long time since you underwent surgery Helen, but presumably it was rather earlier still that you started to realise that you felt uncomfortable as a male?

HL   (Helen Lovell)   Yes, my first memories of things not being quite right were in my childhood. Up until the age of seven I had been brought up in India, in the care of a local ayah (a house servant). My parents were very busy people and around my seventh birthday I began boarding school in England. As my parents were still abroad I spent most of my holidays with various aunties. One of these herself ran a school, and it was there I came into close contact with girls. I realised that I wished I was a girl, and up until the age of nine or so, regularly played with dolls.

BP   And how did this develop?

HL   Well, later I went on to senior boarding school, which was for boys only. The lack of female companions highlighted my earlier impressions. I took an interest in girls as members of the opposite sex, but I was also keen to be near all things female. I started to take dance lessons to this end.

BP   During those years and later, did you ever start to question whether others shared your feelings or convictions?

HL   Yes, I did, but for many years I was totally convinced that there was nobody else who felt like me. I would think to myself, 'why am I the only idiot who felt like this?'

BP   After school I know that you joined the Indian army, and returned to the sub-continent.

HL   Yes, that was before the war. I was posted to Poona. You know, the place where one imagines all those frightful 'blimp colonels' come from!

BP   How did the rather masculine world of the military affect you?

HL   Well, the contact with women was slighter, but of course there were games where mixed company was common. I would go and play tennis, rather than pig sticking for instance. At this time I acquired a suitcase in which I would store female clothes. I started to wear these in private.

BP   There was no opportunity then to examine others' reactions to your dress?

HL   No, other than when there was a fancy dress party. I would then go as a dancing girl. It was a legitimate way to practise wearing female clothes, and being able to dance didn't do the image any harm either.

BP   Living so many secrets must have felt isolating. Were there any opportunities to relieve that isolation?

HL   No. The earliest I gained any relief from the isolation was through a magazine article much later in 1953. It was an account of an American GI who had undergone transsexual surgery, in Denmark I think. That came as a tremendous relief, to know that I was not alone in how I felt. By this time we had moved to Egypt and the war was underway.

BP   Did the article offer technical details about surgery?

HL   No, I recall it was more a human interest piece, but consoling nonetheless.

BP I would imagine that the war must have interrupted your feelings, the opportunity to cross-dress?

HL In the desert there was a lot of time to reflect. On cold nights underneath great coats I, and I suspect others, had to relieve themselves through masturbation.

BP What happened after the war?

HL My life started to change. Circumstances were such that through travelling I was able to start going out in women's clothing a little more publicly.

BP How did you feel about these adventure – elated?

HL No, not exactly. There was a feeling of this simply being the next step on. This was what I had to do. I was simply relieved when I wasn't found out.

BP So the secret box of clothes was still in use.

HL Yes. I was also by now starting to keep a diary of my feelings and trips. It seemed important that if I died someone else should understand my experiences.

BP Were you still thinking of yourself as an 'idiot' at this stage?

HL Yes, to some extent. I couldn't understand why I was not happy as a man.

BP Given the GI article, and your diary entries, did you now consider approaching anyone for advice or help?

HL I did. I shared my diary entries with a psychiatrist, but he rather dismissed them saying that there was nothing that could be done. If I did something public I would have lost my position. I had lost around 90 per cent of the sense of isolation, but there still seemed little hope of change.

BP Now after the war you got married and indeed, had three children. How did this affect your developing awareness of your transsexuality?

HL Not as much as one might imagine. I knew that my social role was as a man – that was what was expected of me.

BP Then did you come to a point where you shared your feelings with the family?

HL No, not directly. By the time we were expecting our third child I was coming to the conclusion I should abandon my box of clothes. I got rid of them all and then later regretted it. I simply couldn't change direction. We had been abroad at that point. By the time I returned to England I was able to take weekends away, dressed as a woman for the whole time. My family knew nothing about it.

BP How did you react to male interest on such weekends?

HL I was a little frightened and of course kept them at a distance. There were still some funny moments though. The hotel where I was staying on one occasion had a floor where all the guests were male. Returning there dressed as a woman late one night, I was apprehended by a porter who suspected my intentions! Escorted downstairs to the manager's office it took some brisk footwork to evade them and reach the sanctuary of my room! I had to take risks.

BP   Yes, it seems that you faced two sorts of risk regularly. One was in being found out, in the cross-dressed identity, the other when you had to deal with the reactions to you as a woman from men in particular.

HL   Yes, on two occasions in cinemas men tried to 'hold hands'. I agreed to meet one of them at the cinema on a later date. It was a lie but necessary.

BP   By this stage you were spending increasing time in women's clothing – was there a temptation to broach difficult feelings with your wife?

HL   No, I'm afraid you don't know the half of it! I could not imagine how any family could deal with the news that its husband and father was transsexual. At this stage I was running a business in Scotland. After weeks of pre-planning, I got to the point where I confided in a close girlfriend, and then one day I simply disappeared.

BP   Just vanished!

HL   Yes, I had no idea how they could come to terms with my plans for surgery. I had already separated from my wife and then two years before disappearing I started seeing a psychoanalyst and undergoing a course of sessions where I became quite sure I was transsexual. He agreed that I was, so I then sought out a surgeon who had been recommended to me. The operation would be done privately, and would include later facial, cosmetic surgery to hide my identity. I had also started to take female hormones nearly a year before surgery.

BP   So the facial surgery was to protect your previous identity.

HL   Partly yes, but also my eyebrows and nose were hardly satisfactory. I wanted them to look less severe.

BP   How were you preparing for the surgery?

HL   Well, I started my diary again, writing in it for nine months prior to surgery. I also gained a great deal of solace from my girlfriend, whose shoulder I could cry on. Eventually I travelled as a woman to the Midlands, where I was to undergo the operations. Whilst there I was seen once by a psychiatrist and then after a short and rather lonely stay in a hotel, I was admitted to hospital.

BP   And was there a lengthy stay in hospital, getting ready for the operation?

HL Oh no. I was admitted in the morning to a private room and later that afternoon I went to theatre.

BP How had the nurses reacted toward you? You were after all one of the very earliest patients in Britain to undergo such surgery?

HL They were very good and quite matter of fact about it all. Of course there had not been much time to talk pre-operation.

BP Did you have any last minute fears or doubts?

HL No. This was the last step in a long journey. When I looked under the sheets after the operation I felt no sense of loss, no regret at losing penis and testicles.

BP And was it painful or embarrassing?

HL I remember that there was a lot of blood and I had to wear a thick pad down below. I was tender and of course walked a little gingerly; but I did not feel embarrassed when I first went down to the ward sitting room.

BP So how long did you spend on the ward?

HL I think about a week. Soon after that I had to start thinking about very practical matters. I would have to make a living, I was no longer the executive of my own company. I would have to find a new identity and deal with a lot of paperwork.

BP You sound as though you had a very practical attitude towards it all.

HL I had always been like that. My education, upbringing, previous military life had always made me an organiser. Now I knew I had to think about how I would account for some fifty lost years.

BP I imagine that these problems would have arisen almost daily?

HL At first. I began to realise that if I made up a story about my earlier life, it would be very difficult to sustain and embellish it. That was a major problem.

BP Did you come to any conclusions about accounting for your past life?

HL Yes, I had to. I had taken up residence in the south of England and was starting to socialise more. In the local golf club there was every chance that over time someone would come to learn that I was a transsexual. I decided to tell the secretary honestly all about it and they accepted me wonderfully.

BP And what of your family?

HL After my operation I still longed to have contact with them. I had started to work as a sculptor near Coventry and to arrange my legal documents with the appropriate authorities. When my wife later tried to claim widow's pension rights she was told that she could not as her husband was still alive.

BP That must have come as a great shock.

HL Yes, although I later learned that my children had rather suspected that I had not died. Eventually I was traced to the Midlands and we tentatively began to rebuild relationships. It has not been easy for anyone and now I am working out how a grandchild can be helped to deal with the idea of a transsexual grandfather.

BP   Obviously the body image changes have left you with lots of challenges. Not only did you have to consider a new body presentation, but there were difficulties to get over in social relationships as well. Some years after your surgery you started to help other transsexuals didn't you?

HL   Yes. Initially I trained as a counsellor for the Samaritans, and had helped a few transsexuals in that way – by chance really. I did however feel that I was not making the best use of my experiences. Because of that the Self Help Association For Transsexuals was born. At a practical level I also learned to practise electrolysis – a painful but necessary process for removing facial hair.

BP   And what has been the most important work of SHAFT?

HL   Through a series of regional contacts we have tried to help transsexuals with the practical and emotional problems of their surgery and relationships. At first it was a shoe-string affair, but now I think the association has an average membership in excess of 300. People come and go.

BP   So what of the future?

HL   I've stood down from a lot of organising work now. I hope to continue to help and advise and of course there's a great deal of work to do in the sculpture workshop. All along its been important to have a sense of humour, and the confidence to get things done. That's still important for me today.

Review questions

The review questions posed below are in many respects unlike those of other chapters within this book. They are designed for personal reflection and then perhaps group discussion. There are no 'right answers'. Instead it is suggested that the following will help you to clarify your own perceptions – to develop an appreciation of patient needs, different perspectives.

1 Helen's first realisation that she wanted to be female rather than male occurred during school years. Childhood is a time of developing body image and some of this is linked to our notions of sexuality. Think back to your own childhood, the first time you remember holding feelings about being either male or female. What part did the following play in that feeling:
(a) body reality (such as changing contours, early puberty)?
(b) dress?

(c) toys and pastimes (stereotypical or otherwise)?

(d) social expectations of boys and girls respectively?

(e) role models, (such as parents)?

2 It seems likely that even today a transsexual will be faced with periods of isolation or doubt while slowly coming to realise his or her own sexual orientation. What factors contribute to this isolation and fuel the doubt?

3 In the pre-surgical period the transsexual must undergo counselling, hormone therapy and live in the clothing of the opposite sex for a considerable period of time. To what extent is this a good and prudent way to prepare patients for surgery? Is it possible that concerns over making a grievous surgical error, may limit the transsexual's opportunity to get on with life in his or her desired gender role?

4 An important aid in adjusting to a new body image is the social support network. In the case of transsexuality this may be strained to the limit. A spouse, children or parents may not be able to accept the patient's plans or new identity. What effect do you think this will have on:

(a) the patient's preparation for surgery?

(b) the nurse's care for the patient while in hospital?

(c) the patient's new body image during the first months post-operation?

5 Looking back over Chapter 21, can you identify any coping strategies used by Helen Lovell?

6 Transsexual patients may face prejudice, either amongst the general public or health professionals. For some people a sex change operation is interfering with nature, or what God has intended. Try to identify the factors which might lead an individual to adopt a negative transsexual position.

7 Caring for the transsexual patient might require a very special sort of nurse. What personal and professional qualities do you think he or she requires?

Suggested exercises

Exercise 1

Arrange to borrow a copy of Jan Morris's *Conundrum* from the library (for details see References). Critically read through the book, bearing in mind that the book has been written by a very articulate journalist, and that the operation in this instance was performed abroad, in the very infancy of transsexual surgery. Then in discussion with others address the following questions:

1. What personal coping strategies were used by this author to overcome her body image challenges? Are there any parallels to be found in Chapter 21?

2. Both Jan Morris and Helen Lovell are extremely intelligent, well educated people. What difficulties and disadvantages do you think would accrue to a patient from a less privileged background?
3. Having broadened your reading into transsexuality, share your current feelings about sexuality in general. Do you think that you have become less prescriptive on such issues? Are you now more, or less, sure of 'normality' as this pertains to body image and sexuality matters?

Suggestions: you should assign yourself at least two weeks to read the book and two hours for group discussion. These are issues that require a lot of thought, and time for all members to work through their ideas and feelings.

Exercises 2 and 3 are designed to develop your 'empathetic imagination'. Because comparatively few nurses will care for transsexual patients during gender surgery, you will need to consider their care over the widest possible circumstances, be this for routine surgery or when they are injured, old or infirm.

Exercise 2
In this exercise you are asked to make a careful spot review of one mass media presentation of sexuality. To do this you will need to take the following steps:

1. Choose a central television character, of the same sex as yourself.
2. Choose an appropriate film, drama or series episode when you will study the character in depth.
3. Prepare notes, expectations on actions, dress, or manners which will typically represent the character's sexuality (body presentation) – these are your working guidelines.

Then, notes before you, watch the programme or film. Jot down your observations about the character's behaviour or appearance. Bring these along to the discussion group. In turn, report your findings to colleagues, being sure to identify the character, and address these questions.

1. In terms of body presentation, is there a sharp divide between that which is masculine and that which is feminine? If not, could you subscribe to a continuum explanation of sexuality, with extreme masculinity and femininity at either poles?
2. To what extent does the character epitomise a body image that you can personally identify with?
3. Starting from an empathetic viewpoint, does this help you to imagine how a transsexual may experience his or her own sexual feelings or identity? (You may achieve this understanding precisely because you closely identify with the character who expresses your sexual norms strongly. A case of contrasts highlighting alternative perspectives.)

Exercise 3

In this exercise imagine what the following situations would mean for a patient who has recently undergone transsexual surgery. Remember that by this stage the patient will have 'cross-dressed' and may have felt relief at achieving surgery after a considerable wait.

1. A developing series of dinner and theatre dates with a suitor of the new 'opposite sex'.
2. A prospective admission to a general hospital for an urgent abdominal or perineal operation.
3. Going for an important job interview, when the interviewing manager is of the opposite sex and appears to have very conservative ideas about most matters.

Tackle these questions individually at first, then bring them to group discussion after. If a transsexual counsellor, specialist nurse or psychologist can share in the discussion, this would be most helpful. Each situation involves a mix of body presentation and interpersonal challenges. Collectively decide what these are, and then suggest solutions which might be constructive.

Suggestions: timing for both exercise 2 and exercise 3 depends upon the size of the group and the number of contributions to be made. As a guideline however, allow a whole afternoon session for such a discursive topic, especially if being joined by 'experts'. Remember that sexual issues always raise strong feelings in groups of nurses, doctors, or other health professionals. It is important to raise the issues, allow all an empathetic hearing, and then a time to re-establish group unity and support when feelings might have 'run high'. As with many other exercises, it seems important to allow nurses to opt in or out of such discussions, provided that they have given careful thought to why they feel as they do. The exercise is only constructive to the extent that it helps participants.

References

Hodgkinson L., *Body Shock: The truth about changing sex*, Columbus Books, London, 1987.
Morris J., *Conundrum*, Faber & Faber, London, 1974.

Unit 6
Evaluating body image care

22 Evaluating body image care

Study of this chapter will enable you to:

1 Reconsider why care evaluation is perhaps inadequately carried out in the area of body image.
2 Define the term evaluation, with due reference to the five stages suggested by Luker.
3 Describe briefly what is meant by *outcome evaluation, process evaluation* and *structure evaluation*.
4 Argue why evaluation must be planned for at the outset of care planning.
5 Suggest strategies for gathering evaluation data, by which body image care may be judged.
6 Outline some of the strengths and shortcomings of the various strategies.
7 Suggest the ways in which a thorough evaluation of one patient's body image care may benefit later patients' care.
8 Discuss with teacher or colleagues, the outline questions that can be usefully posed about the body image care delivered.

Of all the five stages of the nursing process (assessment, diagnosis, planning, implementation and evaluation), the last is by far the least understood. This is especially so in the context of body image care, which is itself in its infancy as a field of nursing. The limitations upon our understanding, and practise of, care evaluation come from misconceptions about the nursing process and the misunderstanding of body image concepts. For many nurses, evaluation is the last stage of a linear nursing process. It is seen as a review of what has already gone before, a hasty act that often coincides with the patient's discharge from hospital. Because the nursing process has been graphically represented by a series of boxes, evaluation has been confined as a final step and not seen as an ongoing and concurrent process.

Equally, because body image has been seen as an abstract subject, nurses have found it difficult to plan and evaluate body image care. The

269

purpose of this book has been to create body image terminology which is usable in nursing care. The concepts of body reality, body ideal and body presentation, of coping strategies and social support networks act as signposts for care planning, delivery and evaluation.

What then is evaluation? How is body image care evaluated usefully. Griffiths and Christensen define evaluation as a planned, systematic, comparison of a patient's health status with the prepared nursing care outcomes (Griffiths and Christensen, 1982). Through this comparison the nurse may judge the effectiveness of her nursing actions, and plan future care or support. Luker sees evaluation as being itself a five stage process. Firstly the nurse selects observable, recordable criteria which represent the attainment of a desired patient goal. The nurse then collects a range of observations, patient history or experiences by which she might draw inferences about his progress. A comparison is made between the patient observations (data) and the selected criteria (usually expressed as standards) which represent attainment of the patient goal. Judgement is then passed as to whether the two match. Have the patient's behaviour, knowledge and attitudes met the selected standards set in the goals? If not, to what extent do they fall short? Is there any discernible reason for the shortfall? It can be imagined that in some instances the nursing care goals might have been too ambitious – nursing resources, skills and the patient's motivation may have been overestimated. At other times events might have intervened after goal setting, for instance a post-operative infection. Finally, Luker suggests that these conclusions should be used to further modify the nursing care plan. Evaluation is not an end in itself, but the linking step to a new care plan cycle (Luker, 1979).

Care evaluation may be described at both the 'micro' and the 'macro' level. At the micro level the nurse daily, even hourly, reviews whether single care acts meet the standards that she sets when planning them. This process of reflection upon, and adjustment of, care may be recorded retrospectively. This is evaluation taking place while the nurse gives care – its notation is usually a second reflective act.

At the macro level, the nurse plays a part in a unit or institutional evaluation of care provision. The nurse is after all only one health professional caring for the patient. She works in a team of carers. When nurses participate in such a large scale exercise they are taking a role in quality assurance (Lang and Clinton, 1984; Van Maanen, 1984). The growing discernment in nursing care shown by patients, a need to prioritise care provision and fears of litigation have all encouraged the provision of quality assurance programmes, especially in the USA. To date, body image care has not been the most prominent area addressed in such programmes.

Each evaluation of body image care involves a careful review of three components. Firstly, and in some depth, whether patient body reality, body ideal and body presentation goals have been met. This is, 'outcome evaluation'. Secondly, the manner in which body image care was delivered must be considered. Did the nurse establish an appropriate, trusting relationship and atmosphere whereby body image problems might be understood? This is 'process evaluation'. Thirdly, the nurse considers the ward or institutional resources with which care was delivered. Were these appropriate, adequate, flexible? This is 'structure evaluation'.

Setting standards for body image outcomes

Despite the fact that body image care may extend over months, and may be judged in terms of the patient's and others' body ideal, it is still pertinent to set up standards by which body image outcomes can be judged. Many of these standards will be qualitative – that is, described in terms of patient satisfaction, comfort and social facility. A standard is a statement defining the level of a patient outcome. Look at the following goals:

1. The patient will be able to describe, without show of embarrassment, his stoma to intimate acquaintances.
2. The patient will be able to express appreciation of personal body attributes above and beyond those associated with faecal continence.

In the first of these a body presentation goal has been described. The standard by which the goal is judged is 'without show of embarrassment'. Can the patient at the time of his leaving hospital care, describe his stoma in a confident way to intimate others? The second is a body ideal goal. Here the standard by which the goal is judged is 'express appreciation'. If the patient feels appreciative about his personal body attributes (eg mobility, strength), but does not freely express these feelings, then it cannot be said that this goal has been fulfilled. These are qualitative standards and they look unscientific. Nevertheless, they are statements which might be discussed by nurses seeking to decide whether care has been effective.

It will be important to include similar standards in each of the body image goals planned. The standards chosen should take realistic account of the resources to hand and the length of time that the nurse will be caring for the patient. The nurse should also try to allow for the patient's perceived motivation, coping strategies and social support network. Successful rehabilitation usually starts from a basis of limited, realistic goals. The evaluation of these over a period of care enables further, more ambitious goals to evolve gradually.

It will be seen then that evaluation is actually anticipated during care planning. In preparing nursing goals the nurse will build in the standards of achievement by which she shall later measure the success or failure of care. She decides upon the arena of care (for example, body presentation) and the criteria which describe the standard (for instance, patient behaviour, clothing, grooming). Each evaluation will have to be tailor made for individual patients. This said though, you may find the questions arranged in Table 22.1 to be of value. They are intended as sample concerns which may be common in many body image situations.

Table 22.1 Evaluation – some outline questions worth asking

Body reality
1. To what extent has body reality been disrupted initially, and through treatment or surgery?
2. Have aseptic techniques, wound care, contributed to a successful body image rehabilitation?
3. Have body tubes, drains and dressings been reduced, or removed, as quickly and as safely as is possible for the patient?
4. Has physiotherapy contributed to body recovery, and been a comfortable experience for the patient?
5. Has pain been adequately controlled?
6. Has medication, and its side effects, been taken into account when reviewing body image care?
7. To what extent has the patient's normal ageing affected the matter?
8. Has alteration in body reality now ceased, or will it continue (for example consider the burn victim or cancer patient)?

Body ideal
9. Was it possible to establish a clear picture of the patient's normal body ideal (prior to surgery or injury)?
10. To what extent is this patient's body ideal vulnerable to past, present or future change in body reality (for instance is body ideal strongly founded on the skin)?
11. Have patient or relative coping strategies been recognised and accommodated in the plan of care?
12. Does the patient recognise realistic limitations on the creation of a new body ideal?
13. Have staff, relatives or friends who are influential upon the patient been identified and has this resource been built upon?
14. Are facilities for patient counselling and support available and adequate?

Body presentation
15. What challenges to body presentation have been recognised by patient and nurse?
16. Have these been viewed with due regard to the patient's normal pattern of body presentation?
17. Has the patient been tactfully assisted with practical body presentation concerns (for instance breast prostheses and use of makeup)?
18. To what extent has the patient been assisted to 'rehearse' body presentation to account publicly for body reality change?
19. Have relatives and friends been assisted to understand the importance of body presentation as a part of rehabilitation?
20. To what extent have you felt comfortable in providing practical body image care?

Standards for process evaluation

Unlike outcome evaluation, process evaluation does not usually refer directly to nursing care goals. These are expressed in terms of what the patient will be able to do, to express or to experience. Evaluating the process of body image care must therefore rely upon less direct measures of success or failure. The nurse will have to set standards which have been informed by a code of practice or conduct, for example the UKCC *Code of Conduct*, and which embody local protocols for body image care. To this extent a parallel may be drawn with the principles of good research practice. Ethical body image care must be devised, starting from a philosophy that views the patient and kin as partners in rehabilitation. The means of effecting care must start from a thorough assessment of the patient's normal body image, his habitual coping strategies and normal level of social support. It must proceed to identify the nature of the body image alteration and its impact upon the patient's body reality, body ideal and body presentation. It can be argued that care which does not follow the steps of the nursing process is likely to be disorganised care. The nursing process does after all offer the means to provide planned, rational care.

Other areas of process evaluation concern patient education, patient counselling and communication. Many of these activities are not solely restricted to body image care but they do offer areas in which standards may be more successfully described. When examining the level of the patient's knowledge, his mastery of body image problems, it may be possible to gain an indirect impression of the process of patient education. During ward reports it is often noted how patients respond to the nurse's guidance. All nurses have encountered 'difficult' or 'bad' patients, perhaps even created them through misunderstanding of what the patient has tried to communicate. It is healthy for the nurse to question herself, examining whether past interactions with patients have really been constructive, empathetic and ethical?

Evaluating the process of giving care should then, be a regular occurrence. It can be summatively worked through, in a group discussion or workshop. Daily review of care giving is still the foundation of professional care. It is what separates out nursing as a profession – an ethical practice by nurses who critically review whether they are establishing the right care atmosphere. Without the bond of trust, the professional relationship, it is not possible to approach body image care. Without the patient's consent, the nurse would never learn about his intimate body image worries.

Structural standards

Neither patient outcomes, nor the process of care, can be evaluated outside the context in which the nurse practices. For each patient's care, the nurse draws upon the material and staff resources of the hospital, clinic or health centre. This involves reviewing what resources were available, and which choices the nurse made from these. Because the nurse acts as an important liaison officer for the whole patient care team, it is she who often draws staff attention to patient needs. The nurse should question whether she has found enough, or the right resources and whether she has requested the right help, from the right professionals at the right time?

Given that nurses are accountable for the care delivered, it seems important to review the resources provided by the hospital. Without adequate logistic support, no single nurse can effect a complete plan of body image care. It is as much a professional as a political issue to advocate adequate staffing and resources for a ward or clinic.

Gathering the data – the patient's progress

Having established the standards by which body image care shall be judged, the next step is to consider how to gather data on patient outcomes. A combination of strategies can be employed, adjusted to patient circumstances and needs.

Photographs

On burns units, the taking of periodic patient photographs has become a familiar way of judging the patient's progress. The sequence of instant snaps show the gradual rise and fall of burn oedema, the formation of keloid tissue and the benefits of subsequent treatment. If the photographs are in colour and appropriately lit, so much the better. Using photographs tactfully can help motivate the patient and family. The nurse should highlight the areas of improvement and provide a rationale for the altered physiology under way.

Reviewing the photographs, either with the patient or professional colleagues, the nurse is able to identify longer term changes in body reality and body presentation which have gone unnoticed in day to day care. This may be especially important if the patient has been supported over an extended period of time, or if there has been succession of carers. When looking through the photographs with the patient it is useful to listen carefully to his comments:

Patient I can't believe how swollen and ugly my face used to look....
Nurse Do you think there's been an improvement then?
Patient Only partly. I've swapped the swollen for the scarred. My skin texture is important to me.

This patient is giving information about his progress toward a new body ideal. The central concern with smooth skin texture remains, the hurdle of facial oedema has been replaced by that of scar tissue.

Diaries

A body image diary may be kept by the patient, the relatives, the nurse or all three. The diary is a means by which the trauma to body ideal can be recorded. It may reflect the trials and tribulations as the patient struggles to adapt to a new body ideal and tackles body presentation. Because a daily diary requires conscious reflection on altered body image, the patient will have a chance to start coming to terms with painful feelings. It is suggested therefore that daily patient diaries are best suited to situations where the pace of body image change has not been abrupt. A patient admitted for a planned radical mastectomy might benefit from this approach.

Having decided just who will be keeping diaries, it is important to agree with the patient who will have access to them. A weekly meeting where nurse and patient share diary thoughts seems a good idea. Such a forum helps the patient to ask questions, to unload irrational fears and to start to understand the body image changes. The meeting should take place in a private environment, with relatives or other carers invited as the patient feels comfortable. When the diary is solely maintained by the nurse it approximates to 'field notes'. Ideally, such a diary is controlled by the patient's primary nurse. It forms an in-depth evaluation of how body image care has been delivered and may be used to brief the patient, or colleagues, on suggested changes in care.

Observation

Critical to all the preceding techniques, are the nurse's observation skills. It has been emphasised in earlier chapters that noticing what the patient wears, how grooming and skin care is dealt with, may offer hints about the patient's current body image state. The nurse uses her observation skills widely. Visiting times, consultant's ward rounds, group discussion in front of the television, all afford opportunities where note can be made of patient posture, his comments about his appearance, and apparent comfort in company. Try to record the patient's behaviour, and the circumstances of that behaviour. Both may offer clues by which care can be evaluated.

Because body presentation is such a key issue in patient rehabilitation, it will be necessary to observe other's reactions to the patient's new appearance. The interplay of conversation, body language, the expressed concerns of relatives, help in anticipating how social support will develop or fail after the patient's discharge from hospital. The range of observations should be extended to include these social support networks.

Patient interviews

A summative patient interview often occurs just prior to the patient's discharge home. This provides an opportunity to gain final impressions of the patient's coping strategies and to offer further advice or education. The success, or otherwise, of patient interviews as an evaluation method depends upon the quality of the nurse–patient relationship. An unfamiliar nurse, who invites the patient to share a review of traumatic body image events, is unlikely to form an accurate evaluation of care. The patient may be tempted to offer a limited insight, an account which it is assumed will please the nurse. The interview may be limited by the patient's grief reaction. A patient experiencing denial is unlikely to furnish a conscious, clear account. Patient interviews are far more effective when the patient is repeatedly readmitted to hospital. In these circumstances there is a need to evaluate patient progress, as a result of professional or lay support. The nurse has gaps in her knowledge of patient history, of what others might have done. The interview is a cogent and efficient way of filling in these gaps. As with patient diaries, it seems beneficial if the interview is conducted by a primary nurse, or at least one who has been trusted by the patient in the past. Diaries, photographs or a review of the patient's last consultation with the doctor may form a focus for discussion. Patient interviews should start with the least invasive questions and proceed to more intimate concerns. It is useful if the nurse prepares a quiet environment, some notes, spelling out the areas which she is especially concerned about. The interview questions act as prompts, an aid to discussion, not an inquisition.

Patient questionnaires

Patient satisfaction questionnaires, from the most informal to the most sophisticated, are increasingly used to evaluate the patient's experience of care. Two questions are pertinent when considering such questionnaires. Firstly, has the questionnaire taken a balanced sample of questions associated with body image into account? Because body image concepts are still strange to the lay public, the question terminology will have to be very clear and simple, with perhaps a few key definitions. It should be remembered that patient tolerance of questionnaires rests upon their clarity and brevity.

Secondly, consider when to administer the questionnaire. Will it be at point of discharge home, a few weeks later or even a year hence? Will it be repeated? It cannot be expected that patient reactions to care will be constant. Personal opinions on care may either deteriorate or improve over time.

At the present time, it seems that patient questionnaires have a role at two levels. At their simplest, they are a means to spot sample patient satisfaction short term – 'gut reactions to care'. At a more complex level, questionnaries which have been researched, properly piloted and tested, may be used to advise the institution about its total package of care. Both involve the nurse in planning and updating a long term tool as part of quality assurance.

Making judgements

Using one or more of the preceding teachniques, it should now be possible to start comparing goals and results, standards and outcomes. Making judgements about the effect of body image care could simply mean that it is concluded to be a success or a failure. Usually however, the nurse will wish to conclude that there has been a degree of success, which is more or less satisfying for the patient and nurse alike. Finding that there has only been a limited achievement is currently common because firstly, the tendency is to create very optimistic goals, and secondly, body image rehabilitation is often long term and nurse–patient contact time may be lamentably short.

Judging the care is often best carried out in an informal meeting, where the patient's primary nurse may report on detailed observations. The care plan is referred to regularly and additional factors affecting care noted. In the light of findings, future care is planned, or adjusted or abandoned. The hope is that much care will have become redundant, the patient once more substantially in control of body image matters. If the body image outcomes have not been achieved, and the patient is soon to be discharged, a hand-over to community colleagues must be planned. The transfer of whole care plans to a health centre may not always be practical. A discharge summary should therefore include outstanding goals, together with notes on the patient's progress towards the same. Alongside these notes, it may be use-ful to offer points about factors which have either promoted or inhibited rehabilitation.

Before the notes are finally despatched and the patient discharged, it is constructive to record those body image goals which regularly prove dif-ficult to meet. This collection of 'unsolved mysteries' can then be used as discussion points for in-service workshops or seminars. It may be appro-priate to plan more limited goals, or to introduce additional expertise into the team to maintain the original goal. At this level, attempt to learn useful lessons that may be transferred to future patients' care. While it is true that all patient care is individualised, there are some common dilemmas posed by specific operations or treatments. It is important to anticipate these regular problems.

Conclusion

There are good reasons to suppose that many patients will leave the care of the nurse without an adequate evaluation of body image interventions. This is a loss to the patient (future advice and counselling might have been based on the evaluation) and a loss to the nursing team which may be planning other patients' care. Evaluation is an important part of total care, and not an optional extra which may or may not be explored.

Evaluation is made possible by drawing up measureable nursing goals. This is achieved by ensuring that the goals include a standard, a clear patient behaviour that can be identified during observation, interview or similar. Accurate evaluation is facilitated when the nurse chooses an appropriate data gathering strategy. In this chapter some of the possibilities have been set out, with comments upon their use. Finally, it is essential to judge candidly the nursing care and to adjust future care in the light of the results. Clearly this must involve an investment of nurse's time, thought and energy. It is however the best way to ensure that body image care is delivered professionally and sensitively.

Review questions

1 Why do you think evaluation of nursing care is not completed as often as it should be?
2 Name the five stages of the evaluation process.
3 Define what is meant by 'structural' and 'process' evaluation.
4 Offer strengths and weaknesses of the following strategies for evaluation:
   (a) patient questionnaires
   (b) patient interviews
   (c) use of photographs
5 Why is it important to anticipate evaluation, when care is being planned?
6 What is meant by an evaluation standard?
7 Which type of evaluation is likely to address patient education?
8 What professional – ethical concerns should be taken into account when using patient diaries for care evaluation?

Suggested exercises

Exercise 1
Co-operating with one or more colleagues, decide which of the following represent outcome, process and structure evaluation.

1. The nurse examines details from a patient interview, in which she learnt that he felt unsure about dealing with the odour from his stoma.
2. The day and night shift nurses discuss the anxiety that Mrs Brown has been showing during the last few days. It appears to be getting worse the nearer her breast biopsy operation comes. They try to identify Mrs Brown's 'favourite nurse'.
3. The nurse watches the patient adjust her breast prosthesis and then dress in the clothes she has recently bought.
4. The two senior nurses on the ward review how money has been allocated to various ward ventures. They notice that an increasing amount of cash is being allocated to decorating a side room for use in patient counselling.

Suggested time for exercise is 30 minutes.

Exercise 2
This second exercise is designed for use by a small group. Its purpose is to test out the assertions made in Chapter 22, and then to enable participants to form opinions about local nursing circumstances.

Use Chapter 22 to formulate a short survey of about ten questions which you will apply to nurses practising in a local ward or clinic. Try to choose clinical areas where there is a high percentage of patients requiring body image care. Ensure that your questions cover the following areas:

1. The purpose of evaluation.
2. When evaluation takes place.
3. When evaluation is planned.
4. The techniques of evaluation.
5. Areas that evaluation should address (in Chapter 22 this was defined under headings such as outcome and structure).

Try to word your questions so that they may be answered in short phrases, or, offer alternative definitions which ask the nurse to choose a correct response.

Explain the purpose of your survey to all potential respondents, assuring them that results will be kept confidential, and the purpose of the survey is to 'test out what you have read in nursing texts'. Score your replies and prepare a report, keeping ward and staff anonymous for your group supervisor or tutor.

References

Griffiths J. and Christensen P., *Nursing Process*, C.V. Mosby, St Louis, 1982.
Lang N. and Clinton J., 'Quality Assurance – The idea and its development in the United States', Ch. 3 in Willis L. and Linwood M. (eds), *Measuring the Quality of Care*, pp 69–89, Churchill Livingstone, Edinburgh, 1984.
Luker K., 'Evaluating Nursing Care' in Kratz C. (ed.), *The Nursing Process*, pp 124–46, Bailliere Tindall, London, 1979.
Van Maanen H., 'Evaluation of Nursing Care: A multinational perspective' in Willis L. and Linwood M. (eds), *Measuring the Quality of Care*, pp 3–42, Churchill Livingstone, Edinburgh, 1984.

Further reading

Gordon M., *Nursing Diagnosis, Process and Application*, McGraw Hill, New York, 1982.
McClure M., 'The Long Road to Accountability', *Nursing Outlook*, Jan, pp 47–50, 1978.

Useful addresses and agencies

The following agencies deal with problems or needs that might be considered to include a body image component. In many instances they will be able to offer personal experience in and practical advice about, body image matters.

Anorexic Aid
The Priory Centre, 11 Priory Road, High Wycombe, Bucks HP13 6SL
Telephone: (0494) 21431

Anorexic Family Aid and National Information Centre
Sackville Place, 44–48 Magdalen Street, Norwich, Norfolk NR3 1JE
Telephone: (0603) 621414

Association to Aid the Sexual and Personal Relationships of People with a
   Disability (SPOD)
286 Camden Road, London N7 0BJ
Telephone: 01-607 8851

Breast Care and Mastectomy Association of Great Britain
26 Harrison Street, London WC1H 8JG
Telephone: 01-837 0908

British Colostomy Association
38–39 Eccleston Square, London SW1V 1PB
Telephone: 01-828 5175

British Limbless Ex-Servicemen's Association (BLESMA)
Frankland Moore House, 185–187 High Road, Chadwell Heath,
   Essex RM6 6NA
Telephone: 01-590 1124

Chest Heart and Stroke Association
Tavistock House North, Tavistock Square, London WC1H 9JE
Telephone: 01-387 3012

CRUSE Bereavement Care
Cruse House, 126 Sheen Road, Richmond, Surrey TW9 1UR
Telephone: 01-940 4818

Disabled Living Foundation
380–384 Harrow Road, London W9 2HU
Telephone: 01-289 6111

Doreen Trust MBE
Disfigurement Guidance Centre, 52 Crossgate, Cupar, Fife KY15 5HS
Telephone: (0334) 55746

Ileostomy Association
Amblehurst House, Blacks Scotch Lane, Mansfield,
  Nottinghamshire NG18 4PF
Telephone: (0623) 28099

LINK: The Neurofibromatosis Association
London House, 26–40 Kensington High Street, London W8 4PF
Telephone: 01-938 2222 extension 2226

London Rape Crisis Line
Telephone: 01-837 1600

The Multiple Sclerosis Society of Great Britain and Northern Ireland
25 Effie Road, Fulham, London SW6 1EE
Telephone: 01-736 6267

The Psoriasis Association
7 Milton Street, Northampton NN2 7JG
Telephone: (0604) 711129

Self Help Association For Transsexuals (SHAFT)
BM Box No 7624, London WC1N 3XX
Telephone: 021-3551579 (evenings and weekends)

The Spastics Society
12 Park Crescent, London W1N 4EQ
Telephone: 01-636 5020

Spinal Injuries Association
76 St James's Lane, Muswell Hill, London N10 3DF
Telephone: 01-444 2121

The Terrence Higgins Trust Ltd
52–54 Grays Inn Road, London WC1N 3XX
Telephone: 01-242 1010

Urostomy Association
Buckland, Beaumont Park, Danbury, Essex CM3 4DE
Telephone: 024-541 4294

Appendix B
Manufacturers of body image products

Charles H Fox
22 Tavistock Street, London WC2E 7PY
Telephone: 01-240 3111

Innoxa (England) Ltd
Beauty House, Hawthorne Road, Eastbourne, Sussex BN23 6QX
Telephone: (0323) 639671

Medoxport Ltd
PO Box 25, Arundel, West Sussex BN18 0SW
Telephone: (0243) 544132

Thomas Blake and Co.
Blatchford Close, Horsham, Sussex RH13 5RQ
Telephone: (0403) 54742

Appendix C
A summative exercise: the body image assessment tool

In reading through the chapters of this book, the reader will probably have reflected upon the benefits of using a simple, body image assessment tool. While such a tool would undoubtedly require adjustment for specific clinical settings, for instance in the oncology unit, it might prove a useful first indicator of body image needs. Arriving at an altered body image risk score, should assist the nurse to plan the allocation of limited resources of nursing skills, expertise and time. Until now, most body image assessment scales have been lengthy and complex tools, and many are more suited to research settings, rather than day-to-day clinical practice.

In this final exercise, you are invited to consider just one embryonic, simple body image assessment tool. The purpose of this exercise is to encourage you to discuss the tool critically, and to assess its appropriateness for your clinical environment. You should be asking the following fundamental questions:

1. How valid is it? Will it measure what it sets out to measure?
2. How reliable is it? Will it measure altered body image risks amongst a wide range of patients?
3. How clear are the terms? Will it be easy to use?
4. How long will it take to use? Is it an economical tool?
5. Is it an ethically sound tool to use? How will patients respond to it?

When you have examined the assessment tool, make notes on its strengths and weaknesses, and where you believe it would benefit from adjustment. Bear in mind that any such tool, for practical purposes, must be relatively brief, clear and attractive to use.

You may extend this exercise by negotiating a trial of the tool (perhaps modified), as part of a care study or research project. To do this you should ensure that you follow appropriate local research protocols, gaining clearance from the hospital or health authority ethics committee. You are also advised to take local advice on protocol from your course tutor, or nursing research interest group. Remember to acknowledge all the source materials that you use.

Note to teachers and organisers

This exercise is of necessity open ended and may be tackled at a variety of levels. The exercise is offered in the hope that nurses from varied backgrounds and settings will feel enthusiastic about contributing to a tool which may enhance future body image care. It is anticipated that the exercise will be useful as part of an undergraduate programme or a post-basic clinical specialty course.

Body image assessment tool

This tool is designed to highlight patients at risk of developing a seriously altered body image. Please fill in all sections of the tool, either through observation or patient interview.

Body reality

Place ticks in the boxes against the areas of the body reality affected, or likely to be affected, by the stressor (trauma, pathology etc). Score requisite points and total.

Body area affected	Point score	Tick
Face, hands, sexual organs (external and internal)	5	
Neck, legs and arms	4	
Anterior torso	3	
Posterior torso	2	
Internal organs – no scar, non-sexual organs (for example endoscopy)	1	
Total points		

Tick the relevant boxes and score accordingly.
The body reality change will be:

	Points 2	1	0	
Permanent				Temporary
Painful				Pain free
Daily apparent to patient				Infrequently apparent to patient
Totals				

Score this page:

The body reality change will affect the following functions:

	Points 2	1	0	
Sexual function	A lot			Not at all
Mobility/gait	A lot			Not at all
Limb co-ordination	A lot			Not at all
Body strength	A lot			Not at all
Totals				

Body ideal

Tick the (a) boxes which best describe the patient's position:

(a)   (b)

1. The patient has a clearly formed body ideal which emphasises a good physical appearance.

2. The patient has a clearly formed body ideal which emphasises controlled physical function.

3. The patient has a body ideal with very well defined body space area/boundaries.

4. The patient anticipates that body ideals will have to change in response to his/her current situation.

Now, in the (b) boxes score 4 points for each tick placed against questions (1), (2) and (3). If you have placed a tick against question (4) subtract 4 points from this section total.

Total

Score this page:

Body presentation

Score 1 point for each 'temporary' box ticked, 3 points for each 'permanent' box ticked. The patient as a result of the stressor (trauma, pathology, treatment etc) will have to adjust:

Presentation area	Temporary	Permanent
Mobilising		
Skin care		
Toileting		
Dressing/clothing		
Grooming		
Body smell/fragrance		
Body space (such as aids/attachments)		
Sexual expression		
Verbal account of themselves/history		
Totals		

Section total

Coping strategies

Interview the patient and ask which of the following approaches best describes his/her habitual way of dealing with health or other life dilemmas: (more than one choice permitted)

	Tick	Score
Confront the problem		
Seek and take advice		
Redefine problem as a challenge		
Total		

Score −3 for each box ticked.
Subtract this block total from total on previous page to arrive at total score:

Please tick the appropriate boxes which describe the patient's habitual responses to health or other life dilemmas:

	Tick	Score
Talk problem over with friends		
Make light of the situation		
Use distractions		
Total		

For each box ticked in this block, score −1.

	Tick	Score
Withdraw from the situation		
Blame others		
Feel fatalistic		
Suppress the problem		
Indulge in self pity		
Total		

For each box ticked in this block, score +2.

Coping strategy items adapted from: Weisman A., *Coping With Cancer*, McGraw-Hill, New York, 1979.

Score this page: _____

Social support network

For each statement ticked, score −2.

1. Patient feels that he/she has extensive and supportive family/friend network ( )
2. He/she receives tangible help from helpers (eg transport, financial) ( )
3. A relative or friend helps to take stock of events ( )
4. A relative or friend compares him/her favourably with others ( )
5. The patient has a good array of visitors/enquiries about his/her health ( )

Total ( )

Total this page

Final total overall

Scoring sheet

Gross scores

20+   A major body image problem is either already in existence or in the making. This patient requires early body image care to be planned.

10–19 This patient has a significant body image problem risk, and should, clinical situations notwithstanding, have body image care featuring in the care plan.

0–9   A relatively less significant risk of major body image problems. However, review situation again in the light of changed therapy, surgery, complications and infections.

Body reality scores

If body reality score accounts for more than 50 per cent of total score, attention must be paid to whether physical problems can be anticipated and prevented. High body reality scores are most significant if they feature permanent and sexual body reality problems.

Body ideal scores

High body ideal scores are not easily reduced – they require attitude change over time. Consider assisting patient to value other body attributes or other personal or self-image qualities.

Body presentation

Permanent high body presentation scores are most significant, and perhaps indicate that the nurse should work with professional colleagues to develop new body presentation techniques (for instance working with occupational therapist, stoma therapist).

Coping strategies

Any positive score in the coping strategies area, even in the light of a general score of less than 10, should cause concern. Such patients are extremely vulnerable to future body image change. Look for a useful social support network score to assist such patients.

Social support network

Patients with high body image scores, featuring a zero or low minus score in this area will tend to cope poorly with long term body image challenges. Attention should be paid to directing the patient to support agencies, either voluntary or statutory.

Index